I0815158

STORIES of JOSIE

GROWING UP WITH ABUSE AND RACISM

MARY WENDLAND

Little Creek Press®
5341 Sunny Ridge Road
Mineral Point, Wisconsin 53565

Edited by Grace A. Peters

Interior book design and project coordination:
Little Creek Press®

Reprint (new title)
March 2024

Printed in the United States of America.

For more information or to order books:
visit www.littlecreekpress.com

Library of Congress Control Number: 2021920425

ISBN-13: 978-1-955656-10-8

Disclaimer: This book is a work of creative nonfiction. The author wrote chapters based loosely off the memories and stories of Mary Wendland's childhood. All names and and some identifying details have been changed.

I did it, Mar'.

Love, your husband, Ed

Table of Contents

Chapter One
Requiem

A tiny sliver of gold appeared over the blue-green waters of Lake Michigan. It tiptoed through the neighborhoods, reflecting off the steeples and domes of the churches, illuminating the stained-glass windows set like jewels in gray brick—monuments built by people with callused hands and work-worn clothes to honor their Creator, by immigrants and the sons and daughters of immigrants who clustered together in little towns called "The Neighborhood."

"The Neighborhood," held together by a school, a church, and a corner grocery store, was bordered on one side by streetcar tracks and on the other by a shopping district. Mini neighborhoods touched and overlapped, ever-changing, but always in the same way: touching at the corner store, overlapping at the A&P grocery store, touching at the bus stop, overlapping at the park.

Suddenly, the sun exploded across the sky, urging housewives to get about the day's business. There was water to heat and washing to start. Only a sluggish woman wouldn't have laundry hung before noon. Bread left to rise overnight must be baked; there was breakfast to make, lunch to pack.

"Wake up, sleepyheads!" Mamas called out to their offspring.

"Eat your oatmeal."

"Change that shirt! You want Teacher to think your mama don't care how you look?"

"Hurry! You can't be late!"

The men hurrying to work were grateful that at last, once again, they could provide for their families the way a man should. Grateful that at last they could erase that look their wives had worn for so long—faces puckered so their features pulled downward; mouths once full and laughing now thin-lipped and frowning; eyes empty, hollow—except for the fear.

Fear.

Fear that filled their lives day by day and robbed their sleep by night. Fear of what unforeseen disaster might befall today. Fear of children crying from hunger. Fear that the little they still hung on to, what they had salvaged and scraped and scrimped to keep, might be gone, too. Taken by this unknown, unseen, un-fightable enemy. This Depression that lay over the country like a smelly, moth-eaten, dirty blanket that suffocated everything and everyone.

But now that fear was being chased away! It was banished from the land by smoke from factories, by heat from foundries, by the humming of motors and machines, by the chugging of locomotives and the quiet rumble of boxcars moving down the tracks. And the man responsible for that banishment had promised that it was only the fear itself to be feared.

The sun traveled up the valley that sliced through the city and stopped the natural flow of the neighborhoods. The city divided in half, north and south. Both sides were joined together by narrow bands of steel and cement, of asphalt and streetcar tracks.

"Whad'ya call a bridge from Germany to Poland?" people would shout.

"The 16th Street viaduct!" came the response, in laughter.

A river ran through the valley, a gentle river that had at one time nurtured marsh-grass and cattails, willows and scrub brush and an occasional oak, and offered sanctuary to deer and wild creatures. But man had imprisoned it behind brick and cement and barred its flow with railroad tracks and factories. The gentle beauty of the valley had been replaced by manmade starkness.

Yet there was a beauty to this starkness, too. Sunlight and shadow played against one another with shades of gray in between. Cream-colored city brick and red brick got daily dustings of soot. Puffs of white from towering smokestacks created a study in black and white etched against the blue sky. All of it was framed by the geometric lines of railroad tracks that ran east and west through the valley. This silver frame was kept polished by the steel wheels of the trains that wove their way along spur lines.

The sun greeted the men who had labored all night in the factories. Gray men stumbled out into the daylight, blinking and yawning like ghosts. Men with hands and fingernails that would never be completely clean again and tiny steel slivers that festered before being seen and removed. Men with grease-filled pores and life-etched patterns across their faces. Men with work-weary backs and legs that must climb up from the valley floor to the street level of the viaduct. They gathered at the base of the steps, reluctant to start. Some sat resting, waiting for a surge of energy before starting up. Then, slowly, they began to haul themselves upward. Some counted each step, muttering the number as if it were a prayer, a litany for the laboring man.

As they tired, the gray men sat on the steps, scooting to the left, making room for the climbers. Climbers on the right, sitters on the left. A man sat to the left, sweating profusely despite the cool morning air, wiping his forehead with a grimy red handkerchief.

"Hey, Swede, ya okay?" another man patted his buddy's shoulder.

"*Da,*" Swede gasped and wiped his face once more.

His friend moved to the left and sat behind him. "I need ta sit, too."

The flow of men continued to pass.

"Hey, Tony, the Swede okay?" someone shouted without stopping his climb.

"Yeah, just gotta give up them cigs." Tony roughed Swede's head. "Ya gotta give them things up."

Swede nodded, unable to cough words out. The two sat quietly as other men hoisted themselves upward.

"Yer gonna miss your ride," Swede forced the words out.

"If you can talk, you can walk. Come on, I ain't got all day."

They pulled themselves to their feet and rejoined the gray stream on the right.

At the top, the men waited for the streetcar. Those going south crowded into the three-sided shanty that at least broke the wind and allowed a few lucky ones a place to sit. Those going north straggled across to the other side to wait.

"Hey, here comes our taxi."

The streetcar, traveling full speed, squealed to a halt at the only stop here on the viaduct, and the tired men hurried to find a seat where they could rest, maybe even snooze a bit before getting home for their "supper" that others called breakfast.

Thomas tucked his lunchbox under his arm and started up the viaduct stairs. The mists that seeped into the valley last night swirled around him, but he knew that up at street level, a beautiful day awaited. When he'd first started this job Father Mike had found for him, he would count the steps as he climbed upward. The first sixty were the hardest, but by the time he reached the landing, he always got a second wind and other things began to fill his mind, so the remaining climb was almost easy. The number never changed anyway, no matter how often one counted them.

Yet so many continued to count. Over and over after each shift, the steps were counted and complained about as men puffed and pulled themselves to the 27th Street level. The numbers were muttered under their breaths as though they were saying their rosary.

Along with finding him a job when he'd moved up here to Milwaukee, Father Mike had promised, "It's God's country." But winter had been the coldest he'd ever experienced and spring merely a brief period of mud and dampness followed by a hot, uncomfortably sticky summer that bred mosquitoes.

God's country indeed! Thomas had thought.

Then came autumn.

A glorious fall with a sky so blue it hurt your eyes and air so crisp and clean and clear that each maple, each elm, each sumac stood out in majestic color to become a work of art. It was, indeed, God's country during September and October. The rest of the year remained questionable, but there was no doubt about autumn.

It was as Thomas expected when he reached the top of the viaduct: the sun was chasing the night mists away with a warming glow, and the October sky was bright and blue. The day was just beginning, and it was wonderful to be wide awake and a witness to this brand new morning while others were still sleepy-eyed and unaware.

"Blue skies smilin' at me! Nothing but blue skies do I see …"

The song flitted through his mind. He was pleased with the morning. The sun slanted just perfectly over the stark, man-made panorama of the valley, the fresh smell of Lake Michigan wafted through the air, and the faintest glimmer of the river below was still shrouded by fog. The river down there had long ago been tamed. Why, this river was so tame that a good man could, well, throw a silver dollar across it. If he had a silver dollar.

Thomas inhaled deeply, feasting his senses. Sun-warmed vapors floated upward, growing thinner and thinner like silent, wispy ghosts that disappeared before his eyes. "I love this shift!" he spoke out loud, but to himself.

This shift allowed him to not only witness the miracle of each new morning with its promise of hope, but also gave him the opportunity to bathe the kids each night before he left, to tuck the boys into their beds and get his little Josephine into her nightie and fix her last "baba" of the day, then lay her in bed beside her mother where he'd join them until it was time to leave.

Mother and daughter were so much alike, dark wild curls tumbling together, tiny veins of blue through translucent skin. Mother and daughter snuggling together. Celia's dark eyes twinkled down at her baby's solemn ones, then she'd chuckle deep in her throat, the way she did when she was really pleased. "Sucking a bottle is serious business."

The three of them together were "snug as bugs." Josephine sucking contently on her bottle, unaware of their plans and dreams. He and Celia plotted their future now that he was working every day. Not just an every-other-week job, but a real job. They dreamt of a home of their own with a yard and space for a garden. Prosperity was just around the corner, President Roosevelt had promised.

"Never saw the sun shining so bright! Never saw things going so right …" The music still lingered in his mind.

Thomas reached the street and stood a minute to catch his breath. Some fellow workers were sitting in the shanty waiting for the streetcar, which was nowhere in sight. He fingered the coins in his pocket.

Might as well walk, he decided, and save the carfare.

He turned south and started for home, lunchbox still tucked under his arm. The clasp had sprung open last night, spilling the contents to the ground and shattering the fragile glass liner in the thermos. The box itself was still useable if he found an old belt for a strap, but that shouldn't be a problem, there surely must be an old belt around somewhere. But the thermos would need replacing when payday rolled around next week.

When he reached the south end of the viaduct, he crossed the street to walk along the western edge of Mitchell Park. Breezes rustling through the drying leaves carried the scent of the world reaching its glorious peak before the cold of an oncoming winter. The cicada chorus was warming up, their songs rising and falling, then rising again, peaceful as church chants. Giant elms formed the arches of the Creator's cathedral, a few maples were reddish-orange, and the early morning sun slanting through them created a glow no stained-glass window could match.

How nice it would be to bring Celia here to see them, Thomas thought. Maybe it would help her feel better, stronger, if he brought her here. She loved the trees when they put on their "annual show." She even planned which ones to plant in their own yard someday. Maybe now with cooler weather she'd start to feel better again.

"Noticing the days hurryin' by, when you're in love—oh, my, how they fly."

It seemed at times as though she'd been sick forever. First having Josephine, then too soon, pregnant again, only to miscarry. And now, not eating. She hadn't had all these problems with the boys, and they had been close together, as close as possible without being twins. Just ten months apart. But hopefully, fall with its crisp bright beauty and coolness would have a healing effect and she'd regain her strength.

He prayed each morning at Mass for that blessing.

"Holy Trinity, One God, make Celia well. Holy Mother of God, make Celia well. Holy angels and archangels, make Celia well." His litany.

The streetcar finally clanged past as Thomas neared The Coffee Pot, just a half-block from National Avenue. He'd made the right decision to walk. He'd have been standing back there all this time instead of half way home with an extra nickel jingling in his pocket.

National Avenue was bustling with activity. A streetcar pulling out of the car barn across the street had jumped its trolley, creating a tiny Fourth-of-July shower of sparks that filled the air with an electrical smell. The corner druggist was sweeping his steps as he did every morning. The Italian grocer was stacking crates of potatoes and onions and squash on the sidewalk in front of his store, and Mr. Schmidt, the jeweler, was standing on a ladder tinkering with his tall street clock.

Thomas pulled out his pocket watch and double-checked it.

"Das ist right, yah?" Mr. Schmidt called down.

Thomas grinned and nodded, then formed an "OK" sign with his thumb and fore finger. "To the minute."

"Yah, yah...das ist gut." Mr. Schmidt puffed his way down, ample belly hindering his descent.

Across from the grocery, the bakery already had a steady stream of customers following the enticing aroma of bread and sweet rolls. On impulse, Thomas joined them. After all, he'd saved a nickel. He counted his change.

"A long-john and a crueler." Then on a second thought, he added, "And a jelly-filled."

It was all he could afford, and it meant he'd walk to work tonight, but hopefully one would tempt Celia into eating.

"Women do that sometimes." Doctor Brian had explained to him. "Go off their feet awhile until you can get them goin' again. It's an attention getter. It'll pass."

Celia had never been one to do that sort of foolishness, but then she'd never lost a baby before either. Besides, Doc Brian must know. He was, after all, a doctor.

Thomas put the sweet rolls in the lunchbox and continued home, another block, turn left, and down the alley. His back gate was guarded on one side by three garbage cans, one for each tenant, and on the other side by the newly-built trash bin, painted a remarkable shade of green.

What a color! Thomas thought. Probably just mixed all the paint he had left over!

Mr. Winklemann wasn't the worst landlord Thomas ever had, but he certainly was stingy with his money. He wouldn't even replace this uneven brick walk that led to the back door of the flat. It was a bumpy business to shovel the snow, and each spring loose bricks had to be tapped back into place so no one would stumble. But even the worry of someone falling didn't make Mr. Winklemann listen to their complaints.

Thomas went up the stairs, past the landing to the lower flat where old Mrs. Tiergarten had died last month exactly two weeks to the day after Mr. Tiergarten. It had been such a bittersweet sadness, as though she couldn't bear to continue along, alone without him. The new people who were moving in seemed nice enough when Mr. Winklemann had introduced them.

Death comes in threes. The old superstition popped into his mind and was quickly rejected. Unaccepted! Unthinkable!

He hurried up to the second-floor landing: his flat, his home.

Becka, his sister, had the boys dressed and eating breakfast at the kitchen table when he walked in. Thank goodness she was with them taking care of everyone and everything while he was at work. Without her, things would have been impossible.

"Daddy! Daddy!" His sons greeted him with big sticky smiles and oatmeal dribbling from their mouths.

Unappetizing little buggers, Thomas thought, cautiously kissing the top of each head, one light, one dark.

"Hi, Sissy," Thomas whispered to Becka. "There's sweet rolls, and watch out, the box busted last night."

He hurried into what was supposed to be the living room but was now their bedroom, his and Celia's. The flat's three bedrooms had been enough until the boys and Josephine were born. Then they had moved the kids into Sissy's room and Sissy into their room and the living room had become their bedroom. John had the third bedroom, which Thomas shared whenever he worked a night shift. It was all just temporary, they told each other, until they found a bigger place or until John or Sissy moved out. Then again, it could stay this way. He would never ask his brother or sister to leave. This was their home too, for as long as they wished it to be. Their first real home together since Ma had died.

Celia didn't seem to mind. She understood how, after so many years of being shuffled from one "obligated" relative to another, or living in boarding houses here and there, it was good to have a home. A real honest-to-goodness home where one could raid the icebox or make a batch of fudge whenever they felt like it.

Celia was lying in their bed, Josephine snuggled next to her, sucking hungrily on a bottle. Thomas tossed his jacket on a chair and kissed Celia's forehead. It was dry and warm, too warm it seemed.

"She's such a little piggy." Celia said. "Just look how she hangs on to that baba."

He leaned over to kiss his tiny daughter's head. "It's a beautiful morning," he said. "Maybe you'd like to sit outside in the sun later."

Celia nodded.

"Fresh air will make you feel better. Give you an appetite."

She nodded again. "Sounds good."

"I brought some sweet rolls. Want one?"

"Not now. Later."

Thomas picked up the baby. "Come on, little girl. Let's change those pants and see what Aunt Becka has for you."

Thomas returned, washed and shaved and balancing a plate with three halves of the sweet rolls and two cups of coffee, his black, Celia's laced generously with the cream that Sissy saved from the top of the milk bottle.

"Room service," he announced. Celia chuckled.

"Right here, bellboy," she said, patting the bed next to her.

Thomas sat the plate down on the bedside table, kicked off his shoes and slipped in next to Celia. She broke off a piece of the long-john and ate it, to please him, then gave a long, weary sigh and lay down curling toward him. Her head rested against his thigh, hair tumbling across his lap. She reached an arm over his legs and sighed again, contently.

Thomas sipped his coffee while stroking her hair—wild, dark curls he could drown in. Some days he wanted to just bury his face in those incredible waves and simply drown. Such soft, pliable little springs that never failed to fascinate him. A stray curl fell across her forehead and he pulled it back, stretching it full length and watching as it snapped back.

How lovely she was. A delicate, pale flower, and so fragile. Her eyelids, mere cloud shadows over star pools. A rare frail flower, petals so easily crushed, so easily wilted and lost forever.

His heart constricted with fear. How long could she go on like this? Becoming thinner and thinner each day, barely making a dent in the mattress. She must get better soon. She must. It was his constant prayer. His only prayer each morning at Mass.

"Make her well. Make her well," as he knelt before the alter, begging. "Make her well."

Pleading. "Just this one thing: make Celia well, and I'll never ask for another thing. I promise."

Bargaining. "Make Celia well, and I'll come to Mass every day. I'll always do good things in Your name. I'll say a Rosary every day. I'll never lose my temper, never swear. I promise!"

He lay down too, and she rolled over. He shaped his body to hers, gently pulling her close. His chest pressed against her back, his thighs curled against her legs. A perfect fit. He buried his nose in her hair, and she gave that familiar little shiver she always did when he breathed on her neck.

How could one body fit another with such perfection that it was impossible to tell where one began and the other ended? She had to feel better soon. She couldn't just keep fading away, like the mists drifting up from the valley, slowly becoming thinner and thinner until the quietest breeze simply blew them away. He stroked her shoulder tenderly and ran a finger down her arm. Love for her filled him and overflowed. His eyes brimmed with tears. He kissed her shoulder, so soft to his touch. The mole, that ugly stain she hated so much, was nastier-looking than ever, but there was no point in mentioning it. She would only fret about it, and it didn't matter to him. Nothing could distract from her beauty, nothing could flaw her charm.

"Sweetheart," he said, "I have to leave soon."

"Hurry back," she murmured.

Thomas kissed her once more, lingering, reluctant to leave, yet compelled to go. The feel of her, her scent so strangely sweet, held him. In his mind, it seemed he should be able by sheer force of will to allow his strength to flow outward into her. If only she could absorb it, he would give it gladly.

He waited until the last possible moment before slipping out of bed, tucking and shaping the blanket carefully around her back so she wouldn't feel any draft. Then he kissed her hair, soft against his lips.

Thomas put his shoes back on, grabbed his jacket, and hurried down the front stairs and out the door and across the street to Saint Matthew's Church for eight o'clock Mass, to plead once more to his God.

Chapter Two
Sweet Little Josie

After the men left for work and the children had been sent to school, the housewives combed their hair, put on fresh aprons, slipped coin purses into pockets, and, with market baskets in their hands, walked to neighborhood grocery stores to buy the things necessary for the day.

Shopping lists: Bread, if there was no time to bake, yeast, if there was. Canned goods they hadn't "put up" themselves. Tomato soup for a meatloaf. Pineapple for a Sunday treat. Soap flakes, if they didn't make their own, and a bar of Fels Naptha to really cut the grease in their men's work clothes. And after shopping, a sociable visit with some neighbors. There was always a little time to review the neighborhood news and hear a few comments.

A lady patted back a few wisps of hair that had worked themselves loose from the bun that rode on the back of her head. She sighed and recited her list. A soup bone (that's cheap enough), maybe an onion and a bunch of carrots. And a loaf of bread, if Mr. Schick seems agreeable. "Oh, Lord," she prayed under her breath, "don't let the Baxter sisters be there."

She walked the block-and-a-half and entered the store. The Baxter sisters were on their way out.

"Good morning! Good morning!" Everyone so polite and friendly.

"What will it be today, Mrs. McGuiness?"

"Well, have you a nice soup bone?"

Mr. Schick wrapped the bone in waxed paper and tied it with store string. "Anything else?"

"Well, just this small onion, too. And these carrots." She took a deep breath. "And can I pay you

on Friday?" Her words tumbled out and she felt her face redden. "When Mister gets his check?"

"Sure, Missus. What else?"

"Well, just a loaf of bread."

"Aren't you going to make any of your famous noodles for the soup, Mrs. McGuiness?"

"Well, I'd need a couple of eggs then, too."

"Two eggs coming up. I'll put this on your account, then."

"Thank you, Mr. Schick. Thank you."

Every store had a wooden counter with rolls of paper on metal frames for wrapping, and a huge bolt of string suspended overhead for tying the packages. There was a walk-in cooler for meat, and if the owner was experienced, a well-stocked candy counter with shelves of penny candy.

"Yoo-hoo!" Mamas would call out to the closest child. "You! Can you run to the store for me? Lunch I gotta make, and I don't got any bread! You should get for me a rye. Dark rye. Not that white mush!"

"Okay."

Then, she would hand the child a dime. "And you can get some candy with the change."

To the smallest child, The Neighborhood was also small, extending from the back door, down a brick walk between the rear cottage and an old shed, to the alley where the gate was guarded by three metal garbage cans on one side and a large wooden trash bin on the other. It was the row of narrow back yards and wire fences that could be seen from the back gate leading to the alley. The Neighborhood ran around the house, along the narrow walk that bordered a flower garden to the front sidewalk. It stretched four doors this way and to the corner that way. It was made up of Polish flats with high back porches and tiny bungalows with wide front porches, and flats and the alley cottages, the red brick convent next door, the church across the street, and the corner grocery store.

The Neighborhood, to a little child, was just as far as could be seen from home.

A young woman leaned over the porch rail.

"Yoo-hoo!" she called. "Where are you?"

"Here I am!" The child peddled a rusty tricycle rapidly down the sidewalk. "Here I am!"

The young woman smiled. "That's a good girl. Stay where I can see you."

The aroma of coffee drifted in from the kitchen, nudging Josie awake. She lay listening to the sounds of breakfast being served. There was the *scrape, scrape* of a spatula against an iron skillet and the smells of eggs sizzling in bacon drippings that mingled with the coffee. She could hear Aunt Becka talking quietly to her brothers. "Eat your toast. Want some more coffee-milk?"

"Baby" Josephine, now five-year-old Josie, stretched herself awake, but the sweetness of Aunt Becka's bed overwhelmed the smell of coffee and eggs. No place in the world was quite like Aunt Becka's bed. It was the softest, best-smelling place Josie knew of. And safe. Aunt Becka's bed was safe. Whenever Josie was frightened at night or when she was just cold or lonely, she would tip-toe through the darkness and know she was welcomed. Aunt Becka would always lift the covers so Josie could snuggle in next to her and everything would be warm and right again.

Josie opened her eyes. The sun was peeping through from the kitchen; the curtains were puffing out as breezes gave them gentle pushes. The smells from the kitchen were tantalizing. Josie's tummy rumbled uncomfortably but she didn't get up. It was too pleasant lying here listening and feeling and smelling everything around her. Besides, if she did go in the kitchen, Aunt Becka would give her a hug and say, "Go back to bed, little one. It's much too early for you to be up." So, Josie propped her head up on her arms and thought about how wonderful everything was and how special she was.

She had a mother and a daddy who loved her. True, her mother lived in heaven with God instead of at Josie's house, but that was okay. After all, her friend Barbara's father lived there, too. Sometimes she would picture them there, her mother and Barbara's father, looking down at their two little girls, watching as they gave their teddy bears a wagon ride or rode their tricycles up and down the sidewalk.

Josie knew what her mother looked like from the picture that smiled down at her from the top of the bookcase in the living room. Barbara's father, however, remained vague. Josie supposed he looked like all the other Vanders: blonde hair, sparkling blue eyes, and pudgy pink cheeks.

Josie lay and listened to the noises from the kitchen, smelled the wonderful smells, and dreamt, even though she was awake. She reveled in the pleasure of the moment, happy and content with herself and her little world.

Aunt Becka's voice came in from the kitchen, insistent as it always was every morning when the boys left for school. "You can't leave 'til I get my kiss! Bye-bye now! Be good, now! Bye!"

Then Aunt Becka came into her room. "Who's been sleeping in my bed?" She laughed as she leaned over Josie.

Giggling, Josie pulled the blanket over her head and wiggled down as far and as fast as she could, but Aunt Becka tickled her through the covers.

"Who's been sleeping in my bed?" she asked again. "Why, it's a little girl!"

Her fingers continued to chase Josie. "Why, it feels like a Josie!" Aunt Becka pulled the blanket off. "Why, it is! It's a Josie!"

Josie stood up on the bed laughing in delight to receive her good morning hug, feeling very special because she had an Aunt Becka. A mother, a daddy, and an Aunt Becka. How wonderful it all was.

"Go get dressed, Sweets," Aunt Becka said, "while I start your breakfast."

Josie darted down the hall to the tiny bedroom she shared with Will and Danny. The sweet, pungent odor that greeted her told her one of them, probably Danny, had wet the bed. Sure enough, the blankets on the lower bunk were pulled back to allow the stained mattress pad to dry. Aunt Becka didn't always change the bedding when one of them wet. She could only wash on certain days because Mrs. Lewendoski, the downstairs neighbor, shared the laundry area in the basement and there was room for only one family to wash and hang things out to dry at a time.

Josie dressed quickly, putting on an almost out-grown sailor dress she wore for play only. Each time she wore it, Aunt Becka said it would be the last time, but it was Josie's very favorite dress. So, even though it was snug under the arms and far too short, she managed to struggle into it one more time. Then she hurried to the kitchen, carrying her shoes. Every morning they played a game that had started when she was little that consisted of pretending she couldn't remember which foot a shoe went on. Josie would hold her shoes in front of her and Aunt Becka would nod her approval. Sometimes, just to test her, Josie would switch the shoes around and Aunt Becka would frown and shake her head.

Aunt Becka sat at the kitchen table, watching the toaster carefully so the bread would brown nicely, not burn. When it was just right she opened the toaster and flipped the slice over to do the other side. If she wasn't careful, one side or the other would get too brown and have to be scraped and scraped with a knife to get all the burnt part off. The sound of scraping mingling with the eye-stinging scent of smoke meant whomever had been assigned to watch the toaster hadn't done their job very well.

"Can't cry over burnt toast!" Aunt Becka would say while scraping away, but there still was a strong burny taste, no matter how much jelly was on it.

Josie slipped into her chair and took a napkin from the red crocheted ring, an egg already in front of her. Aunt Becka handed her the toast covered with jelly.

"Perfect!" she said smiling.

"Perfect!" Josie agreed taking a bite.

Josie allowed her thoughts to drift until the familiar step-scuff, step-scuff of Uncle John coming up the back stairs and across their landing brought her back to her breakfast. Josie stared at the door in anticipation. Her morning was about to brighten. Uncle John always brought laughter and silliness with him. He played such fun games like lifting her high on his shoulders so she could feel what it was like to be a grownup. He'd haul her around under his arm "dogpatch style" while asking everyone, "Where's Josie? Has anyone seen Josie?"

"Hi, all!" he greeted them as all the little wrinkles around his eyes and mouth explained themselves and the kitchen seemed brighter. His skin was flushed red, and he smelled of outdoors. He put his battered lunch box on top of the icebox, reached up to remove his striped railroad hat—the brim creased to fit his thumb perfectly—and tossed it there too. Then he ran his fingers through his flattened, stick-straight hair as if to free it after the confines of the cap. He took a step-scuff to the table, plopped down in a chair and stretched out the leg he'd broken years ago as a boy. It was obvious that he was tired and aching and in need of a shave and wash.

He took off the old suit coat he wore over his work clothes and turned to hang it neatly on the chair back. Then he pulled off a gray wool sweater, revealing a faded, collarless blue work shirt buttoned to the top.

"Hey, silly face!" he greeted Josie while unbuttoning the shirt. She wiggled delightedly at his attention.

He stood up, pulling the shirt over his head without finishing the unbuttoning, then took off a sweatshirt. Now stripped to his undershirt and looking his normal slim size, he piled all the clothes on top of the suit coat and sat down again, stretching his leg.

"You'd better stop before you're indecent!" Aunt Becka said as she handed him a cup of coffee with little whiffs of steam rising from it.

"Thanks, Sis." Uncle John grinned, and his eyes twinkled as they always did, as though he always had some private little joke and was about to chuckle at it. In fact, it seemed to Josie the only difference between Daddy and Uncle John was their eyes. And not simply because of the "trick the angels had played" on Uncle John by giving him one brown eye and one gray eye. Rather, it was the sadness that was always in Daddy's eyes.

Poor, sad Daddy. His eyes were dark pools of clouds and rain that sometimes overflowed in quiet, noiseless tears. For no reason at all. Tears running silently down his face, to drip off his chin and leave tiny wet spots on his vest and shirt.

It was scary. Something had to be terribly, terribly wrong to cause Daddy to cry like that while never making a sound. It wasn't right that Daddy had to be so sad all alone, so Josie had to be sad too. After all, if you had some candy or something, and you shared it, well, then you had less. So, Josie reasoned, if she took some of Daddy's sadness, he would have less and that would make him feel better sooner. She would crawl on his lap and start to cry too.

"Why are you crying?" Daddy would ask.

"Because you are," Josie would sniffle.

They would cry together until Daddy dried his tears. He'd hold her close, comfort her, and wipe away her tears. Sometimes Danny and Will came over to hug her too. The four of them clung together for a few moments until Daddy started tickling her, and they'd fall in a heap, arms and legs tangled. After a bit, Daddy would become himself again. Not poor, sad Daddy, but wonderful Daddy. And she'd helped take some of the sadness away. She'd made him smile again. For a while.

If only she could make Daddy happy always, take all the tears away so his eyes would twinkle and laugh too. Always. That would be perfect. Like the toast. Perfect.

Josie giggled at the thought of Daddy perfect like a piece of toast, covered with jelly.

"What's so funny, silly face?"

Josie snapped back to the kitchen and breakfast, surprised to see her egg was eaten. Aunt Becka was frying bacon and eggs for Uncle John while he watched the toaster.

"Hey, don't I get a hug anymore? Aren't you my silly face?" Uncle John tugged her arm, then looked at her face and wrinkled his nose. "Or maybe I don't want a hug! Maybe I should call you sticky face!"

Josie got up as he continued pulling her.

"No, I want a hug, I've decided," he said. "Sticky or not, I want a hug."

"A bear hug, Uncle John! I want a bear hug!"

Uncle John stood up, wrapping his arms around her and lifting her off the floor, and buried his face against her neck, making growling noises like a bear. His whiskers rubbed her cheek as he pretended to be nibbling at her ear. Josie squealed in delight.

"Uh, oh!" Uncle John said, setting her down on his chair. Smoke billowed from the toaster, the odor filled the kitchen. Uncle John flipped the side open, but it was too late. The slice of bread was a blackened cinder.

"Hey, Sis, think you can scrape this off?" He lifted the slice gingerly between thumb and fingers. "What do you think, silly face? Want another piece of toast?"

Aunt Becka laughed that even such a simple job was too much for him, and he whined back that it was still a good piece of toast—for anyone but him! It was such fun when they teased each other. Josie hugged herself, pleased with a mother and a daddy and an Aunt Becka and an Uncle John.

"Hey, silly face," Uncle John interrupted her thoughts. "As long as you don't want any more toast, how about some candy?" He handed her two pennies.

"It's too early, John," Aunt Becka protested.

"It won't be by the time she finds Barbara. And gets to the store. And makes up her mind." He wiggled his fingers into her ribs. "And changes her mind. And changes it again. Right, silly face?"

Josie nodded, agreeing with him.

"Go wash your face first," he said. "Don't want the neighbors looking at you, saying, 'Just look! Josie had eggs and toast and, let's see, yes, grape jelly for breakfast!'"

Then Uncle John attacked the bacon and eggs Aunt Becka had fried for him.

Aunt Becka followed Josie into the bathroom and helped her wipe her face. Then she brushed Josie's hair, gently working the tangles out.

"Your hair is so much like your mama's."

The words made Josie feel close to her mother. There were no memories of her for Josie, so she never tired of hearing even the tiniest details. How much fun her mother had been. How well she sewed. How pretty she was. How she'd said this or done that. It all became real for Josie, almost as though she'd actually known her mother. Only usually, whenever the talk started, Daddy got that sad, faraway look and closed himself in the bathroom. Then everyone who'd been enjoying the stories became uneasy. Aunt Becka or Uncle John would change the subject or try to distract her and the boys with a game, or sometimes just tickled them until they were laughing again. Finally, Daddy would come out and rejoin them, but his eyes would be red from crying, and she'd feel terrible because she'd been unable to take away any of his pain.

Aunt Becka checked Josie over, making sure she was clean, polished, and ready to go. Josie, clutching her two pennies, left, first to find Barbara, then to go to Mr. Schick's grocery for penny candy.

She went down the back stairs, carefully grasping the rail. Danny and Will could race down fearlessly, but Josie was still small enough to worry about falling, especially where the stairs turned sharply. Each step was shaped like the slice of a pie, narrow on one side and wide on the other. The boys could leap down over the narrow part, landing with a thump three or four steps down.

Mrs. Lewendoski from another flat would call out, "Stop running!" or "Stop that jumping!" Once her grown-up son, Warren, had stopped them and yelled so loud that Daddy came out onto their landing to hear what was being said. And that was when Josie discovered that where she was standing, on this certain pie-slice step, no one could see her. Not from the top, nor from the bottom. It was just like being invisible. Sometimes, if she felt like "disappearing," Josie sat there quietly, unseen.

But today Josie didn't feel like being invisible. She was on her way to buy candy. Mrs. Lewendoski's back door was open to catch the spring breezes and allow the aroma of baking to fill the hall. The woman loved baking—cookies and cakes with wonderful Polish names Josie couldn't pronounce. Prune-filled, nut-covered delights generously shared with the children. Mrs. Lewendoski was sitting at the kitchen table, her coffee all "saucered and cooled" and a spoon vase pushed to one side as she listened to her story on the radio: "...that asks the question: can a small-town girl find happiness as the wife..."

Josie tip-toed past and turned down the last four steps and out the back door. She blinked a few times to adjust her eyes to the sun. The smell of spring flowers blended with the distant odor of fresh tar and the damp dust stirred by the street sweepers. A hungry robin searched for worms in Mrs. Lewendoski's flower bed. The "bleeding hearts" in full blossom hung in graceful arches over the sidewalk's edge. Josie loved the way the tiny flowers did indeed resemble little hearts with a drop of blood beneath, just like the picture of Jesus that hung in her room.

Josie's favorite flowers, peonies, weren't open yet, but the ants were busy doing their job, so one day soon they would blossom too. But there was no time this morning to watch the activities of ants. She hurried along the narrow walk next to the house.

It was a wonderful morning. Soft breezes caressed her skin and tickled her hair. Mrs. Lewendoski's flower bed, between the walk and the house, had attracted bees that hummed pleasantly. The sunlight filtered through the leaves of the huge tree in the side yard, creating a dance of light and shadow across the walk. It was a splendid tree that all the boys in the neighborhood loved to climb, disappearing among the shadowy greenery.

Uncle John called it "the monkey tree." When Josie asked him why, he just chuckled and gave her one of his silly answers.

"Why do they call apple trees, apple trees?" he'd ask back.

"That's silly," Josie had answered, "because they have apples."

"That's right! That's absolutely right!"

When Josie got to the front sidewalk, she turned left to call for Barbara, Uncle John's two pennies clutched in her hand. She walked past the big, red brick convent where all the Sisters lived, and past the white house where the "Old Busy Bodies" lived. To Josie they appeared to be two old ladies, and not very busy ones either. They walked so slowly and talked so quietly to each other, no one else could hear. Occasionally, they directed some baffling comment to her, like the time she'd been trying to pin down Will and they said, "Young ladies shouldn't wrestle like that." And Uncle John had called from the front porch, "I know, lady! That's why we're tryin' to teach her to do it right!"

"Step-on-a-crack-break-your-daddy's-back," Josie sang to herself.

Not that she really believed stepping on a crack could hurt her daddy, but it didn't hurt to be careful. And she couldn't step on an ant. Mr. Russell had warned her many times, "Step on an ant and it'll rain tomorrow." And he was so smart about such things.

"Oh, Barbara!" Josie called out when she reached the Vanders' front yard. "Oh, Barbara!"

She never knocked on the door or rang the bell. Grownups always scolded, "Why are you bothering us?" when kids did that, so all the kids she knew simply stood in the yard and called their friends to come out and play.

"Oh, Barbara!"

Mrs. Vanders opened the kitchen window. "In a minute, Josie!"

Josie sat on the bottom step of the front porch to wait. She opened her fist to check the pennies. The coins had been held so tightly that there were little red circles on her palm. She studied them, rubbing a finger across them. They didn't hurt at all, but it was fascinating to see penny marks on her hand.

The Old Busy Bodies came out of their front door and locked it behind them. One was carrying a marketing basket, so they must be going to Mr. Schick's. Just the place she and Barbara were heading soon.

The side door opened and Barbara came out, smiling a welcome, and without a word offered Josie a bite of the apple she was eating. Josie showed the two pennies and, still without a word, the two little girls walked to the back porch. Barbara held the apple between her teeth while pulling a tricycle from under the porch. They walked the trike to the front sidewalk, sharing bites of the apple. Barbara sat on the seat and Josie stood on the back, balancing herself by holding one of Barbara's shoulders with her open hand and laying the other hand holding the pennies across the other shoulder. They rode together past the Old Busy Bodies' house, past the convent, past Josie's home, and past two more flats to the corner store.

Josie studied the way Barbara's hair glittered in the sun like the spun gold in fairy stories. It was so unlike her own dark, tangled curls that, no matter how often she and Barbara were together, her friend's hair was a source of fascination.

They parked the trike where no one would trip over it and, taking one last bite each from the apple, Barbara flung the core into the street where some hungry bird might find it. Barbara held the screen door so Josie could go in first. The light was muted because Mr. Schick had lowered the green-and-white striped awning so the vegetables in the window "couldn't cook 'fore I sell 'em!" Inside, everything was shaded and cool. The ceiling fan kept the air moving with a "thump-thump, thump-thump." The faint odor of onion let customers know that one of them must have spoiled, despite the lowered awning.

The Old Busy Bodies were talking quietly to Mrs. Schick. The huge tube of string, suspended from an unseen bracket, turned slowly as Mrs. Schick tugged a length to tie the package of meat she was wrapping. Josie and Barbara headed to the glass candy counter on their right. The Old Busy Bodies turned to stare at the little girls.

"So early," said one with raised eyebrows.

"Well, she has no mother," replied the other one in a mock whisper.

Josie's ears perked up. Who didn't have a mother? How silly. Everyone had a mother.

"Good morning, girls," Mrs. Schick said in a tight voice. She seemed almost uncomfortable.

The two girls pressed their faces against the glass. Josie handed Barbara one of Uncle John's pennies. It was time to decide. Candy raisins, licorice buttons, peanut butter kits, bubble gum, Tootsie Rolls, a lollipop?

Josie knew the two top shelves were penny candy, but sometimes penny candy was down lower among the nickel candy bars. Sometimes a candy bar was a nickel, sometimes two or three cents. Even a penny. She told Danny and Will that a Butterfinger or a Baby Ruth wasn't always a nickel but they never believed her. Whenever *they* went to Schick's, it cost five cents. But if she was alone, Mrs. Schick would ask, "How much do you have, Josie?" And whatever she had, well, that was the price. It was very confusing.

"... runs wild. Look at that dress. Who takes care of her?"

"No mother! Really, runs wild ..."

The Old Busy Bodies were whispering, whispering, heads close together, hiding their words behind wrinkled old hands, occasionally allowing a word or two to escape from their fingers.

"I'll wait on the children first, if you don't mind." Mrs. Schick said to the Old Busy Bodies and nodded toward Josie.

Both sets of icy eyes turned to stare at Josie. "Yes. Yes, of course," said one.

"Hush," said the other. Her eyes moved over Josie like a spider ready to do its death dance for some unfortunate ant: an old, shriveled, gray spider with cold blue eyes.

Josie squirmed, suddenly hot and sweaty. She pressed her forehead against the cool glass of the counter, trying to ignore the old women and concentrate on what to get. Cinnamon bears, chocolate drops, chocolate covered nuts?

"Dress so short ... no mother."

Josie felt their eyes, their prying eyes, penetrating even though her back was turned. Why did they keep staring at her? They couldn't be gossiping about her. She had a mother. No. No, it wasn't her. It couldn't be her. It must be some other little girl. It had to be some other little girl. She had a mother. A beautiful, young mother. They meant some other little girl.

Her legs trembled unexpectedly.

Mrs. Schick handed Barbara a strip of paper with candy dots on it. "What'll it be, Josie?" she asked.

"Kits," Josie answered in a strained, little voice that sounded strange even to her.

Mrs. Schick gave Josie a package of the peanut butter squares and returned to the two women.

Josie paused, then asked, "Who are you talking about?" Her boldness was so unexpected and unaccustomed that it surprised everyone. Especially Josie.

The Old Busy Bodies gasped. "Listening in, no manners. No mother!"

The words, barely audible, reached Josie's ears.

Barbara tore her strip in half to share with Josie. But Josie ignored her and waited for an answer.

"Oh, um," Mrs. Schick stammered, "just some little girl down the street."

Relief swept through Josie. It was just some other little girl they were gossiping about. Of course! How silly! She had a mother, everyone knew that. But that other poor little girl didn't! How awful for her!

Josie followed Barbara out into the sunshine, banging the door behind them. She'd find that other little girl and be her friend, explain how her own mother didn't live with her anymore either, but far away in heaven. Then maybe that other little girl wouldn't feel so alone and strange for having no mother.

Josie began unwrapping her kits to share with Barbara, half and half, the way they did everything. But where was this little girl? She and Barbara were the only little girls she knew on the whole block. Josie's fingers didn't seem to want to work right. They fumbled and shook as she handed Barbara half of the kits.

They *were* talking about her! It wasn't someone else. It was her. She was the one with no mother!

No, her mind reassured her, *your mother is young and pretty. How dare they say you don't have a mother! How dare they talk about you like that! How dare they gossip about you in the store.* It must be some other little girl.

But who was she?

Aunt Becka will know, Josie thought. *She knows everyone in the neighborhood. She'll take me to meet this poor little girl and we'll be great friends.*

Josie bolted for home and for Aunt Becka, who would know the truth—know that Josie wasn't a freak with no mother like the Old Busy Bodies said. "Of course you have a mother, Josie," Aunt Becka would reassure her. "Your mother lives in heaven, that's all."

Josie let the door slam behind her, not caring if Mrs. Lewendoski scolded. She ran up the stairs as quickly as possible.

"Aunt Becka! Aunt Becka!" She rushed into the kitchen, gasping for air.

"In here, Josie," Aunt Becka answered from her bedroom.

Josie rushed to her, fear and indignation tearing at her. What if she was just a *thing* without a mother? Suppose the Old Busy Bodies were right. Aunt Becka would tell her what she needed to hear—that it was some other little girl.

"Aunt Becka!" Josie gasped. "There's a little girl—" Her breath came in painful spasms. "A little girl—"

"What's wrong, Sweets? Calm down." Aunt Becka dropped Daddy's shirt that needed the collar turned. She took Josie's hands in hers.

"Deep breath," she ordered. "Okay, slowly now. What's wrong?"

Josie had to make Aunt Becka say what she wanted to hear. The question had to be phrased just right, or else the alternative was too unbearable to contemplate, even for a moment.

"In the store," Josie began. "In the store they said, they said there's a little girl down the street with ..."

"Yes, Josie?" Aunt Becka urged gently, still holding Josie's hands.

"They said there was a little girl with no mother." There. She'd said it. Now Aunt Becka would say, "How silly. Everyone has a mother."

"They meant you, Josie."

"No! No!" Josie argued. "I have a mother!"

"Josie, they were talking about you."

"But I have a mother!" She pulled Aunt Becka to her feet and tugged her into the living room. "See?" Josie pointed to the smiling face in the silver frame on the bookcase.

"Yes, dear, but she's dead. So you don't have a mother anymore."

Aunt Becka's wonderful voice was saying the thing that Josie couldn't bear to hear.

"No! I have a mother!" Josie continued to protest. "I have a mother! They were talking about some other little girl! Some other little girl down the street!"

Aunt Becka's voice, so soothing, saying the unthinkable: "They were talking about you." She reached out for her, but Josie stepped back, arms folded tightly across her chest, refusing to be touched. Anger replaced fear.

"I do so! There she is! She's living in heaven, but I have a mother. I do!"

"Josie, oh, Josie dear, that means she's dead. When people say someone is in heaven with God, they mean that person is dead. Your mother is dead, Josie. You're the little girl they were talking about."

Her tears came then, releasing all the anger. Tears running down her reddened cheeks in uncontrollable streams. It couldn't be true. She had her mother. Pretty and forever young. There was her picture smiling from the silver frame. How could there be a picture if there was no mother? It was okay if she had to be in heaven with God. Josie could accept that. But not to have one at all was unthinkable. Unbearable.

Too exhausted to argue any longer, Josie allowed Aunt Becka to comfort her, to hold her close, to hug her and gently rub her hair, rock her slowly, murmuring quietly over and over, "There, there, Josie. It's all right, love. It's all right."

Josie looked over Aunt Becka's shoulder at her mother's picture on the bookcase. "I do have a mother," she told herself. "I do."

Aunt Becka carried Josie into the bathroom, sat down on the toilet seat, and ran water into the sink. She held her on her lap and wiped away the tears, crooning, "It's all right, Josie. It's all right."

The hotness left her face, and Aunt Becka's voice calmed her, easing her pain. How long they sat there Josie had no way of knowing, but gradually she felt better. Only inside there was an emptiness she'd never felt before. A strange, hollow emptiness as though part of her was gone forever. Why couldn't Aunt Becka just say, "Of course you have a mother, Josie. How silly! Everyone has a mother."

For days afterwards, Josie asked the others whose picture it was in the silver frame on the bookcase.

"Well, that's your mother, Josie," Uncle John said. "You know that."

Daddy gave her a strange, cold, faraway look and withdrew into himself, sad and quiet. She knew she had crossed the line of unspoken things, things best left alone, things best left unasked. Untouched. Untouchable. What Aunt Becka had said gnawed at her like an unwelcomed rat nibbling away at her peace of mind. Someone had to tell her what she wanted—no, *needed*—to hear. She tried a different approach with her brothers one afternoon while they were sitting on the floor playing checkers.

"That's our mother," she announced, pointing to the picture. "Where does she live?"

"Sure, it is," said Danny.

"You know that," Will added.

"She's dead," Danny continued.

"She don't live nowhere," said Will.

How can that be? wondered Josie. *Did she just disappear? Vanish?* Her mother had to be somewhere.

"But where is she?" Josie persisted.

Danny scratched his head. "I guess she's buried someplace."

"Buried?" That made no sense. Squirrels buried nuts. Pirates buried treasures. But mothers? No one buried mothers!

"Yeah," said Will. "You know, dead and buried."

Josie tried again. Her pretty mother couldn't be *nowhere,* least of all buried someplace like a dog buried a bone. "But I thought she was living."

"Nah."

"She's dead."

Why was everyone telling her the wrong answer?

"But I thought she was living in heaven with God."

Danny and Will looked at her, then at each other.

"Well," Will said, "that's what the nuns say."

"They mean she's dead though," Danny explained.

"How can living mean dead?" Josie asked, her voice rising unsteadily.

Danny ran his fingers through his hair, then stood up, moving beside her, adjusting his wire-rimmed glasses as he studied their young mother's face in the picture.

"You know, Josie, I think you're right." He slipped his arm around his small sister. "She's living in heaven with God."

Will joined them creating a little triangle.

"Yeah, I think so, too. That's a nice place to live."

Josie's heart fluttered in delight. She had been right all along. The three of them stared at the photo as their mother smiled lovingly back at them.

"Does she see us?" Josie asked.

"It's just a picture, Josie."

"Pictures don't see."

"I mean from Heaven."

Danny shrugged. "Why not?"

Will nodded in agreement. "Sure, why not?"

They continued to stand there, pondering it all until they heard the kitchen door open. Daddy had come home with a basket of groceries. Knowing the sight of them looking at their mother's picture and discussing her among themselves would distress him, Danny and Will returned to the checkers. Josie plopped next to them, pretending to watch.

Daddy settled himself in his corner of the couch. He opened a bottle of beer, took a sip, leaned back, and sighed a long deep sigh.

Poor Daddy, Josie thought as she crawled on his lap. Daddy set the beer down and snuggled Josie close to him. She loved the smell of him, fresh from outside, tobacco from his cigarettes, the soap he washed with. All these things combined to make Daddy smell his special way. Josie snuggled into his embrace, his fingers playing with her earlobe, and felt the scratchiness of his trousers on her leg. Everything was wonderful again. She had a daddy and a mother who loved her. True, her mother lived in heaven with God.

But that was okay.

Chapter Three
Daddy's Story

No one ever ate at the dining room table. The kitchen table was for eating. In the morning, as family members came and went, Aunt Becka fed them. Danny and Will, before they left for school; Daddy, when he went to work or, if he was on third shift, when he came home; Uncle John, if and when he showed up; and finally, last of all, Josie ate her breakfast. Aunt Becka managed bites of toast or bacon in between feeding everyone else.

At lunch the boys came home for soup or a sandwich that they'd gulp as fast as possible, then dart out the door to join their friends on the playground across the street. Josie would finish eating alone. Aunt Becka had her lunch afterwards, while reading a book or listening to the radio. It was her special quiet time, so Josie had to stay indoors and be "a little mouse" for a while.

Sometimes Josie played house under the dining room table. She'd get all her doll babies and pretend the chair seats were their beds. It made a very nice house, but no one ever ate at the dining room table.

There were times when a jigsaw puzzle would be spread out across the table. If anyone walked past and saw where a piece fit, they'd add it to the picture. When it was finally all put together, Aunt Becka would leave it for a few days until everyone had admired it; then she'd push the pieces into a box and trade it with one of her friends for another one. Sometimes they'd end up putting together the same puzzle again, but it didn't matter. By then all would have forgotten where the pieces fit.

The dining room table was for homework, like her brothers did. Figuring and writing: Danny at the end and Will around the corner from him, heads together—light and dark—barely touching as they pondered their important business. Josie could hardly wait until she could join them, putting all sorts of wonderful things on paper.

Daddy and Uncle John used the dining room table for their chess games. Sometimes the game waited days for them to return, and woe to the kid who fussed with the pieces. Even Aunt Becka dusted around them, leaving the pieces untouched.

Josie used the table for coloring or drawing. She much preferred drawing so she could fill the blank pieces of paper with flowers and smiling people. But paper was hard to get. Occasionally she used the backsides of Danny's and Will's school papers, but those were scarce since the nuns always warned, "Waste not, want not." Aunt Becka saved wrapping paper from the store for her, but all too often it would be sticky or torn or waxed and not suitable for drawing on. So, she usually had to be content with just coloring in a book.

She always colored the way Danny had shown her, press the crayon hard around the edge then fill in the rest of the space lighter. But the colors she used were all her own.

"Dogs aren't those colors!" Danny said.

"Whoever heard of a blue dog?" Will added.

Josie didn't listen to them. Her brothers, who were so smart and knew so much, sure could be dumb sometimes! "Dogs that wear aprons and bake cookies are blue!"

They just shook their heads at her foolishness.

Tonight, they were busy at the dining room table doing their homework. Josie sat with them transforming flat white nothings into magical creatures of rare and unusual colors.

The old rocker in the corner *creaky-creaked* as Aunt Becka mended socks from her bottomless basket, needle and yarn reweaving heels and toes so at least one more wearing could be had.

Daddy and Uncle John were engrossed in a chess game at the

opposite end of the dining room table from Danny and Will. Josie loved the little horse pieces called "knights." When she was little, she'd thought they were nights, like night and day. One evening as Daddy and Uncle John played their game, she asked, "Are all the black ones nights?"

"No, silly face," Uncle John answered, holding up a pretty black horse. "These are the knights. Doesn't matter if they're black or white."

Josie studied the black horse. "Why are they called nights? Why not horses?"

Uncle John chuckled. "Good question," he said. "You get to answer that one, Thomas."

"Knights rode horses, sweetheart," Daddy said, "but horses look more ..." He paused. "They look more interesting than knights."

Josie was confused. "Knights?"

"Soldiers," Danny told her.

"From when there were kings and queens," added Will.

"Really, Daddy?"

"That's right."

Daddy lifted her onto his lap and showed her each piece and explained how they worked. There was a king and a queen and a bishop and a piece that looked like a tiny tower but the only one Josie could remember was the knight. And that the knight was different because it could jump over the others.

As Josie colored in the flowers on a baby dog's bib, she heard Uncle John say, "It's your turn."

She glanced at them. Daddy was just staring at nothing the way he did sometimes.

"Come on, Thomas. It's your turn," persisted Uncle John.

Daddy snapped awake even though he hadn't been asleep. "Sorry. Guess I'm not in the mood."

Josie became alert. Something was wrong. But what? She listened carefully.

"You've got to snap out of it," Uncle John said.

Daddy nodded.

"Get on with your life."

Daddy stood up abruptly, knocking the chess pieces about. Josie stopped coloring, crayon paused in mid-air as she listened intently. Daddy walked to the window and stared out into the darkness.

"Easier said than done," he said in a voice that sounded as if something was caught in his throat.

Everyone stopped what they were doing. The boys stopped writing and Aunt Becka's chair stopped creaking. Josie dropped her crayon. Uncle John moved next to Daddy and put an arm across his shoulder.

"I know, brother," he said, "but you've got to get on with your life. Celia would want you to."

"You don't know that!" Daddy turned, pushed the arm away, and glared at Uncle John. "I won't do to them what Da did to us."

"There are nice women around. You'll find one who'll be a good mother."

"No! I won't put my kids through that." He faced Uncle John, his eyes dark with anger. "Have you forgotten?"

Daddy's face filled with pain as tears washed the anger away, overflowing down his cheeks to be brushed away with the back of his hand. Josie got out of her chair and went to him, to take care of him, to share the pain and sadness and make it go away, to make Uncle John stop saying things that upset Daddy and made him cry.

"I haven't forgotten! How could I?"

Josie wrapped her arms around Daddy's waist and let his pain seep into her, tightening her throat and making her chest ache. Only she understood the depths of it. Only she could help ease it. *Be quiet, Uncle John,* she thought. *Be quiet and let my Daddy alone!*

But Uncle John continued. "Just because Da made a mistake, doesn't mean—"

"Can't divorce if you marry a mistake," Daddy interrupted Uncle John. His hand, still damp from tears, stroked Josie's cheek gently. Josie's eyes brimmed too, tiny drops ready to join his. Poor sad Daddy.

If he didn't want to marry a "Miss Take," he didn't have to. Why would Daddy want to marry her anyway? Someone no one had ever heard of before.

Daddy bent and kissed the top of Josie's head.

"Thomas, I'm—"

"I'm going for a walk!" Daddy announced, removed her arms, grabbed his coat from the hook, and bolted out the door.

"Thomas," Uncle John repeated softly. "Thomas, please."

The sound of Daddy's footsteps echoed down the front stairs, growing fainter and fainter, followed by a slam and a click as the lock snapped tight.

Uncle John looked at Aunt Becka. "I'm sorry, Sis. I didn't mean to upset him."

"I know, Johnny," she said. "It's not your fault. No one's fault, I guess."

"He's got to get on with his life. It's been almost five years! For God's sake, how long—"

"I know. I know. I worry, too."

"He's got to get over it."

How could Daddy "get over it?" They didn't even understand his pain. Only Josie could understand. Only she had that ability. To understand, and with that, had the responsibility to take it away. And now she'd failed to absorb enough of his pain. The tears that had been lurking in the corners of her eyes overflowed and trickled down her cheeks.

"Don't cry, Josie," one of her brothers said.

"Come on, Josie," Uncle John scooped her up under his arm, "dog-patch style." "Let's go color." He pointed to the boys' school books. "Get to work," he said.

Dutifully, her brothers returned to their papers while Josie, arms and legs dangling, was hauled back to her place at the dining room table and plopped in her chair.

"Whatcha got there, silly face?" he asked. "Pink dogs! When did you ever see a pink dog?" He poked her ribs, tickling her. Unable to help herself, Josie responded with giggles. Uncle John continued to tease her with wriggling fingers until her tears were chased away by her laughter.

"That's better. Can I color, too?" Uncle John asked, pulling a chair next to her.

Josie turned the page so two uncolored pictures showed. Uncle John began coloring some dogs making sandcastles. She used her blue crayon to start outlining a dog-child holding a small shovel and filling a sand bucket. Uncle John teased and chatted, and the old rocker began to *creaky-creak* as Aunt Becka returned to her mending.

Josie fretted to herself as she colored. *Well,* she scolded herself, *I'll just have to try harder*.

Later, Aunt Becka put her in bed, heard her prayers, and kissed her. "Goodnight. Don't let the bedbugs bite."

Josie worried about Daddy. Was he all right outside, all alone in the dark? She missed him when he wasn't there to tuck her in. She felt guilty because she hadn't been able to stop his sadness, so, when she finally fell asleep, the "Spiders-of-the-Night" engulfed her and she woke, shaking with terror, her heart beating wildly. She listened cautiously. Were there spiders there in the darkness for real, waiting for her to move so they could find her? Find her and suck her dry, leaving only her empty shell?

Danny's and Will's quiet breathing from their bunks on the opposite side of the room was a comfort, in and out. The house settled itself like an old woman in a rocking chair, wheezing and sighing, creaking the way it always did at night.

Then she heard the muffled sounds of the radio playing. Quietly, Josie slipped out of bed and tip-toed to the door to peek and see who was up. The lamp was lit in the living room, so she took a step out into the dining room. Daddy was slumped in "his corner" of the couch, head resting on his propped up right hand, seemingly half asleep. A cigarette smoldered in his ashtray and a bottle of beer sat on the table next to the radio. He looked so lonely. Josie crept to him, shivering as the night coolness invaded through her thin pajamas. Daddy opened his eyes.

"Well, sweetheart," he said, "can't sleep either?"

He lifted her to his lap and she snuggled close. Daddy's touch, Daddy's voice filled her with such love and comfort, it was almost unbearable. Even his odor was special: the soap he washed with, the cigarettes he smoked, the faint whiffs of sweat. Tonight, she noticed a new smell, sour and unpleasant. She buried her face against his chest and tucked her nose between his shirt and vest where the sourness couldn't penetrate.

"You're so cold," Daddy said.

His jacket lay next to him on the couch, so he covered her with it. Everything was so warm and wonderful, safe and cozy, surrounded by Daddy and his love. Quietly, Daddy began speaking, almost as though to himself.

"My mother. You're named after her, in part." He gave a small nudge, and Josie nodded in acknowledgment. He continued. "My mother died years ago when I was almost twelve. There was this terrible flu epidemic. 1918. And Mama caught it. No one would come in the house. They were so afraid. They'd knock at the door and when Da answered, they'd back away holding handkerchiefs over their nose and mouths. 'How is she?' they'd ask. The only one who came in was Auntie Claress. She wasn't really our auntie. She was an old black woman from down the block. Mama had us call her 'auntie' to show our respect. 'She's lived too long, been my friend too long for you children to just use her first name.'"

He paused, leaning his head back, and, for a moment, Josie thought he'd fallen asleep.

"Most people, even kids, just used a black's first name in those days, but we always called her 'Auntie Claress.'"

Josie nodded again, enjoying the story even if she didn't understand all the nuances of courtesy.

"Anyway, Old Auntie Claress came every day to help out. She cooked and cleaned, even bathed Mama to lower the fever. And once when Da tried to pay her, she got real angry. 'Ms. Delight, she comes when I'm down and feeling poorly. Brings me whatev'a I need. Never asks for no money! Never! Now it's my turn to do for her. Don't you be cheatin' me outta returning her kindness!'

"Da never offered again. After that he'd just say, 'Thank you, ma'am.' Just that. 'Thank you, ma'am.'

"Then Johnny got sick, then me. We lay together in the big bed, Mama across from us in another bed. Auntie bathed us and spooned soup down us and fretted to Da. 'Get them boys outta that room! They gonna suck the strength from their mama!'

"But Da didn't listen.

"I remember Da asking, 'Want some soup?' I did, and as he left, I saw this tiny black dot up in the corner near the ceiling and wondered what it was. It started rolling toward me, getting bigger and bigger. When it hit my feet, I remember yelling. When I woke up, it was three days later and Mama had died. I couldn't even go to the funeral. Couldn't see her one last time."

Daddy stopped, reaching for his beer, and took a long drink, then lit another cigarette. The smoke drifted pleasantly to engulf them. The movement disrupted her comfort, but soon he leaned back and resumed his story.

"After Mama died, Da hardly ever stayed home. We lived at home, John and Becca and me, but Da dropped Sissy and Danny off to live at Aunt Rebecca's and Grandma's. Sissy was five, maybe six, and Danny hardly more'n a baby. He looked just like Mama, Danny did. Blue eyes. Sparkling blue eyes and golden red hair. Just looking at him made you think of Mama, her smile on Danny's lips. Her laughter.

"Then one day Da comes home with this, this *woman*! All painted up like a new outhouse. A real 'uptown' woman. Know what I mean?"

Josie shook her head.

"No, I guess not," Daddy said.

"'This is your new mother,' he said. As though anyone, especially one like her, could ever be our mother! Take Mama's place! The 'new mother' never fed the men who came to the back door, or tried to find a piece of work for 'em so's they'd keep their pride. She refused Auntie Claress' gifts: vinegar pie, peach cobbler. 'Won't eat no food from no burr head like her.' Tried to stop us from even seeing her. But John and I, we'd go there anyway. Auntie Claress fed us, hugged us, fretted and fussed over us. God bless her. I think we'd have died ourselves without her. 'Your poor Mama,' she'd say. 'Hardly cold and her boys runnin' around all raggity and hungry! Shame! Shame! Shame!'

"Da brought the little ones, Becka and Danny back. Danny, the image of Mama. That's why that woman didn't like him."

Josie listened carefully. She'd heard bits and pieces of this story before, but never from Daddy who rarely talked this much.

"She never watched him. I told her and told her, 'Danny's too little to be outside alone, unwatched.' She just ignored me, like I was nothing. Just kept filing her nails or reading her fancy books. I told her, 'I found Danny in the road again!' She looked at me all icy. 'If ya yell at me again, I'll tell your pa to lick ya good!'

"He would've too. All he cared about was her. 'Mind your mother,' he'd say. 'She ain't our mother!' I'd answer. 'She ain't fit to be a dog's mother!' And Da took his belt and whipped me. But I never called her mother!

"Then Danny got hit by a car. Three blocks from home! Dirt ground into his little face. Even the undertaker said he'd cried himself at this pretty child brought in all broken and dirty!

"'Three blocks!' he'd said. 'What was a little fella like him doing three blocks from home?'

"'I was takin' a nap,' she'd whined. 'I get tired takin' care of all the kids.'

"'Well, you wasn't takin' care of Danny!' Da finally saw what he'd done. 'Married a mistake,' he said after that. 'A real big mistake.' She never did care at all about Danny. He was too much like our mother and she knew it. Couldn't stand it."

Daddy took another drink and leaned back, silent now. The story was over.

Josie felt the lump in her throat grow, crowding her heart, making her chest hurt. She swallowed, not wanting to move and break the spell. Poor Daddy. First his mother, then Baby Uncle Danny. Everyone died on him like that, even her mother. That's why he worried about marrying a mistake. Maybe Danny or Will would get killed. But she'd never leave him. Even if he did marry a mistake, she'd never leave him. Never!

Josie closed her eyes and matched her breathing with his. The next morning, she was surprised to find herself in bed. She stretched herself awake and wondered if the night before had only been a dream. Just a dream.

How could it be that such sweetness and sorrow could be so intertwined, like a spider web covered with dew drops, sparkling in the early morning sunlight? Yet, still lurking somewhere, was the spider.

Chapter Four
The Naughty Boy

One morning, Aunt Becka spread a newspaper on the floor and emptied the garbage into the center. Then she wrapped it all in a tight, neat bundle tied with a store string and handed it to Josie to carry out. Josie went down the back stairs slowly, holding the rail with one hand and the bundle with the other, past Mrs. Lewendoski's back door, then outside.

She walked down the brick path to where three garbage cans stood in a row near the fence next to the alley. Josie thought this walkway was wonderful, almost magical. Daddy and Uncle John both complained that its unevenness made shoveling snow a bumpy business, and her brothers whined that skating on it was impossible. Josie knew from experience that one couldn't run on it without risking a skinned knee. Even Mr. Russell grumped in the spring when he re-tapped all the bricks winter had loosened. But Josie loved the way the tiny, green plants grew up between them—so fragile, yet strong—pushing upward against the worn gray bricks to spread their tiny leaves and occasionally, a delicate blossom.

She took a deep breath and held it while the lifting the lid from their can and peered in. Flies— black and shiny green, fascinating and repulsive—crawled around the smelly contents. Josie watched until she could no longer hold her breath, then dropped the bundle in, quickly slamming the lid back on before the swarm rose up to escape. She heard them buzzing and pinging as some hit the lid, and all sorts of questions began to form in her mind.

"Where do flies come from?" her mind raced with questions to ask Aunt Becka later. "Can flies see in the dark? Why do they like garbage?"

"Hey, girl!"

Josie jumped, the harsh wind of fear blowing her questions away. Her heart seemed to stand still. Suddenly the beautiful morning was gone and she felt cold. Cold and afraid. The Naughty Boy from down the alley was right outside her gate, grabbing at her. Reaching through the gate and grabbing at her.

"Hey, little girl!" he yelled wetly through his oversized tongue. Thick, disgusting slobber ran down his chin. His strange little eyes glittered at her. His grubby paw-hand reached for her. How could he be here? His mother knew how naughty he was. Didn't she always keep him locked safely away from the rest of them? Didn't she keep him home from school so he couldn't hurt any of them? How could he be here, right outside her gate, yelling at her, grabbing at her, frightening away the beautiful day?

Josie ran back along the brick walk, praying she wouldn't fall and be caught, hoping he wouldn't pick up a rock and throw it, like he did whenever any kid walked past his backyard. She ducked around the corner of Mr. Russell's house and leaned back to catch her breath before cautiously peeking around. The Naughty Boy was still there, trying to open the gate by pushing at it instead of sliding the catch. He threw his whole body against the fence, just like he did to his own fence whenever any kid walked past, yelling and heaving rocks or mud clots at them in the summer, snowballs in the winter. Once Josie had seen him throw the toy soldiers he had been playing with at her brothers. They had run down the alley yelling, "Retard! Retard!" over their shoulders until they were safely away and the Naughty Boy's voice could barely be heard in the distance.

Josie judged the distance to her back door and decided even if the Naughty Boy managed to open the gate, she would still be able to make it to safety.

"What's the matter, Josie?" Mr. Russell had come out on his porch and her terror eased now that a grownup was there to chase the boy away. But all she could do was stare, speechless.

"Josie, what is it?" Mr. Russell repeated.

Josie blinked and cleared her throat. "It's him! That Naughty Boy!"

"Naughty boy? Who? What naughty boy?"

Mr. Russell stepped carefully off the porch to look toward the alley.

"That Naughty Boy from down the alley. I can't remember his name. Re—Re—something."

"Oh, Josie. It's just Francis. He won't hurt you. Come on."

Mr. Russell started walking back to the alley, picking his way along the brick walk with his cane. Reluctantly, she followed behind him.

"Hello, Francis!" he said, opening the gate. Shifting his cane to his left hand, he held out his right one. The Naughty Boy hesitated a moment, then reached to shake hands. Mr. Russell gently pulled him through the gate into the yard. Josie stepped backwards, bumping into the trash box.

"Josie, this is Francis. Francis, this is Josie," Mr. Russell introduced them.

The Naughty Boy stared with his strange, scary little eyes. Josie returned his look, her eyes wide with fear. She stepped a little closer to Mr. Russell.

"Say 'hello,' Josie," Mr. Russell said.

"Hello," Josie answered obediently.

"'Ello, Jodee," Francis said wetly, at the same time.

Josie peered from behind the safety of Mr. Russell's leg, thinking if he'd just keep his tongue where it belonged, he wouldn't look so bad. Mr. Russell led the Naughty Boy back along the walk to his front porch. Josie followed along, making sure not to get too close.

The three of them sat down on Mr. Russell's front steps, Mr. Russell in the middle with a child on each side.

"Say there, Mrs. Russell!" he called out to his wife. "We'd like some cookies out here!"

Mr. Russell always called his wife "Mrs. Russell" and she always called him "Mr. Russell." They never used pet names like "dear" or "honey" or even first names like other grownups did. Perhaps Mr. and Mrs. Russell never had first names like other people did. Perhaps "Mr." and "Mrs." *were* their first names. Josie had reasoned it all out.

Mrs. Russell came to the screen door to see who the "we" was, then disappeared into the shadows of her living room, only to reappear in a few minutes carrying a small plate of cookies.

"Mr. Russell," she said, handing him the plate.

Josie only took one. Mrs. Russell's cookies were often stale, so she had learned it was best to take one at a time, just in case. The Naughty Boy took two, one in each hand. Sure enough, the cookie was stale. Even the raisins were hard, but the Naughty Boy didn't seem to notice, he ate them so fast, then took two more when they were offered.

"Francis is a good boy," Mr. Russell assured Josie. "He's not naughty, just different. It's okay to be different. We're all different in some way or 'nother. Makes us more interesting, don't you think, Josie?" Mr. Russell patted Francis softly on the head. "Francis shows his difference more'n the rest of us. That's all."

Josie looked across as Francis, cookie crumbs scattered down his shirt front, began to lick his fingers, seemingly unaware that Mr. Russell was talking about him. He smiled and laid his head on Mr. Russell's knee.

"Nice man," he said quietly, wrapping his arm around Mr. Russell's leg. "Nice man."

Josie nodded. Now that she looked him over, Francis didn't seem quite so scary: a bit messy eating cookies, but not too unlike other boys she knew.

Mrs. Russell came to retrieve the plate and handed Mr. Russell a damp washcloth. "Sure you don't want another cookie, Josie?" she offered.

Josie shook her head.

Mr. Russell wiped Francis' mouth off. "Here, wipe your hands,

Francis," he said, handing him the washcloth. Francis rubbed each hand awkwardly, then gave the cloth back to Mr. Russell.

"Come on, Josie." Mr. Russell stood. "We'd better walk Francis back home 'fore his mother gets too worried."

As the children stood to leave, Francis reached for Mr. Russell's hand, but upon noticing his cane, moved to hold the other hand. He then reached to hold Josie's. She pulled away, hands quickly thrust behind her.

Then she looked into his smiling blue eyes and slowly allowed him to take her hand. It felt like any other hand, warm and slightly damp from the wiping. She looked at his stubby little fingers with dirt under the nails, like boys have sometimes, and smiled back.

Together they walked down the alley towards Francis' backyard.

"Francis! Francis! Where are you?" a lady's voice called out, shrill and urgent. "Francis, answer me!"

"He's here, Mrs. Holliday, right here," Mr. Russell answered.

"Oh, dear," Francis' mother sounded out of breath, almost as if she were about to cry. She came half running to her back gate. "It frightens me so when he ..." Her voice trailed off when she saw Josie holding Francis' hand. She kept staring while taking a key from her apron pocket to unlock the padlock and remove the chain.

"It's okay, Mrs. Holliday," Mr. Russell said. "Francis is a good boy. He wanted to meet Josie, that's all. But he's a good boy, aren't you, Francis?" He nudged the boy.

Francis giggled, shyly rubbing his face against Mr. Russell's arm.

"You're so kind, Mr. Russell, but ..." Francis' mother glanced nervously around and lowered her voice. "But not everyone is, you know," she whispered. "Not everyone is."

Francis pulled away from Josie and Mr. Russell, and flung himself into his mother's arms, hugging her around the waist as tightly as he could. She returned his hug and kissed the top of his head.

"Say goodbye to Mr. Russell, Francis," his mother said. "And thank him for bringing you home."

Francis thanked Mr. Russell and gave him a hug. Then before Josie could react, Francis hugged her too. A tight, warm bear hug that almost took her breath away.

"Bye, Jodee," he said in his funny, wet sort of way. His mother wrapped the chain around the post and locked it again. Francis waved shyly over his shoulder and followed his mother to the house.

Josie and Mr. Russell turned to go home.

"Why is he like that, Mr. Russell?"

"Well … well … outside he's growing up, but inside," Mr. Russell paused, seeking the right words. "Inside he's still just a very little boy. Always will be. Sometimes, when the inside can't … well, can't do what the outside should be able to do, *wants* to do, he … well, he seems strange to us."

"He scared me."

"He didn't mean to, Josie. You know that, don't you?" Mr. Russell patted her head. "You know that now, don't you?"

Josie nodded. Mr. Russell opened the gate and hand-in-hand they walked up the brick path. Josie looked down at the frail, little plants sticking up between the rock-hard bricks. How wonderful they are, she thought, growing so bravely there, where they aren't expected and don't belong. ♡

Chapter Five
Barbara Moves

There were so many wonderful things about Aunt Becka that it was hard for Josie to decide just which one thing was the *most* wonderful. Aunt Becka made sure Josie ate when she was hungry. She fixed Josie's hair, making sure she was clean and pretty. She gave hugs and kisses along with Mercurochrome and Band-aids. She made Josie feel like the most important, special little girl in the whole world. She turned tears into smiles. No wonder she always had so many friends "popping in" to visit her.

Aunt Becka's best friend Theresa Ryan would come over, and sometimes Beth from across the alley joined them. They laughed and giggled together, fixing each other's hair different ways, like movie stars wore theirs, or painting each other's nails. All sorts of grownup things. And best of all, they included Josie in their "girl talk."

Both Beth and Theresa had known Josie's mother, and occasionally they mentioned her. How beautifully she'd sewn, how clever she'd been, how smart. How much Josie resembled her. Josie felt so warm then, proud of her mother. She never heard enough, never tired of hearing more, no matter how trivial. She feasted on these tidbits, savoring each tiny detail. At night, lying in the darkness of her bedroom, Josie relived the memories of others as though they were her own. She wove them together with a few photographs and the picture on the bookcase to get a shadowy substance of her mother: a dreamy, gossamer understanding of who and what her mother had been.

Aunt Becka, Theresa, and Beth also talked a lot about boys: not boys like Danny and Will, but men like Uncle John and Daddy. Only they called them "boyfriends" or "admirers." Not surprisingly, Aunt Becka had the most admirers.

There was J.D. with bright red hair who called everyone "Kiddo." He was nice enough, Josie supposed. When Aunt Becka's friends had built a huge snowman in the side yard, J.D. went with her to find small pieces of coal in the dark, spooky, old bin, and then lifted her to put them in for eyes and a big smiling mouth.

There was James, who was tall and quiet, never saying much to Josie except a disinterested "That's nice," to whatever she told him. James didn't visit often since he'd moved away because of his job. As everyone knew, "You've got to go where the work is." Even if you didn't want to.

And there was Del, so tall. He was taller than either Daddy or Uncle John and had tiny wrinkles around his eyes and a brown mustache that tickled when he kissed her ear. He'd tease, asking, "You gonna marry me someday, Cutie Pie?" Everyone knew it was Aunt Becka he really wanted to marry.

He'd talk baseball with the boys. "How about them Bums?" he'd ask.

Del had given Aunt Becka the little bunny-fur kitten that always sat on her bed after she made it. Josie loved to bury her face in its softness until her nose tickled, pretending it was real and not stuffed.

Josie and Aunt Becka agreed, Del was their favorite admirer.

"Only, he's not Catholic," Aunt Becka said.

Josie didn't really understand exactly what "Catholic" meant. She knew *they* were Catholic, which was good. So, "Not Catholic" must be bad. Del wasn't bad in any way she could see, but maybe he was in some grownup way she didn't know about. So, she listened carefully whenever the subject of Del came up. It wasn't always easy because sometimes his name wasn't mentioned, so Josie wouldn't know who was being discussed.

"Maybe he'll convert," Daddy said.

Aunt Becka shook her head. "No. He was very adamant about that."

"Does it matter?" Uncle John asked. "As long as your children are baptized. Raised Catholic."

Aunt Becka just shrugged and looked unhappy.

Josie, not understanding the words and their meanings, knew only that her aunt was sad, all because of Del being "Not Catholic," so it must be a terrible, terrible thing.

It didn't matter for long because Del stopped coming, and Josie missed him. She knew better than to ask about him; it might make Aunt Becka sad again, the way Daddy got at the mention of her mother. And maybe she wasn't supposed to wonder where Del was or why he didn't visit any more. He was "Not Catholic" and that was a bad thing.

Like Aunt Becka, Josie had a best friend of her own. Her friendship with Barbara was wonderfully simple. They were the only two little girls on this end of the block, so they played with one another as often and for as long as the grownups allowed. If a grownup called one of them to come in, no matter how much fun they were having, the game ended. But as soon as one little girl was allowed outside again, she'd "call" for the other.

They shared everything they had. One half of anything Josie had was Barbara's, and in turn, one half of everything Barbara had was Josie's, equally and without question or discussion: cookies, pennies, apples, or raisins. Half and half. Always.

They shared their toys too. Barbara's tricycle was newer than Josie's old, rusty one with the wobbly seat. So, Barbara peddled up and down the sidewalk while Josie rode, standing on the back. Then, without a word, Barbara would climb off and they reversed, Josie doing the peddling now.

Josie's wagon was the largest, so when they gave their teddy bears rides, it was always with her silver and blue coaster. Sometimes they tied the wagon to Barbara's tricycle, using an old jump rope, and took turns peddling and riding back and forth between Barbara's house and

Mr. Schick's on the corner.

They talked very little and then only about what they were playing, so whatever Josie knew about Barbara, she learned from Aunt Becka or other grownup conversations. She listened carefully, absorbing and analyzing each bit of information.

Barbara's father was in Heaven too. In fact, Aunt Becka remarked once how he had "passed on" before Barbara had even been born. *Poor Barbara!* Josie thought. *At least my mother waited until I was born before leaving.* The knowledge that her mother had held her, stroked her, bathed and fed her, even though there was no memory of it, was very important to Josie. But poor Barbara had never even felt her father's touch at all.

Barbara had four older brothers, but only one still lived at home.

"Jimmy takes such good care of his mother," the Busy Bodies said. "Not like those other rough- necks of hers."

Josie had seen all of Barbara's brothers at one time or another and their necks looked just fine to her, like any other neck. Unless there was something under their collars that she didn't see.

Mrs. Vanders was older and Barbara had been a "surprise." This was very confusing to Josie. How could a little girl be a surprise? Presents were surprises. Candy bars in Uncle John's jacket pocket and sweet rolls Daddy brought home for breakfast were surprises. Sometimes Aunt Becka made chocolate pudding for dessert as a surprise. But little girls?

It took a while but Josie finally figured it out.

Whenever the doorbell rang and it was someone unexpected, Aunt Becka would say, "What a surprise!"

Josie pictured Barbara as a tiny baby, yellow hair glowing in the sunlight, stretching on tippy-toes to ring her mother's bell, and Mrs. Vanders opening the door to see Barbara, exclaiming, "Why Barbara! What a surprise!"

The latest information Josie was trying to understand was what Aunt Becka meant when she told Daddy, "Someone's going to be unhappy when Barbara moves."

Daddy nodded in agreement and said, "She'll get over it soon enough."

Aunt Becka answered, "I know. Still, I feel bad for her."

Who was going to be unhappy? Why should Barbara's moving hurt anyone? She moved all the time, riding her tricycle, running, and jumping ... all kinds of moves and the only time anyone was unhappy was if she fell and skinned her knee or elbow. And then that "someone" was Barbara.

Josie thought and thought, but, unable to figure out what the grownups meant, forgot about it.

An extraordinary day began for Josie when Aunt Becka woke her, saying, "Get up, Sweets. Barbara's mother is dropping her off here while she moves."

There was that mysterious "move" again, but Josie had no time to ponder it. She dressed quickly. In spite of their close friendship, Barbara had never actually been in her house, nor had Josie ever gone beyond Barbara's back hall. It was so exciting, brightening up an otherwise gloomy morning that normally would have been boring, with Josie just waiting for the clouds to lift.

"Thank you so much for having her," Mrs. Vanders said to Aunt Becka. "It makes moving much easier."

"I'm glad to do it," Aunt Becka answered. "It's too bad that you've got to move in all this rain."

"Well, there's really no choice. And my boys have some tarps to cover things. Does make a lot of mud tracked in to be cleaned up."

Since Barbara had never been in the house before, she had to be shown everything: Josie's dolls and doll bed, her books in the bookcase, and the picture of her mother sitting on top, even the chess game on the dining room table. Then the two little girls played paper dolls, dividing them into two families that visited back and forth from their homes under opposite ends of the cedar chest.

At lunch time, the boys came crashing through the door, starving like they always were. Aunt Becka made toasted cheese sandwiches and heated some tomato soup for them all. That was the second thing that made the day so special. Barbara and Josie had never eaten lunch together. Aunt Becka cut a sandwich in half and they shared it. The cheese was gooey and runny, just the way Josie liked it, and it turned out, so did Barbara.

When the sun came out and the sidewalks dried, they went outside and took turns riding back and forth in Josie's wagon. One girl would sit, holding the handle to steer while the other ran, pushing the wagon. The wheels made pleasant little *bumpy-bumps* over each crack in the cement.

The sun slowly sank behind the big flats across the alley, and in the approaching darkness she heard the forlorn *beep-beep* of fog horns. Her tummy rumbled uncomfortably and she was getting tired. But Barbara's mother wasn't back yet.

"There must be fog moving in from the lake." Josie repeated the words Daddy used when he explained the noise.

"I'm moving too," Barbara said. "We're moving someplace with cheaper rent."

Josie knew that already; she'd heard this all before from Aunt Becka. Meaningless words.

"Barbara! Oh, Barbara!" her mother called. "Come on now, Barbara. It's time to go."

Barbara looked up, acknowledging her mother's presence.

"Say good-bye to Josie, dear. You won't be seeing her again."

Barbara turned to Josie. "Good-bye," she said.

Josie nodded, relieved Barbara was going home now. The day had been so long and she was so tired and so hungry. Aunt Becka must have forgotten her out here in the dark.

"Bye," she answered, watching Barbara skip off toward her mother. *She moves just fine,* Josie thought, wondering what all the fuss was about.

Josie walked dreamily to her back door. Fog crept up the street and filled the yard, making ordinary buildings and trees appear mystical, muffling every noise and wrapping itself around her, hiding her and making her invisible.

She went slowly, quietly, up the stairs, still unseen. No need for a light, she knew the way perfectly. The darkness held no threat or unexpected terror. She was so tired, so hungry, each step an effort. And yet, not wishing to end this feeling of magical detachment, she sat for a moment on the invisible stair to ponder all the questions beginning to fill her mind. Were you really invisible if no one saw you? How did the horns know fog was coming, and why did they want everyone to know? And of course, why had Aunt Becka forgotten her?

The kitchen was bright and full of activity. Aunt Becka was getting supper on the table. Danny and Will were ready at their places, pushing each other the way they did. Daddy was pouring coffee into big white mugs.

"Go wash, Sweets," Aunt Becka told her.

Josie washed quickly, then hurried back to the kitchen and slipped into her chair just as Daddy began, "In the name of the Father," right hand to forehead, "and of the Son," hand to heart, "and of the Holy Ghost," hand crossed from left shoulder to right. Josie made hers backwards but no one seemed to notice.

"Bless, oh Lord, these gifts which we are about to receive. Amen."

The words were barely done when Danny and Will ripped their napkins from their colored rings.

"Settle down!" Daddy said, dishing up mashed potatoes for each of them.

"How come we're eating so late?" asked Danny.

"Yeah! I'm starving!" Will added.

Josie wondered too. She was hungrier than she'd ever been before.

"I thought I'd let the girls play as long as possible," Aunt Becka explained. "Barbara's moving and today's their last day."

Josie listened. There was that "moving" again. And what did Aunt Becka mean, "last day?" She ate her supper, waiting for another clue from the grownups, but none came. Maybe she could coax something out of them.

"Tomorrow, Barbara and I are …"

"Barbara moved, dear. She won't be here tomorrow." Aunt Becka said.

How silly, Josie thought. *Where else would she be?*

The next morning, as soon as she was allowed outside, Josie headed to Barbara's house. "Oh, Barbara!" she called over and over, but no one came. *Barbara must not be home,* Josie thought. She went back to her own yard. She tried a little later: still no answer.

"You're wasting your time!" One of the Busy Bodies called from their front porch. "They've moved!"

Josie stared blankly. There was that "moving" again! The Old Busy Body returned Josie's stare with her own icy glare and said, "Barbara doesn't live there anymore! She moved!"

Barbara was gone? The realization of what "moving" meant swept over Josie, filling her with a nameless dread. She looked at the house. There were no curtains in the windows, no chairs on the front porch. It was empty. Josie started walking around back.

"You can't go back there! I told you! They've moved!" yelled the Old Busy Body.

Josie ignored her, walking on numb legs that quivered with each step, to find out for herself, to be sure. Barbara's tricycle wasn't parked in its space under the porch. There was only an old candy wrapper lying on the hard-packed dirt. It was true. Barbara was gone!

In a trance, Josie turned toward home. What was she going to do? The lump that had been slowly forming grew so rapidly she felt like choking.

"I told you, didn't I?" The Old Busy Body yelled once more.

Josie hung her head so the tears that were forcing their way out couldn't be seen. They were *her* tears, not to be gossiped about later at Mr. Schick's. She wanted Barbara to be there so they could ride the tricycle, pull their wagon. Without Barbara, how could she play? What would she do all day?

Inside she hurt so terribly, she wanted to run to Aunt Becka for comfort, but something held her back, told her not to. No one wanted to hear about her sadness. Everyone had enough sadness of their own: Daddy with her mother, Aunt Becka with Del. More wasn't needed, wasn't wanted, wasn't allowed. Josie's sadness had to be hers alone, not to be given to the others, forcing them into still more unhappiness.

Instead, she crawled through the bushes to the opening under the front porch, that quiet haven where grownups didn't fit because the hole was too small. The sunlight filtered between the cracks of the steps, turning the dust particles floating in the air into a golden glow. She and Barbara had played house here, using their teddy bears as "babies." There was the round, flat rock that had been their table, still set with jar-lid dishes and sticks for spoons and the pretty rock they'd found in Mr. Russell's garden for a centerpiece. And all the tiny rocks that were their play food.

Josie tucked her knees up under her chin, wrapped her arms around her legs, and slowly rocked herself back and forth, back and forth. The tightness in her throat was almost unbearable until the tears came in full force, running down her cheeks and dripping off her chin. She let them flow, not bothering to wipe them away.

The mailman came and went up the steps on his morning delivery, unaware she was under there and in such terrible pain. She patted her right upper arm with her other hand, saying, "There, there," in her mind like Aunt Becka said whenever Josie scraped her knee and needed comfort.

"There, there. There, there."

How long she rocked to comfort herself, she didn't know. But slowly she felt better, becoming aware of where she was and that Aunt Becka was calling her. She wiped the last of her tears off on the skirt of her dress and crawled out from under the porch and through the bushes, blinking at the brightness of the sunlight.

"There you are, Sweets," Aunt Becka said. "I've been looking for you! I have to go to the A&P for coffee. Want to walk along?"

Josie nodded and grinned, trying to appear okay. She hoped Aunt Becka wouldn't notice that she's been crying and ask questions too difficult to answer.

"Let's go wash up, then."

Aunt Becka's expression seemed to change slightly. Had she seen the hurt Josie was feeling? Would she expect to be told what was wrong? How could Josie explain how she felt, simply because Barbara was gone, when Aunt Becka already had such grief because of Del, and Daddy suffered every day because of her mother?

Josie turned away quickly. Aunt Becka followed her up the back steps.

"What do you say we stop at the park on the way?" She called to Josie.

Later at supper, Daddy asked how the day had been.

"Josie and I went to the park," Aunt Becka said. "We had a fine time, didn't we, Sweets?"

Josie nodded, feeling a tiny tightness starting again. "May I be excused?" she asked, folding her napkin to fit in its red ring.

"Sure," Daddy answered. Then he looked at Aunt Becka. "I told you she'd get over it soon enough," he said. ♡

Chapter Six

The New Neighbors

After Barbara moved away Josie began to hang around with her brothers, tagging after them as they played their "boy games." She had never thought about what Danny and Will did while she was playing with Barbara, so now a whole new world opened up for her: a world of Cowboys and Indians, baseball (or rather, "Peggy," as there was no room for bases in the alley), kick the can, and all sorts of exciting new adventures.

The only problem was Danny and Will didn't want her sharing their world. They complained about it at supper one night.

"She's a pest!" grumbled Danny between bites of macaroni and cheese.

"Follows us around," said Will, agreeing with his older brother.

"All our friends say she's a baby," continued Danny.

"Yeah! They laugh because 'Baby Josie' is always with us!" added Will, using a silly little kid voice, mimicking their friends.

"She's a real pest," Danny repeated, sighing deeply as if in pain.

Josie hung her head, red-faced, figuring out how to defend herself.

Instead, Daddy reacted in the most remarkable way.

"What do you mean?" he said, glaring at the boys. "She's your sister and she hasn't anyone else to play with!"

"But …" Danny whined. "All our friends even …"

"No buts!" Daddy exploded. "She's your sister! *Friends*!" Daddy made the word sound like swearing. "*Friends*," he repeated, "can disappear like that. Poof!" He snapped his fingers. "But your sister is always your sister. In ten years' time, you won't even remember their names, but your sister will still be your sister."

Josie, who'd been preparing to cry and whimper her way out of a scolding, sat with mouth open in amazement at Daddy, who seldom scolded and never showed much passion. He moved quietly, almost remotely through their lives, and now he was angrily tongue-lashing her brothers.

Both boys slumped in their chairs, trying to appear smaller, their faces red and embarrassed. Then Daddy turned to Josie, pinning her with his stare. It was her turn to shrink in her chair.

"And you!" he said harshly, almost threatening. "If you're gonna play with the big kids, you can't be a baby anymore. Understand?"

It was true; she had whined a lot to her brothers when she'd been unable to keep up, complaining in front of their friends, begging them to wait for her, to let her have an extra turn just because she was smaller and inexperienced.

I'll never do that to them again, she vowed to herself. *I'll do everything they do, and I'll do it better.*

In the weeks that followed, Josie kept her promise and found she could do much of what Danny and Will and their friends did and, in some cases, even surpass them. When Aunt Becka saw her hanging from the "monkey tree" in the side yard, dress way up around her waist, she took some of Will's old blue jeans and cut the legs down so Josie could wear them.

"Just until your daddy buys you something more appropriate."

What a difference jeans made! When she climbed trees, the bark no longer scratched her legs, so she could "shimmy" up easier. There was no tree Josie couldn't climb. If she could wrap her legs around the trunk, it didn't matter if there were branches low enough to grab hold of or not. She could climb it (a talent all the boys she now played with admired)!

"Wow! Look at her go!" they remarked, while Danny and Will

glowed in her reflected glory.

She found she could walk fences that swayed and sagged under her weight, but didn't break as they might have for bigger kids. She jumped these same fences and hedges too, tucking her legs under and hurling herself through the air, "like a cannon ball," her brothers said.

Even when she couldn't keep up, she never stopped trying, never cried when she failed. She just kept going with such determination, that slowly, Danny and Will began respecting their small sister, accepting her as one of them.

Inside, Josie still missed Barbara: playing quietly under the porch, riding the tricycle together, the complete sharing of all they had. So, one morning when Aunt Becka told Uncle John, "Someone has moved into the Vander's house," Josie interpreted that "someone" to mean Barbara. Her heart leaped with joy. Barbara had moved back! How wonderful!

She bolted breakfast down, hurried Aunt Becka through hair brushing, then rushed outside. Skipping down the walk, past the convent, past the Old Busy Bodies to Barbara's house, she was excited at the thought of seeing her friend again. How wonderful to see curtains on the windows and some furniture piled on the front porch.

"Oh, Barbara!" she called happily. "Oh, Barbara!"

As the front door opened, Josie ran up the steps to greet her, but instead of Barbara, a big girl, bigger than Danny and Will, with long, brown braids that needing re-doing, stepped out. A strange girl, wearing bib overalls and a nasty expression.

"Hey, ya little jerk!" she snarled at Josie. "Whadda doin' here?"

Confused, Josie just stared at her, shocked that a stranger was in Barbara's house. Surprised, speechless.

"I asked ya a question! Ya stupid or somethin'?"

The girl stepped closer to Josie, who backed away, still too surprised to answer.

"Do I look like a *Barbara* to ya?" She said "Barbara," like it was a terrible name to call someone.

Josie shook her head dumbly, backing down the steps as the girl advanced toward her. Two boys about Danny and Will's age came out the door, snickering to each other.

"Ya chicken s—," the girl swore, grabbing Josie's shirt front and thrusting her face close. "Come back here again and I'll fix ya good."

Josie hadn't said a word. Her brain was refusing to work, to comprehend this nasty girl with scummy teeth and fetid breath, breathing in her face.

"You should brush your teeth," Josie blurted out unexpectedly. She regretted the words as soon as they had left her mouth.

The girl gave a snarl and shoved Josie away with such force that she went flying backwards, landing on her bottom, shaken and terrified. No one had ever treated her this way before. The big kids might not like her tagging along, but they would never hurt her. There was no glory in fighting a little kid; her small size was usually her best protection.

The nasty girl stood over her, glaring as the two boys sauntered down off the porch to join their sister. The three of them surrounded her, laughing without joy or humor. The cold, mean laughter sent a chill quickly through her.

And, just as quickly, the terror was overcome by rage. *How dare they treat her this way?* Josie picked herself up, determined not to cry, willing herself not to flee. Her pride prevented it.

Slowly, she brushed off her jeans. Slowly, she turned her back on these, these *what*? Josie couldn't think of a word bad enough for them. She said nothing. If she tried to speak, they would hear the tremor in her voice and know how frightened she was.

Slowly, and with as much dignity as could be mustered, she turned to leave. Slowly, nonchalantly, she strolled away, pausing to stick her butt out and brush it off with deliberate slowness. An ultimate insult.

Then the girl said a curious thing. "Nigger Hair!" she shouted. "Get outta here, ya Nigger Hair!"

Josie had never heard that term before. It made no sense at all, but she knew it wasn't nice. Not the way the girl yelled it.

Josie wanted to run home to Aunt Becka for comfort, to tell her about this terrible, nasty girl, to ask her what "Nigger Hair" meant. But she didn't dare. Daddy had made it very clear about her not being a baby any longer. Not crying about every little thing. About being a big kid, handling her own problems and not whining to everyone else.

She went back to her own yard and pulled herself up into the lush greenery of the "monkey tree," with all its branches that made it such fun to climb.

"Just see if I ever let you climb my tree," she muttered to herself as the leaves folded protectively around her.

It was Saturday. Danny and Will didn't have school, and now that chores were done, the day was theirs. And Josie's. The three of them sat on the huge, old trash bin next to the alley. It had been painted green years ago, but was now worn to a soft gentle texture, wood grain blending with color. When Josie ran her finger over it, she could feel the circles and swirls, smooth and soft. On the yard side it sloped down at an angle, allowing residents to lift the hinged lid and toss in their ashes from furnaces, old tin cans, and broken jars. Josie could easily scramble up that side. On the alley side, it was almost as tall as Daddy and Uncle John, and being almost six feet long gave the children plenty of room to sit, or even lay down on it.

But the really wonderful thing about the bin was how Josie's imagination could transform it from an ordinary receptacle for unwanted discards into a boat, a car, or even (like today) a high cliff overlooking a wild river, where she casually dangled her feet, cautious not to fall into the swirling waters and be swept away.

The boys were discussing what to do with this, the only day that belonged just to them. All week there was school, and on Sunday, "God's Day of Rest," there was church, then all afternoon they had to stay dressed in stiff, uncomfortable clothes and play quietly indoors or take walks with the grownups if the weather was nice.

But Saturday was all theirs alone.

It was always her brothers who chose what to do. Josie, while welcome to come along, had no real voice in the decision, so she only half-listened to them talking, while carefully removing an Ovaltine label Danny needed for a de-coder ring.

"Well, well, well. Look who we have here!"

Josie's tummy did a little flip at the sight of the nasty girl who now lived in Barbara's house, approaching, with her two brothers following behind. She had on the same overalls as before, now much dirtier, with one strap hanging undone. Her braids looked like what Aunt Becka called, "a rat's nest," all tangled and snarled. One of the brothers was barefoot, a foolish thing to be in an alley.

Danny's eyes moved slowly up and down, looking the three over. "You move in the Vander's place?" he asked.

"Yeah. I guess that's who they were," she answered. "What's your names?"

The girl was smiling and seemed friendly. Maybe she was sorry about the other day and wanted to be friends now, Josie thought uneasily. Hopefully.

Will spoke next. "I'm Will, that's Danny, and she's Josie," nodding toward the other two.

"What's your names?" asked Danny, following the correct courtesy.

But the girl ignored him, coming closer, smiling pleasantly.

"Ya live here?" she asked.

Will nodded.

"Where ya go ta school?" she asked, relaxed and smiling, hands casually stuck in her pockets. She came to a stop in front of Josie.

"St. Matthew's," answered Danny.

"Are you going there?" Will asked.

"Na. We ain't Catholic."

Suddenly, the girl grabbed Josie's ankle and jerked it. Josie dug her fingers into the boards and Danny clutched at her, stopping her from crashing six feet down to the ground.

"Hey!" Will yelled, jumping down just as Josie, in desperation, thrust out her other leg, striking the girl in the chest with her foot. The force of the blow sent the girl flying backwards to fall on her bottom in exactly the same position Josie had a few days earlier. Josie scrambled to her feet, stepping back safely out of reach, Ovaltine jar held over her head, ready to be thrown if necessary.

"Creep!" Will yelled, standing over the girl. Her face was red with fury. Both brothers hurried to help her up, but she shook them off in rage.

"Don't touch me!" she screamed. "Get them!"

She picked herself up, but without the deliberate slowness and dignity Josie had managed to maintain.

"Ya hit me!" the girl roared, a vein swelling in her neck. "Ya chicken s—, Nigger Hair! Ya hit me!"

Josie suddenly began giggling uncontrollably, which seemed to incite more rage.

"Nah!" Will laughed at her outrage. "She *kicked* ya!"

"Yeah, stupid!" Danny added, jumping down to join Will in the alley. "When it's done with a foot, it's a kick!"

The girl glared at him. "Who asked ya, four eyes?" she snarled, advancing toward him threateningly.

"Let's get 'em," she ordered her brothers.

"She's sure got her monkeys trained!" taunted Will.

"Hey, Cheetah!" Danny laughed, making monkey sounds. "Uh! Uh! Uh!"

"Come on, monkeys," Will put his fists up. "Here, Cheetah! Here!" he called.

The girl swung her fist at Danny, a real "hay maker" that Danny dodged easily.

"Hey, Ugly! Ya missed me!" he sneered.

That made the girl wilder. She screamed furiously at her brothers to help her, but they seemed uncertain, trying to figure out why these kids didn't seem afraid of them.

"Ugly! Ugly! Ugly Face!" chanted Will, while jumping around her, laughing at her fury.

"Bet your ma puked all over the place," Danny said, circling to her other side, so she was between them. "When she saw your Ugly Face!" they both sang out together, again moving away so quickly the girl couldn't touch either of them.

Red faced, the girl was out of control. She swung, first at Will, then at Danny, growing more agitated.

Josie watched the scene in amazement. She'd never seen anything like this.

Then the girl began to swear. Words flowed out of her mouth like a backed-up toilet.

"Ya Chicken S—s! You G—d-mn turds! You little s—heads!"

Josie's knees buckled and she plopped down on the trash bin, staring, as the dirty words kept coming. If this was what being "Not Catholic" meant, no wonder Aunt Becka had been so upset about Del.

Even Danny and Will seemed horrified as the profanity continued.

"You asses! I'll kick you asses good! Just wait, you s— brained, lousy ..."

Suddenly, Mr. Russell appeared at his back door. "What's going on here?" he yelled. "Who's talking like that?"

Josie had never heard Mr. Russell scold, much less holler at anyone.

"What's it ta you, Pops?" the girl yelled right back at him, eyes flaring.

Josie was dumbfounded. No one talked to a grownup that way.

"Go on! Scram!" Mr. Russell shook his cane in the air. "Get! Before I take a stick to you!"

The girl hesitated a moment, glaring, then spitting toward them, turned to join her brothers, running down the alley toward their house.

"I'll get you!" she shouted over her shoulder. "Nigger Hair!"

Will jumped up and down, scratching himself under his arms, mimicking a monkey. "Run, monkeys, run!" he called after them.

"We'll be right here, ya jerks!" Danny yelled furiously, his face as red as a beet.

"Enough, children." Mr. Russell said, opening the gate for the boys.

"It's over now. Enough."

"Come on," Danny called to Josie. She slid off the trash bin, Ovaltine jar still in her hand, the label almost completely loose.

Josie had never experienced anything quite like that before. She had never had another kid deliberately try to hurt her. She'd never seen her brothers ridicule and taunt someone, completely fearless, ready to fight and, so it seemed, loving it! She'd never heard Mr. Russell sound so angry. And she'd never struck out in real self-defense before. All her other "fights" had been just fooling around with someone who'd never dream of really hurting her, or her them. Her knees were quivering, but the rest of her felt exhilarated.

Will put his arm around her shoulder. "Come on, Josie," he said quietly. "Let's go."

The three of them walked up the brick path together, and Josie handed Danny the label.

"Thanks, Josie," he said as he folded it and stuck it in his pocket.

That night someone dumped the garbage from the cans.

In the morning when Josie carried out the day's bundle of trash, there was a smelly mess all around Mr. Russell's back door. He had spread a thick layer of newspaper on the ground and was piling on the egg shells, potato peels, and slimy old chicken bones that had been strewn about. Mrs. Russell was sweeping up coffee grounds.

"Such a business," she kept muttering to herself. "Such a business."

It didn't take long for the antics of the newcomers to become the talk of the neighborhood. Whenever Josie went to the store to buy candy, or was out with Aunt Becka, she'd overhear some grownup complaining about the latest outrage. The Old Busy Bodies were especially subjected to all sorts of abuse.

"We can't even hang our wash outside," lamented one.

"Mud!" clucked the other. "Mud all over our clean sheets!"

"And the language! Oh, dear!" The first Old Busy Body puckered her face in disgust. "Terrible!"

"Yes, terrible!" agreed the other. "Just terrible!"

"Maybe now they realize all their fuss about the Vanders boys was uncalled for," commented Daddy unsympathetically when Aunt Becka related the tales to him at supper.

Mr. Schick refused to allow all three of them in the store together. When he saw them approaching, he'd call his wife to wait on customers while he stood at the door to let only one in. Then, after locking the other two out, he'd "stick like glue" to that one until a purchase was made and the kid was escorted out.

"They just about cleaned me out before I wised up!" he'd explain to everyone in the store, then with a nervous laugh add, "I can't afford their business!"

The other customers nodded, understanding.

When Mrs. Lewendoski's flowers were torn out and thrown all over her front porch and walk, Warren complained to their father, who apparently was as nasty as his kids.

"He don't care. They're all no-goodniks!" Warren told Uncle John.

The nasty girl and her brothers continued their reign of destruction on the grownups, and bullying on the kids. They threatened or beat up just about every kid on the block. And each morning some unfortunate neighbor discovered the fly-covered, maggot-infested, smelly contents of a garbage can dumped in front of their door, waiting to be cleaned up.

Even the nuns weren't spared. After one of the Sisters scolded the girl for climbing over the fence and trampling through their garden, a rock was thrown, smashing the music room window where Sister Luke gave piano lessons.

That was when the police were called.

Josie squatted between the fence and her front porch, watching the desperate struggle of an ant she'd just dropped into a spider's web. She was torn between remorseful pity for the ant and irresistible horror at the deadly skills of the spider.

She feared spiders. She dreaded their intrusion into her dreams that caused her to wake, sweaty and shaken, afraid to move for fear that giant spiders lurked for real in the darkness of her room. Perhaps if she offered them ants as a sacrifice, they would leave her in peace. She watched the spider do its death dance for the ant, darting in, biting again and again while the ant grew weaker and weaker, struggling less and less as the poison took effect.

As she gazed, spellbound, she heard a police car pull up in front of the convent. Very few people in the neighborhood owned cars. The Priest, of course, had a car so the last rites could be rushed to dying people, insuring entrance into Heaven. And Mr. Schick had one so he could deliver groceries. But naturally the sound of a car drew Josie's attention. She had never seen a police car before, except in movies, and everyone knew that didn't really count. She watched curiously from her hiding place.

The policeman walked slowly up to the convent's small front stoop and rang the bell. One of the Sisters let him in, and a few minutes later he reappeared with Mother Superior, who showed him the broken window and handed him a rock about the size of a softball.

"Glass everywhere!" Josie heard her tell him.

The policeman nodded seriously.

"If one of the children had been taking a lesson ..." Mother Superior shuddered. Josie strained to hear more.

"I'll go have a word with them," he said.

The policeman walked past Josie again, this time carrying the offending rock. At the front walk, he turned left toward the nasty girl's house.

At last, Josie thought with relief. The policeman was going to put a stop to all the trouble. The neighborhood could go back to being the same old, comfortable place and she could once again move around freely without care or concern. After the incident in the alley, Aunt Becka made her stick close to home unless she was with Danny and Will.

"I can't imagine what those hoodlums would have done if the boys hadn't been there," she said.

But now it was over. Josie decided it would be fun to walk down and watch the policeman "give it to 'em." Several others in the neighborhood seemed to think so too. Mrs. Lewendoski was peeking through her front window, carefully holding the starched curtains back so they wouldn't be crushed and wrinkled. Mr. and Mrs. Russell had walked out to the front yard. The Old Busy Bodies were watching from their front porch. Even some of the Sisters were peering out of windows.

Josie crawled between her fence and the porch, through the bushes and to the walk, arriving just as the policeman returned to speak with Mother Superior.

" …deny it." Josie heard him say. She couldn't hear Mother's answer, but it was obvious she was upset.

"I know," he continued. "But you really gotta catch 'em in the act."

"In the *act*!" Mother Superior repeated in an astonished voice. "Ask the neighbors," she waved her arm toward everyone standing around, watching. "They can tell you we never had such goings-on before!"

"Of course they done it, Ma'am," the policeman paused. "They was nothin' but trouble where they lived before." He shook his head and rubbed the back of his neck. "But there's nothin' we can do unless someone sees 'em do it."

He turned to leave, then stopped to look over his shoulder. "I'm sorry, Ma'am," he said. He walked back to his car and drove away.

Everyone stood a minute, staring at each other in disbelief, then slowly, one by one, returned to their homes.

Josie sat on the bottom step of the porch, elbows propped on her knees, chin on her cupped hands, and worried. Their parents didn't care, the grownups couldn't stop them, and even the police weren't able to do anything. "*Sees* 'em?" she thought. Whose gonna see 'em when they purposely wait 'til no one's around to see 'em?

After that the nasty kids seemed even more bold. It was as though they knew not much could be done about their behavior. For Josie, things continued pretty much the same. She stuck close to home or stayed with her brothers. Whenever the girl spotted her, threats and insults were shouted, including the puzzling, "Nigger Hair" or sometimes just, "Hey, Nigger."

Josie would lie in bed, surrounded by the darkness, trying to figure out what in the world that meant. It made her feel so strange, sort of unclean. It had to mean something! Sometimes all the kids piled on top of one another and the bottom kid had to wriggle out, over and over until everyone was tangled up and laughing so hard they couldn't move anymore. Some of the kids called that a "Nigger pile." But what did that have to do with her hair?

Some mornings Josie was tempted to ask Aunt Becka as her hair was being fixed, each curl forced to behave by brushing it carefully around a finger. Only, suppose Aunt Becka gave the wrong answer again? Suppose Aunt Becka looked at her in disgust and said, "You know, I never thought about it before, but they're right! You *are* a nigger hair!"

So, the only thing she could do was just keep trying to figure it out on her own.

Some of the neighborhood kids discussed the three intruders one Saturday morning, sitting in the little nook at the back of St. Matthew's School. Mike McGuiness was there with his little brother Frankie, who was Josie's age. Both Donnys, Al White, who lived kitty-corner from Mr. Schick's, and his older (by two months) Uncle Glenn, that all the kids called Unc.

"It's that girl!" declared Big Donny Puluski, who was Mrs. Lewendoski's grandson. "She knows we can't hit her back."

It was true; no matter how terribly she behaved, if a boy hit a girl, the grownups always yelled at him.

"Yeah. Too bad Josie ain't big enough to take her," quipped Little Donny Ryan.

"She did okay!" bragged Danny.

"Sat that ugly monkey on her tail!" said Will, chuckling. "Right on her tail!"

"They're chicken s—," Mike McGuiness sneered. "Notice how they only go after the little kids? Girl or no girl, if she touches Frankie, I'll kick her ass good!" He laughed, punching Frankie affectionately on the arm. "Nobody hits my little brother, 'cept me!"

Josie shuddered at the idea of what Mike McGuiness could do. That girl was at least head and shoulders taller and had two brothers, but Mike was the toughest kid Josie knew. And he was very protective of Frankie. It was rumored that even their old man wouldn't touch Frankie, because of Mike.

"They'll be moving soon," said Unc. "My Pa says them kind always moves a lot."

"Well, until they do, we'll just have to watch out for the little kids," said Big Donny, playfully rubbing Little Donny's head.

"And my mean old uncle can watch out for me. Right, Unc?" said Al.

"Right!"

"Right!" they all chanted.

Then each of them pretended to spit on their right hand, stuck it out in the middle of their little group and, piling one hand on another, shook hands. "Right!" they said again in unison.

It was comforting to know that, now, not only her brothers were looking out for her, but the whole gang had taken an oath to do so too. While she appreciated their protection, it was stifling and annoying too. She missed the freedom to just move around without fear. If only Barbara hadn't moved, everything would still be fine. Those awful kids never would have come to the neighborhood.

Later that evening while walking home with Danny and Will, Josie relaxed and accepted the new situation completely. She decided to find out once and for all just what that mysterious "Nigger Hair" meant.

"Why do they call me that?" she asked. "You know, 'nigger hair.' What does that mean?"

Will shrugged. "Guess it's just something mean to say."

"Yeah. They call me 'four eyes,'" said Danny.

"That's 'cause you wear glasses. But what does 'nigger hair' mean?"

"Beats me."

"Never heard it before."

"It must mean something!" Josie persisted.

"Well, when Old Man McGuiness ran electricity out to his shed … he said he was 'nigger rigging' it."

"What does electricity have to do with my hair?" she asked.

"I don't know."

"Nothin' I guess."

As they crossed the street, Danny shouted suddenly, "Last one home is a rotten egg!" He took off with Will right behind him. Josie, being the smallest and usually last, didn't even try to race. She walked along, still confused and bothered by the name calling.

The grownups always said, "Sticks and stones may break your bones, but names can never hurt you." This was true in a grownup way, but in her way Josie knew names meant a lot. And those kids said the name like they knew something awful about her that even *she* didn't know. Like somehow she wasn't quite right, but was too dumb to even be aware of it.

Josie was across the street from home, bouncing her tennis ball against the wall of St. Matthew's School. All the kids were gone now for the summer, so Josie could play there undisturbed. She threw the ball and caught it. Over and over. It was a great game, even when she failed to catch the ball as it bounced back. It was when she ran to retrieve it that she saw the nasty girl walking down the alley in back of St. Matthew's, on her way home from the public school. Josie looked around, alarmed. She was alone and if the girl spotted her, there was no one else to help her.

She snatched her tennis ball and darted under the steps only the priests used that led to the rear entrance of the church. It wasn't much of a hiding place, but there were some broken cement slabs she could fit behind. She crouched there, watching the girl stroll along, carrying some books and whistling to herself. Josie had never seen the girl in a dress before.

Suddenly, Mike McGuiness came running up from behind the girl and tackled her. She went sprawling, her books scattered. Before she could respond, Mike was straddling her, fists pumping into her stomach. The girl let out an inhuman roar like an angry animal, and started swearing. She pulled Mike's hair with both hands, sending his cap flying. She wrapped her legs around his body, locking her ankles so he couldn't escape as she squeezed him. Only Mike didn't try to escape. He just kept punching and punching, like a machine. Methodical.

Mike shifted his position so he could sock her right in the face. Blood spurted from her nose. She dropped her hands and covered her face, trying to protect herself. Josie could hear her sobbing now, and felt a brief flash of pity for the girl.

Mike just kept punching, even though it was obvious the girl was licked. He was breathing hard now, out of breath from the punching. Then he stopped, reached into his pocket, pulled out his jack knife, and opened it.

"No!" gasped Josie in horror.

Mike turned when he heard her, staring blindly, as though he didn't recognize her. His eyes, strange and unseeing, sent a wave of cold fear through Josie. Was he going to kill *her* too?

Instead, he turned back to the girl who lay defeated beneath him. He grabbed one of her braids, viciously jerking it, and proceeded to saw it off with his knife. He stood up, folded the blade of his knife, and stuck it in his pocket.

Then, nudging the girl with his foot, he said, "Don't you never touch my brother again."

She just lay there, sobbing. Mike nudged her again, using more force this time.

"You hear me, B—-?" he asked. "Don't you never touch my brother again!"

"Yeah," she muttered between swollen lips.

Mike glanced at Josie, trembling under the steps. His eyes seemed to belong to him again. He moved his head slightly, warning her to hide once more. He wrapped the braid around his fist, turned, and ran down the alley without another word.

Josie squatted down behind the cement slabs and watched the girl get up. Her face was tear-stained and red. Blood ran down from her nose and dripped onto her dress. Painfully, she limped over to pick up her books, letting some papers blow away across the playground. Her knees and elbows were dirty and skinned. Blood trickled down one leg, soaking into her sock. Slowly, she headed home, sobbing quietly, one hand feeling her hair where Mike had chopped off the braid.

Josie waited until the girl turned the corner of the school and disappeared before she crept out from her hiding place. The quietness was overwhelming. All traces of the awful violence were gone except for a few of the girl's school papers fluttering in the breeze, and Mike's old blue baseball cap lying in the dust.

No one else had seen what had happened; Mike hadn't been "caught in the act." Josie picked up the cap. She couldn't read, but knew the letters printed inside spelled Mike's name. She stuck it in her shirt and ran for home as fast as she could, trying to put as much space between herself and that place as possible. She headed for her special safe haven under her front porch.

She sat a minute to compose herself, catch her breath, and allow her wildly beating heart to slow down. She pulled Mike's cap out from where it was hidden under her shirt. No one had seen her with it. Josie moved to the large flat rock she and Barbara had pretended was their table. It seemed so long ago. She scooped out as much dirt from under it as she could, and stuffed the cap into the hole.

After it was safely buried, Josie peered out between the cracks. No one was around, so she crawled out and hurried around to the back door and safety. She needed the comfort of Aunt Becka and her brothers, yet she knew she could never reveal the terrible violence she had witnessed that afternoon.

Chapter Seven
The End of the New Neighbors

One day the nicest thing happened. Just as the grown-ups had predicted, the nasty girl and her brothers moved. Not that they'd been too much of a problem lately. Mike McGuiness' attack seemed to have had an effect on the girl, whose hair was now cut rather short all around. And the garbage dumping and window smashing had slowed considerably.

Every time a neighbor found trash dumped by their back door, the next morning the girl's father could be seen cleaning up a mess by *his* door. For a while it seemed he cleaned up every other day until there was no more dumping at all. It stopped.

A week or so after the police said they couldn't do much about the window smashing incident, someone smashed the girl's window too. For a while Josie thought perhaps someone else had done both deeds. Maybe the girl was innocent of this particular crime. But then, someone threw a rock through a window a few houses down on the other side, and sure enough, the next night, another window was smashed at the girl's house. It was clear to everyone that someone was doing to those kids whatever they did first.

And, of course, they hadn't bothered Josie or Danny or Will since that night Daddy and Uncle John had chased the girl and her brothers home.

They had gone to a movie that night. All of them: Uncle John, Daddy, Aunt Becka, Danny, Will, and Josie. It was a Gene Autry movie at the Mozart. Then, they stopped for ice cream cones and walked home slowly, enjoying the night air. If Danny or Will even talked loud, a grown-up shushed him. “Folks are sleeping.” So, as they walked around to their back door, the sound of muffled snickers could be heard.

Daddy and Uncle John put their fingers to their lips to warn everyone to silence, then ran down the brick walk to investigate. What they discovered was garbage being dumped by the girl, of course, and her brothers. They started to run for home, with Daddy and Uncle John closely following behind.

Danny and Will darted off to see what was going to happen, leaving Josie and Aunt Becka alone in the dark.

Aunt Becka took Josie’s hand and said, “Come on!”

They too hurried to the alley to see what was happening. Everything was so black, there was no way to see anything. Josie shivered with excitement.

“Boys,” Aunt Becka called in a whisper. “Boys! Come back!”

A few minutes later Danny and Will appeared out of the darkness.

“It was them,” Will said.

“Dad and Uncle John chased ‘em!” Danny added. “Their dad said they was in bed.”

“But Dad and Uncle John said they wanted to ‘have a little talk with him,’” Will laughed. “A little talk.”

Then they all laughed.

Chapter Eight

The Fourth of July

It was a summer Josie would always remember. Afterwards, alone in the darkness, she'd reach into her box of memories, sorting and sifting, inspecting each golden moment to relive and enjoy them again and again.

Two or three times a week Josie put on her old sun suit. Aunt Becka had added material to the straps so they'd be long enough, and the boys wore old corduroys, cut off and hemmed neatly. They'd walk across the street, through the playground, down the short alley in back of St. Matthew's church, past Mike McGuiness' house, and then turn left after another block to reach Square Park.

Square Park was just that: one square block cut diagonally by two sidewalks. Tall trees shaded every inch, except in the center, where its only attraction for kids was located. The swimming pool was always bathed in sunshine.

There was a changing room they never used. It had toilets with old-fashioned, ceiling-high tanks that occasionally overflowed, creating a "waterfall" that delighted everyone until an attendant carrying his ladder chased all the excited, squealing girls out so he could fix it. There was a room in which Josie could see old men, bundled in sweaters and hats even on the hottest days, smoking their pipes and cigars and playing endless card games, oblivious to the splashing, laughing children on the other side of the window.

The pool was very shallow around the edge. Mothers sat here, with their tiny children close by. It sloped gradually to the center, where a fountain sprayed water up in the air to splash down on the bigger, braver kids. There were park benches surrounding the pool where Aunt Becka sat, reading her book or visiting with friends while Josie, Danny, and Will pretended to swim. There was never any embarrassment about how they were dressed; very few kids had clothes just to swim in. Most wore faded and frayed things the way they did.

Danny and Will dunked each other good-naturedly, even swam under water with their eyes open: something Josie never seemed able to force herself to do. Occasionally Aunt Becka would call out, "Boys! Stop that! Stop foolin' around!" or "Josie! Don't get your hair wet!" How good it felt when the water soaked through her hair to cool her scalp, but re-combing was such a snarly, tangled business, it wasn't allowed.

Afterwards, they'd walk home, leaving wet footprints on the sidewalk that dried in three or four steps as if they'd never walked there. They put on shoes only as they approached the alley.

Then back through the alley, through the schoolyard, across the street, to their home: cool, refreshed, usually dry, and always hungry. Aunt Becka had buttered slices of bread sprinkled with sugar waiting for them after they dressed.

For some reason, Daddy worried about them swimming there. He thought they might catch something from all the kids using the pool. Aunt Becka just laughed and assured him, "No one's ever gotten anything there that I've heard of. Besides, we only go on days they put in fresh water." Sometimes, just to tease him, she'd add, "If I notice the water is turning yellow, I'll be sure to make them get out!"

Daddy would chuckle then, and shake his head at such foolishness. He knew as well as Josie the water would never do that. Why should it?

The Fourth of July came, and for the first time, Daddy allowed Josie to join her brothers to march in the parade. All the kids were in front of St. Matthews, churning around, chattering and excited, seeking out special friends to walk with, while two ladies passed out American flags and tried to organize and straighten out the lines of children.

Danny and Will pushed through the noisy mob, dragging her along, to join both Donnys and some boys they knew from school. Josie stood in front of them, wriggling in anticipation. Just when she felt she couldn't stand still another moment, the children surged forward, moving at some unheard command. Walking and turning, walking and turning again to join other kids from other schools, more kids than Josie could have ever imagined, an endless river of children, most carrying small American flags, being cheered by people on both sides along the way.

Up ahead, an unseen band played. Nothing looked familiar and an unexpected wave of terror washed over her, but a quick glance back reassured her that her brothers were still there. Now recognizable landmarks appeared, and as they turned a last time, Josie realized they were entering Mitchell Park and each child was being handed an ice cream cup and wooden spoon.

Josie clutched her ice cream as Danny and Will tugged her along.

"Don't open it ..."

" ...until we sit down."

They found a quiet spot under a tree where Frankie McGuiness sat, eating ice his cream. Two more cups lay on the ground next to him. Mike, face flushed with excitement, joined them, carrying two more cups.

"Eat up, kid," he said, handing one to Frankie, who had started on his second. "There's plenty more where them came from!" He tossed the other one to Josie.

"Here, kiddo," he said.

Then, not even bothering to sit a minute, he ran back to push his way into the line of children waiting to get their reward for marching. This time a man passing out the treats stopped him. Josie could see Mike pointing out into the crowd and the man reluctantly handed him another ice cream.

Mike laughed as he flopped down, digging into the cold whiteness with his wooden spoon.

"I hadda really talk to get this one. The old guy's finally gettin' wise ta me!" He licked his spoon. "Told him my little brother was all tired out," he whined, "so I was gettin' his for him."

He nudged Frankie affectionately as Frankie started his third ice cream.

"Go on, kiddo." Mike said to Josie. "Eat up before it melts." He pointed to the extra cup tossed to her.

Josie opened it and began eating, reluctantly at first, knowing Daddy wouldn't approve of Mike's tactics, but feeling such generosity shouldn't be offended, and ice cream was a rare treat not to be wasted.

"Hey, kids!" Daddy squatted next to them. A slight look of disapproval flickered across his face when he saw the pile of empty ice cream cups surrounding Mike and Frankie.

"Come on, Pokey. You can finish while we walk," Daddy said to Josie.

As she stood up and he saw the extra cup, the same fleeting look appeared in Daddy's eyes. He was ashamed of her. Danny and Will ran ahead, darting in and out between the trees in one of their private, spontaneous games. Josie walked slowly, scooping ice cream with the wooden spoon, each bite weighing heavily on her tummy, until finally she said, "I can't eat anymore."

Daddy ignored her.

"It's sour," she whined. "I can't eat it."

Daddy stopped at a trash can and motioned her to throw it away.

"Seems a shame to waste it," he said.

Josie silently studied her sticky fingers. Daddy pulled out his handkerchief and knelt in front of her.

"Here, spit."

Obediently she did, rubbing her tongue across her teeth to make enough. Daddy wiped her mouth gently.

"How would you feel if you were the last little girl in the parade, and there was no ice cream

waiting for you?"

Josie hung her head. The shame that had been building overflowed, along with the tears that had been threatening. She knew how she would feel. Cheated. Left out. Just because others had been piggy.

"I'm sorry, Daddy."

"Here, wipe your hands." He handed the hankie to her and she carefully wiped the stickiness away.

"Come on," he said, taking her small hand in his. "Let's go find the others."

Josie's hand felt so good in Daddy's big strong one.

"I'm sorry, Daddy," she repeated, needing his forgiveness, his approval. Daddy squeezed her hand.

"I know," he answered. "I know. 'Nuff said."

His tenderness flowed to her, through her hand, down her arm, filling her with such love she thought her heart might burst. All was right again and she could once again enjoy the day.

The picnic table was covered with an old oil cloth, its once bright-red cherries now faded, almost invisible from all the wiping and rubbing endured while on their kitchen table. The picnic table was under a towering old elm tree that shaded them protectively like a huge umbrella. The market basket, transformed for the day into a picnic basket, sat on one end alongside of a chipped fruit jar filled with water and a sliver of soap for washing hands. The blue coaster, holding a box of "necessaries," was parked at an angle close by. And sitting at the table was boring, old, dull James who greeted her with his familiar, disinterested, "Oh, hello."

Danny and Will were anxious to be off and running.

"Can we go …"

" …to the playground?"

"Me too, Daddy!" Josie added quickly.

"Go on … stay together!" he called as they tore across the grass, down the hill, and past the lagoon on their left filled with rowboats that could be rented by the half hour. They crept through bushes and along paths worn by the feet of hundreds of children. Josie's imagination immediately took hold as she watched cautiously for Indians or wild animals that might be lurking anywhere.

The playground was surprisingly empty. A few, small kids dug in the sandbox under the watchful eyes of their mothers, and a couple of swings were already occupied. Josie claimed another for herself, and Danny, without being asked, gave her a couple of pushes. Will raced to the teeter-totter.

"Keep pumping." Danny said as he did an under-duck and dashed off to join Will for a game of "Farmer Brown."

Josie stretched her legs out as she sailed forward, and tucked them under when she dropped back. Forward and back. Higher and higher. Her feet kicked the low hanging branches of the maple shading the swings. Higher and higher until she actually accomplished clamping her feet together to tear off a few leaves. Satisfied, she tucked her legs tightly under the seat, wrapped her arms loosely around the chains, hands on her lap, closed her eyes, and relaxed as the breeze through her hair cooled her, and its softness caressed her skin. Forward and back. Forward and back.

Off in the distance Will and Danny on the teeter-totter called, "Farmer Brown, let me down!" and giggled as they bounced each other to the ground and then yanked up again. Josie didn't like that game. Its only purpose was to bounce the other kid off, its only rule: not to just get off and cause the other kid to crash down. It wasn't a game she played; she was too light, so bouncing her off was easy and she wasn't strong enough to control her side of the teeter-totter. Besides, it scared her to be bounced like that; not everyone followed the rules, and they'd roll off as soon as their side touched the ground.

Kids were always telling of someone they knew, or someone who knew someone who'd broken an arm or cracked their head open during a game of "Farmer Brown." She shuddered at the thought of a cracked head, the worst possible injury a kid could get. Worse than cutting your hand between thumb and pointy finger, and everyone knew that meant you'd bleed to death in minutes unless someone bandaged it right away. "You'll crack your head open!" Grownups always warned when they saw kids doing dangerous things. Did your brains seep out? Josie wondered if they did, could you ever be fixed? No one ever explained, they just warned.

The swing was slowing; soon she'd have to start pumping again or stop.

"Josie! Hey, Josie!" Danny's voice intruded into her thoughts. Reluctantly, she opened her eyes to see her brothers approaching with a big kid she didn't recognize.

"Stop the swing." Will tried grabbing the chain.

Annoyed, Josie dragged her feet, stopping.

"This here's Floyd." Danny pointed to the stranger who was scratching at his nose. "We told him how you can climb ..."

" ...anything! He bet us you couldn't ..." Will continued.

" ...climb one of those trees." Danny finished.

Floyd stared at her, rubbing his nose with the back of his very dirty hand. He probably has worms, Josie thought. Grownups always said if your nose itched, you had worms. Josie shrugged.

Floyd sneered at her. "Little s— like you can't climb no tree. A girl too! Hah!" He closed one nostril with a finger and blew hard, spraying snot across the ground, then proceeded to do the other side.

Danny grabbed Josie's shoulder and pulled her aside. "Listen, he's betting two sticks of gum you can't."

"Yeah, Josie," Will said. "And Danny bet a nickel you could."

"Danny has a nickel? Where'd he get a nickel?"

If he had a nickel, why didn't he just go buy his own gum? Why bother with this dirty, trashy kid? Danny jingled his pocket. Sure enough, there were a couple of nickels in there.

"What's the matter, little girl? Scared?"

"I could, but I got a dress on." Josie answered, red-faced from the unaccustomed attention.

The boys stared at her, incomprehensibly.

"The bark scratches my legs," she explained.

"Yeah, right! Pay up!" Floyd held out a grubby paw.

"No, really. Feel how rough it is." Josie patted the tree. "I can climb something else," she blurted out, not wanting Danny to lose his nickel. "I can climb … I can climb …" Her mind raced.

Floyd looked at the swings: narrow, slippery poles at least ten to twelve feet high. "The swing," he demanded. "Let's see her climb the swing."

"All the way to the top?" asked Danny.

"Gee, that's pretty high." Will said, worried.

"All the way to the top," Floyd repeated. "Or …" He tapped his open palm with a finger, meaning *pay up*.

Josie grabbed the pole as high as she could reach and pulled herself up. Then, holding herself with her legs, she reached up again and kept pulling upward.

"All the way to the top and sit there," Floyd added to the bet.

The smooth, cool, slippery pole didn't scratch her legs, but was really high. And there were no tree branches reaching out to catch her if she did fall. She scrambled to the cross bar to sit, as Floyd had demanded. It really had been quite easy. Down below Floyd was arguing.

"What's so special about that? Anyone can do that!"

"Then let's see *you* do it!"

"Yeah! Pay up!" Danny demanded, scratching *his* palm now. But Floyd continued grumbling.

"I thought I was gonna see something special!"

As the argument heated, Josie decided if he wanted something special … fine. *I'll give him something special all right,* she thought. She eased herself upright on the cross bar and, slowly, with arms extended, began walking across. It was not much different than a fence, only higher.

Will noticed first. "Oh, no!"

Danny followed his gaze.

"S—!" they said in unison.

Danny sprang into action. "Stop the swings!" he ordered. "Stop swinging!"

Even Floyd ran to block the swings, grabbing the chains to prevent the motion from distracting Josie as she stepped cautiously over the first set of bolts that held the swings.

It was harder than she had anticipated, requiring intense concentration. Carefully, she stepped over the next set of bolts, unaware that Danny was holding the swing below completely still so the boy on it couldn't move. One more to go and then she could slide down the middle brace pole. There was no way she would be able to get any further. She stepped over the last set of bolts, the ones holding the swing in which she'd been so relaxed.

Sweat trickled down her back, causing a distracting, irritating tickle she could barely ignore. Her knees began to quiver uncontrollably, and as she felt her feet slip away, she flung herself in desperation towards the branches she'd been kicking just minutes ago. Knowing full well the branch wouldn't hold her but at least might break her fall, her hands grasped at the leaves. She closed her eyes and rode the branch until it dipped down, and at the instant it stopped, she dropped off in an undignified plop in the dust.

Floyd's mouth hung open. Danny and Will seemed frozen, dazed. Josie sat, unable, unwilling to move, amazed she was still alive and as far as she could tell, unhurt. Suddenly, it seemed everyone began to move. Danny pulled her up. Will brushed the dust off her legs and dress, checking for injuries.

"You're okay," Will's voice shook. "You're okay."

"God, Josie!" Danny checked her over, turning her around to make sure. "God, that was … that was …"

"Yeah it was!" Both boys were lost for words.

"That was *something*!" Floyd fished a pack of Black Jack gum from a hip pocket, pulled out two pieces, and handed them to Danny. "Kid," He turned to Josie. "Kid, ya got moxie!"

"Ain't nobody gonna believe this!" he said as he walked off. "A *girl* too!"

Uncontrollable trembling caught Josie by surprise. Her brothers continued checking her, fussing at her in disbelief.

"Ya sure you're all right?"

"Nothing hurts?"

"Were ya scared?"

She grinned up at Danny. "I get some gum," she said, not asking, but telling them as an equal.

Danny broke each piece into thirds. "We each get two."

The sweet licorice flavor flowed over her tongue, relieving the dryness. It was the best gum she'd ever tasted.

"Where'd you get a nickel?" she asked Danny.

Danny jingled his pocket and pulled out two washers. "Sounds like nickels don't it?"

"That dumb Floyd never even asked to see our money!" Will laughed, punching Danny playfully on the shoulder. "He'd 'a killed us for sure if ya'd paid him a washer or two!"

Danny put an arm around Will's neck. "Let's get the merry-go-round." He put his other arm around Josie, pulling her close. "Ya sure scared us when ya said ya couldn't climb no tree on account of an old, dumb dress."

Josie moved stiffly. The fall had hurt some, but the gum was worth it and she'd saved Danny from a fight. She sat gingerly as her brothers pushed her round and round until Daddy showed up to get them.

"What happened to you?" he questioned Josie's dusty appearance and stiff gait.

"I fell."

"Fell? Fell down where? Off a mountain?"

Josie giggled. "No, Daddy. I fell …"

"Off the swing set," cut in Danny.

"Yeah. The swing set," confirmed Will.

"Well, be more careful in the future," Daddy said. "Guess we better swing by the boathouse and clean you rascals up."

He took Josie's hand. "Little girls are supposed to stay clean, you know. Clean and neat and ladylike." But he squeezed her hand to let her know he was only teasing.

Aunt Becka had fried chicken and potato salad, pickles and hard-boiled eggs, and baked beans with hunks of bacon jowl. Uncle John was there next to Theresa Ryan, who had brought a beautiful chocolate cake with fluffy frosting and coconut sprinkled all over it.

The boys filled their plates and sat cross-legged on the blanket. Josie sat at the picnic table next to Aunt Becka and dull old James. Daddy sat across from her next to Uncle John and Theresa Ryan. Instead of fussing over her or helping her, Aunt Becka snuggled close to James, asking him if he wanted more of this or that as though he were a spoiled child to be coaxed into eating.

Josie moved as far down the bench as possible and tried to ignore them, dribbling pickle juice down her front and licking her fingers. But no one noticed. Daddy stared, unseeing, into space like he did sometimes, and everyone else chatted and laughed together as if they were the only ones at this picnic.

"Let's see your ring."

Beaming, Aunt Becka held her left hand out to Theresa Ryan. A new ring was on the finger

between the tall man and little pinkie. In spite of her irritation, Josie scooted over to have a peek.

"See what James gave me," Aunt Becka said, smiling, pleased to show it off.

It was a tiny, silver ring with a small, white stone that seemed to have a pinkish luster.

"It's a pearl," Aunt Becka explained.

"A pearl," Josie repeated, studying it. Light seemed to glow from it.

"Clams make them," James added.

"Clams?" Josie was baffled. She'd always thought them interesting, but somewhat disgusting things she found in the mud surrounding the lagoon. How could they make rings? They had no fingers, no way to handle tools. Josie giggled. He was teasing her. Dull, old James was actually making a joke! None of the grownups seemed to realize how silly he was being. *Clams making rings!* What a funny thought! Josie laughed at the picture her mind was forming.

James just stared at her, not comprehending her amusement. Then, he returned to his lunch, quiet and dull again.

"Sand gets in 'em," Uncle John explained. "Causes an itch, and since clams can't scratch, they form a pearl around the sand."

"Really?"

"Really. Pretty pearls are rare. Not all clams make 'em, and not all that are made are pretty."

Josie leaned closer to inspect the ring. To think some icky mud-creature had made such a lovely thing.

"James and I are engaged," Aunt Becka said. "That's why he gave me this ring."

"Oh." Josie had no idea what "engaged" meant, but it must be okay if it made Aunt Becka happy. She was smiling a lot, even if her gray eyes seemed cloudy.

"When's the big event?" Theresa Ryan asked.

Aunt Becka shrugged. "We have to talk to Father. Have banns posted. Probably late summer." She smiled again at James and squeezed his arm.

Josie glanced at Daddy, across the table from her. He'd drifted off into that unseeing, unhearing world of his, unaware of them or their conversations. All alone in his thoughts.

The grownups went on to talk of other things and Josie soon lost interest. Soon, they stopped talking altogether to watch what was happening down at the band shell. Whenever anyone finished a speech, Uncle John applauded happily.

"Best speech I never heard!" he commented, to everyone's amusement.

Afterwards, while Aunt Becka and Theresa Ryan packed away

leftovers, Josie lay on the blanket, savoring whiffs of tobacco smoke from Uncle John, James, and Daddy who were sprawled on the grass nearby. Below, some girls danced on the stage: graceful, long-legged birds in pink ruffled dresses, bowing and bending to unheard music. Danny and Will were trying to measure a huge elm by joining hands around it.

The smell of cigarettes, her brothers' snickers, and the quiet voices of her family became a lullaby too seductive to resist.

Chapter Nine

Playing with Daddy

She woke gently. Someone had removed her shoes and folded a corner of the blanket over her bare legs. It was warm and quiet. Josie stretched, rolling over.

"Well, hello, sleepyhead," Daddy brushed his finger along her cheek. "Have a nice nap?"

Josie sat up, nodding groggily. There were just the two of them.

"They all went for a walk," Daddy answered her unasked question. "Want to catch up?"

Josie nodded, fully awake now. Daddy handed over her shoes and she slipped them on, extending her feet so he could tie them. When she stood up, Daddy stuck out a hand, pleading, "Help me up!" As she tugged, he bounded up quickly to give a tickle, but she darted away. They frolicked their way through the elms, Josie hiding and peeking, Daddy chasing and sneaking until at the road they joined hands and crossed to the Sunken Garden.

It was a grownup place: a quiet place where noisy children weren't allowed. Wide stairs led down a sharp slope to the stone path. The slope was planted with flowers to resemble colorful curtains tied back with golden cords, and every so often a bed of flowers encircled a huge century plant. All the flowerbeds sloped down to the centerpiece of the garden: a long, narrow pool, dark and quiet, with no movement except goldfish swimming silently between water lilies. Even the occasional frog, perched safely beyond the reach of predatory boys, didn't seem to make any ripples in the still, dark water. The only movement was the reflection of clouds, drifting high in the sky.

Kids told tales of people slipping down the steep slopes and drowning in that still water, their bodies sinking down, down, down, never to be seen again. It was said that the men who planted the flowers near the pool were paid extra because of the danger, and that they watched each other protectively in case one of them fell in.

Josie shuddered at the thought. She'd never take that job! No matter *what* the pay!

There were balconies on each end and along the sides below were stone lions, spitting water into basins which, in turn, overflowed into the pool.

Uncle John and Theresa Ryan walked silently, fingers entangled casually, admiring the garden. Dull, old James and Aunt Becka, whispered quietly with their heads bent together, her right arm under his left, his hand reaching over to cover hers possessively, sharing secrets as they moved. Danny and Will were taking the tiniest of baby steps, pretending to be dignified and impressed by the flowers.

"Oh, my! Isn't it lovely!"

"My gracious, yes! It's simply divine!"

They stopped at one of the balconies. Aunt Becka and James sat together on a bench overlooking the pool. Theresa Ryan sat next to them while Uncle John lounged against a baluster, facing her, enjoying a smoke. Daddy sat to the side, a bit away from the others. Josie curled up on his lap, listening to the boring grownup talk about "bans to be posted" and whether Roosevelt could, or would, "keep America out."

Danny and Will leaned over the railing, engaged in a contest to see who could spit the farthest into the pool. Not hearing anything interesting from the grownups, Josie joined them, dangling over the rail as far as she could and scraping her tongue across her teeth to make enough spit, a problem boys never seemed to have. They seemed able to spit at will. It was rumored that Mike McGuiness could crack a sidewalk just by spitting on it, although Josie had never seen it happen.

Uncle John checked his pocket watch and announced, "Well, there's a 3:40 I have to catch."

Theresa Ryan stood to join him. "You keep the cake," she told Aunt Becka. "I'll pick up the plate tomorrow."

"We're going to the conservatory," Aunt Becka said, "then meeting J.D. and some new girl he met at the Eagles. Want to come along?"

Daddy shook his head. "No, I think we'll just explore around the park. Check out the log cabin."

Danny and Will immediately began whooping and yelling, chasing each other in circles. James stared at them as though they were some sort of strange creatures he'd never seen before, but Aunt Becka chuckled.

"Best be doin' it then," she said. "The Indians are restless."

The log cabin stood at the top of a hill overlooking the valley, a panorama of man's industry combined with natural beauty that stretched as far as Josie's eye could see. Mr. Russell had told them about hunting squirrels and rabbits and even an occasional deer down there when the river was free to meander at will. A plaque set in stone near the cabin said that Solomon Juneau use to trade with Indians in this very spot.

How wonderful it must have been back then! Josie's mind's eye saw the thick woods, dark and mysterious, strange animals lurking, exotic birds flitting from tree to tree, and Indians, silent and restless as a summer breeze, approaching to trade.

Trade what? She wondered, her mind buzzing with questions.

But now the valley was fenced in, the river long imprisoned by railroad tracks and factories. The only things running down there now were trains, and Uncle John was on one of them.

Which one? She thought.

A few clouds drifted by in a wispy race with one another. Josie drifted along with them, wondering where they were going and why some days herds and herds of clouds filled the sky and other days there were none at all.

"Cut it out, fellas!" Daddy's voice snapped and Josie returned from her daydreams.

Her brothers turned, newly prohibited from climbing the cabin's corner points to the roof, and began rolling down the hill, then scrambling up, grasping the grass like monkeys. Down they rolled: Will, with his arms above his head, and Danny, covering his glasses with his hands to protect them. Josie joined them, holding her hands to her sides to keep her skirt from rising too high. It was a wonderful feeling: over and over, faster and faster, light-headed and dizzy, giggly and exhilarating. She scurried up to go again.

To their delight, Daddy stuck his squashy cap under his belt, folded his arms across his chest and rolled down too, just like another kid. Over and over they raced up and rolled down until they were too tired for even one more climb to the top, and the four of them lay in a happy, exhausted row as clouds whirled in the sky and the ground rocked gently beneath.

The children finally rose, but Daddy still lay helpless at their feet. "Here," he pleaded, holding up his hands. "Help up your poor old Da."

Danny and Will each took a hand, tugging him upright. But as soon as he got to his feet, he grabbed them, one arm in each hand, and dragged them down in a heap.

"Josie," Daddy said, motioning to Danny's glasses. She unhooked them for safekeeping.

A grand wrestling match began: Daddy against both boys. Josie hopped up and down in excitement. "Me too, Daddy! Me too!" she begged until, unable to bear it a moment longer, she flung herself on his back, grasping his shirt with one hand and still holding Danny's glasses with the other.

"What? What the ... I think I threw my back out!"

Daddy handed Danny his glasses and stood up, Josie dangling behind him.

"I feel this weight on my back ..." He turned this way and that. "Where's Josie? Where did Josie go?"

She clung to him, stifling her giggles.

"There she is!" Will said, pointing and hopping. "There she is!"

"Where? Where?" Daddy acted puzzled, turning again and again.

"On your back!" Danny cried.

"Oh, my poor old back." Daddy plopped down. My back feels so ..." He reached over his shoulder to grab Josie, and flipped her, head-over-heels into his lap. "Here's my back problem!" He buried his face in her neck below her right ear and blew. She squealed and struggled, giggling.

"There's no escape!" Daddy chuckled, holding her tight. "Don't even *think* about escaping!"

"We'll help you, Josie!"

Her brothers joined in the fray, tugging at Daddy's arms until Josie managed to squirm free. Then, all three piled on him, pinning him down: Will on his chest, Danny holding one arm, and Josie holding the other.

"Uncle!" Daddy cried. "Uncle! Uncle!"

They let him up and retrieved the cap that had worked its way out from its place under his belt. He used it to whack the dust off his clothes.

"Make sure I didn't lose anything. Wallet, knife, comb ..." He recited the inventory of his pockets. Satisfied, he put on his cap again. "Whadda say ... you rascals interested in an ice cream and a boat ride?"

Paint and varnish, combined with old wood and dampness, gave the boathouse such a distinctive smell that Josie felt even if she were blind-folded she would know where she was. Daddy bought "paddle-pops all around" and a ticket for a rowboat. They munched the crunchy, chocolate-covered vanilla ice cream while his strong, swift strokes moved them across the murky waters of the lagoon.

When Danny and Will were done eating, Daddy motioned them to change places with him. Eagerly, each grabbed an oar and began to row, or at least *tried* to row. All the boat did was wobble in half circles. Will, being stronger, forced his oar into the water, while Danny's just skimmed awkwardly across the surface.

"Work together. Will, ease up. Danny, come on, you can do better," Daddy said, urging them on. "Atta boys! Work together. One, two. One, two."

Daddy leaned back comfortably, lit a cigarette, and returned their proud grins.

"Once around the park please," he said, counting out, "one, two," every once in a while, so they wouldn't lose their rhythm. "Great team!" he praised, and they glowed.

After they passed the small island in the lagoon's center, Daddy had them change places again.

"Come on, sweets," he said to Josie. "No free rides."

She sat between his knees, grasping each oar, small hands next to his larger, stronger ones.

"Just move along with me now."

Josie leaned back against his chest, her arms moving with his, but not really using her muscles. One, two, one, two. Daddy's rhythm never changed. She felt the rhythm of his heartbeat, his muscles flexing under his shirt. His familiar odor blended with the special, weedy aroma of the water. The air, cool and breezy, gently brushed sweat from her skin, raising tiny goose-bumps. Her brothers sat at the other end of the boat, admiring new red calluses forming on their palms. A swan flowed effortlessly past, ignoring their intrusion into her watery world.

Josie looked at Daddy's face.

That sad, faraway look had crept back. He was staring straight ahead, unseeing, unaware, moving automatically: one, two, one, two, as the boat slid silently across the water. Her happy Daddy of moments ago had slipped away once again to that dark, sad place. All alone. Her happy Daddy had vanished like a pleasant, sweet dream upon awakening. She leaned against him, trying to absorb his strange sadness like a little sponge, willing the sadness to leave him alone so he could once again be her regular Daddy.

Aunt Becka and James sat with J.D. and a pretty, blonde girl who giggled quietly at everything he said. The children ran back to the picnic table to join them for a supper of leftovers. As dusk turned to darkness, everything was packed back into the basket and box and put in the wagon, the blanket folded neatly on top. All the grownups except Daddy left, and he and the children set off to find a spot near the park exit to watch the fireworks. Excitement and anticipation stirred through the crowd.

A bang! A hush.

The sky blossomed with fiery flowers of gold and blue and red and green. The crowd sighed its approval.

"Whoo! Ahhh!" They breathed and roared in appreciation.

"Let's go," Daddy nudged them.

"It's not over!" Danny protested.

"Almost," Daddy picked up the blanket. "I don't want to get caught in the crowd."

Daddy pulled the wagon, Josie close at his side, while the boys lingered, walking slowly backwards to watch the sky explode with each bang.

Daddy parked the wagon by the back door. "Don't go empty-handed," he said, handing Josie the blanket. She started up the stairs with no need to turn on the light as she turned right at the invisible step. Suddenly, the light was snapped on anyway, and Danny and Will came struggling behind her, lugging the picnic basket. Daddy followed, carrying the box under one arm and fumbling for the house key.

The flat was stifling, like walking into a solid wall of heat.

"Go wash up," Daddy told them. "You can sleep in just your underwear."

He moved through the rooms, opening windows and the small, upstairs porch door to let in whatever cool, night breezes that might be stirring, then came to tuck them in, sitting next to Josie.

"You won't need this." He pulled the blanket down to the foot of her tiny cot and kissed her forehead gently. "Have a nice day, sweetheart?"

She nodded, sleepily.

"Good." He kissed her again as he stood up. "Good night, fellas." He leaned to kiss them and patted Danny. "Stay dry," he said, encouragingly. "I'll leave the door open; maybe it'll help cool things off a bit."

Josie listened as Daddy worked in the kitchen, emptying the pan from under the ice box, heating water to wash the picnic dishes, putting away all the things used today, and returning the picnic basket to an everyday market basket, just like Cinderella's pumpkin after the ball. She heard him walk past her door to the living room. He clicked on the radio and settled himself into his corner of the couch. She stretched out on her little bed as the tiniest of breezes puffed through her curtain to caress her body. She savored the fresh, sweet, clean sheets. The faint urine smell of her mattress wasn't terribly unpleasant. It had been at least three weeks since she last wet, so there were no unexpected damp spots left to surprise her.

"I'm not a baby anymore," she smiled proudly to herself as muted music from the living room lulled her to sleep.

The first bang, followed closely by the second, jolted them from sleep. Josie sat upright, heart pounding. The room was pitch black.

"What was that?"

"I think it was just the door," Danny's voice came through the darkness.

They crept through their room and opened the door. A light in the living room allowed them to see the curtains whipping furiously in the wind and, indeed, the door to the porch had blown shut. Danny opened it again, propping a dining room chair under the doorknob.

Josie crouched by the screen door as the night air washed over her: warm, heavy air with the distinct scent of unfallen rain. The sweet scent of flowers in the dark filled her soul with a strange restlessness.

"Storm's coming," Danny said, standing behind her.

"Fireworks cause 'em," Will quoted Mr. Russell's wisdom.

They watched the night sky. Lightening reflected off St. Matthew's steeple, each flash growing closer and closer, the winds' force increasing. Josie felt an urge to stand, arms outstretched, daring the lightening to harm her, while at the same time felt a need to curl in a protective ball of fear and plead to God to spare her from his terrible wrath. Her brothers went into the living room and she hurried to be with them.

The floor lamp, flickering with each rumble of thunder, created harsh, malevolent shadows, turning familiar chairs and tables into scary, dark monsters of the night. The radio on the table next to the couch was caught between two stations and static played in time to the thunder's tune. A half-empty bottle of beer sat on the table, surrounded by several sticky rings and an overflowing ashtray.

Will flicked the radio off and all was quiet except for the sounds of the approaching storm and Daddy's wet breathing. He was slumped on the couch, asleep; his shoes lay where he'd pushed them off, the laces still tied. He had taken off his shirt and opened his belt and pants. His right arm was extended, an unlit cigarette between yellowed fingers.

The pasty white of his upper arms and shoulders contrasted with the warm, familiar tan of his lower arms and neck. A wispy tuft of chest hair protruded above his sweat-soaked undershirt. His head lolled to one side, the hair sweaty and sticking to his forehead. His mouth sagged open with a bead of drool glistening along his drooping lower lip. Josie watched as it grew larger and larger, eventually rolling down the stubble on his chin like a tear.

Her brothers exchanged one of their secret, knowing smiles, and Danny removed the cigarette from Daddy's fingers. He squatted down to place it under the couch where it might have rolled if it had been dropped. When she started to question this, the boys cautioned her with a finger over their lips.

Suddenly, Daddy bolted upright, glaring out of wild, unseeing eyes, a mad stranger. "What … what the hell …"

Just as suddenly, he slumped asleep again, moaning as he settled. He shifted to one side and passed a long, noisy "puffy" which filled the room and caused Danny and Will to giggle appreciatively. Revolted,

Josie gasped and scurried to Aunt Becka's room, to the safety of her bed and arms and gentle voice.

But the bed was empty. In the dark her hands grasped the soft chenille spread, finding only the furry kitten where Aunt Becka had placed it this morning, as she always did when she made her bed.

Josie ran to find her brothers, now back in the safety of their room. Danny sat on his bed and Will sat on the floor, leaning against the door to keep it open. She leapt into her little bed, shivering uncontrollably.

"Aunt Becka's not here."

"Probably out with James," Danny said.

Josie pulled her legs up under her chin, hugging them to her chest.

"Put your top on," Will suggested, pulling her blanket so she could reach it.

She reached under her pillow for her P.J.s, and slipped on the top, allowing the bottoms to drop to the floor.

"It's still early for them," Danny explained. "Probably out kissy-kissying."

"Yeah. Think they'll really get married?" Will asked.

"Married? Aunt Becka and dumb, old James?"

Had she really said that out loud? Called a grown-up *names*? Out loud! Her brothers didn't seem to care; in fact, they both nodded, agreeing with her opinion.

Danny shrugged. "'Fraid so," he answered.

"Can they do that? Can she really do that?" Josie asked.

"Get married? Sure!" Danny answered.

"All grownups get married," Will added, "eventually."

"Except priests," Danny was so smart.

"And nuns," Both her brothers were.

"And Daddy," Josie said, remembering the story of Uncle Baby Danny.

They stared at her.

"He should," Will spoke softly.

"But he won't," Josie said, knowingly.

"No, he won't," Danny agreed.

Will left his shoe under their door and climbed into his upper bunk.

Josie snuggled under the blanket, her shivering slowly subsiding. Had her brothers noticed how scared she'd been? Why had she felt such fear, such disgust? How could she think Daddy disgusting? How could she, even for a minute, think her wonderful Daddy disgusting? *She* was the disgusting one for even thinking such an awful thing! Blaming Daddy when it was really all her fault because she'd let Daddy down.

Somehow. Someway.

It must be her. It had to be her. It certainly couldn't be Daddy. He was wonderful!

She deserved punishment for her awfulness, her disloyalty, the repulsion of her wonderful, poor, sad Daddy who needed her help to ease his pain. She'd been scared and disgusted. In the darkness of her room, she slapped herself across the face. But it seemed to not hurt at all, certainly not enough to punish her properly like she deserved.

Dejected and guilt-ridden, Josie curled into a ball and fell asleep.

Chapter Ten
The McGuiness Family

She woke as Danny pulled his sheet back to allow his soaked mattress to dry, and winced at the wetness in her own bed. Josie crept out from under the blanket, her PJ top and panties clinging coldly, grabbed clean underwear from her drawer, and headed down the hall to the bathroom to wash. Aunt Becka insisted they, "Warsh real good, so you won't smell!" whenever they wet.

Aunt Becka's door, usually open, was shut tight: an unspoken "do not disturb."

Daddy still slept on the couch, only now he was lying down, covered with the old peach-and-white quilt some old auntie had made years ago. The beer bottle was gone and all the sticky rings wiped away. Even the ashtray had been emptied and his shoes neatly tucked under the radio table. Everything that had frightened her last night had been cleaned up. Perhaps it had only been a bad dream.

Will watched from the dining room as Danny knelt, searching under the couch to retrieve the un-smoked cigarette, which he tucked in his shirt pocket. Their exchanged looks told Josie they were sharing one of their private secrets she was not a part of.

After dressing, she found her brothers had gone, their dirty dishes still on the table. One of them had filled her bowl with corn flakes and poured a glass of milk. She cleared the table as she usually did every morning under Aunt Becka's guidance, stacking all the dirty dishes in the sink and wiping the table clear of sticky spots and crumbs. Then she went to the bathroom to wash her face and fix her hair.

She carefully brushed out each curl with a dampened brush and tried shaping it around her finger just the way Aunt Becka did each morning, but all she could get was an untamed mess. As it dried, her hair became fuzzier and fuzzier until it was practically standing on end, wild and kinky, almost with a life of its own. Unwilling to wait until Aunt Becka woke up to help, Josie put away the brush, slipped on her shoes, and tiptoed down the stairs and outside to search for her brothers.

It was a bright, lovely morning. The storm from the night before had washed everything clean; even the air seemed fresher. Mrs. Russell's laundry was already on the line, gently stirring as breezes nudged it. Mrs. Russell always prided herself on having her wash done and hanging out early. "No sense doin' it if you wait half a day to get to it," she would say to anyone who would listen.

She found her brothers across the street, behind St. Matthew's school, sitting in the alcove by the back door. Danny and Mike McGuiness leaned against the brick on one side of the door, chewing on a wooden match. Will and Big Donny leaned on the other side. Big Donny's cousin Casimer, who lived way over on Cherry street but often took the number 27 streetcar across the viaduct to hang out here, was nearby, throwing pebbles at the brick wall where he'd scratched a target with a piece of chalk rock.

Josie scuffled over awkwardly to join them, shoes untied, hair all fuzzy and unkempt.

"You look like a jungle bunny," Casimer said.

Josie sat on the low slab step, sticking her feet out so Will could tie her shoes. Danny handed her his squashy cap.

"Here. Maybe you can cover it, at least."

She stuffed her hair under the cap and pulled it down tight as far as she could.

"Now ya look like a boy," Big Donny said.

Josie beamed. A cute, little bunny was nice but this was the finest compliment: to look like "one of the guys." She settled down, listening, as they decided how to spend the day.

"Me and Cas gotta help Grandma clean the basement," Big Donny said. "I was hopin' maybe you guys would be around too to help."

That sounded fine to Josie. Whenever they helped Mrs. Lewendoski, she always fed them cookies or sweet rolls and sometimes even gave them a few pennies too. But her brothers didn't seem to care much for the idea. Instead, Danny pulled Daddy's cigarette from his shirt pocket and held it up.

"All right!" Mike breathed. "All right!"

He removed the match from between his teeth and, with elaborate flair, struck it on the sole of his shoe, cupping his palms around the flame to prevent a stray breeze from blowing it out, and leaned toward Danny. Danny inhaled deeply and passed it on to Will, who also puffed, letting the smoke out through his nose. Josie watched, enthralled. Mike fidgeted, ready to grab it when his turn came, relaxing as he inhaled, then offered it to Big Donny.

"Nah. My grandma's got a nose on her."

"I know where there's a mint patch," Mike McGuiness offered.

"Nah. She'd smell it and tell my ma."

"Ya scared of your mommy?" Mike asked.

"Ma'll tell my pa."

Mike had to nod, understanding Big Donny's dilemma. His pa was big as a doorway, with huge hairy hands, capable of who knew what, and a voice that could be heard upstairs in their flat, even when he was just laughing or talking.

Mike passed it back to Danny, but Josie impulsively grabbed it.

"Hey! Girls don't smoke!"

"*Josie!*"

"Aunt Becka will kill us!"

It was true. Neither Aunt Becka nor any of her friends smoked. In fact, the only women she ever saw doing it was in the movies. But Josie's curiosity was aroused. Everyone seemed to enjoy it so much.

Besides, if she looked like a boy and hung around with the boys, and they smoked, she reasoned she could too.

She put the cigarette between her lips and inhaled, expecting perhaps something sweet tasting, like a candy cigarette. Instead, she got a mouthful of nasty, pungent smoke that burnt her tongue and throat, causing her eyes to water. To her embarrassment, she began choking and coughing, gasping for air. This seemed to amuse the boys.

Mike took the cigarette from her hand. There was barely enough left to hold on to, so he took the match stick and gently speared the butt with it. Holding the stick, he inhaled one last time and passed it to Will.

"I gotta go," Big Donny announced, breaking up the conference. "You guys coming?"

"Nah. It's too nice to be inside," Will answered, tearing up the tiny remnant of cigarette butt to scatter the evidence of their deed.

"We're goin' to the park," Danny said. "Mike says you can find all kinds of change laying around."

"Yeah. Last year I picked up 20 cents," Mike repeated what he'd been telling them all morning. "Only I gotta pick up Frankie first."

The children walked down the narrow alleyway that ran from the back of St. Matthew's church to 24th Street. There was a row of Polish flats so close together that a man standing between any two could reach out his arms and touch them both. Each had a high back porch, overlooking tiny back yards that were separated from each other and the alley by wire fences. Each also had a narrow sidewalk, leading to trash cans at each back gate.

The McGuiness family lived in the third house down. The unpainted clapboards were weathered to a soft gray, while the porch showed remnants of having once been painted dark green. Worn by years of McGuiness feet, the stairs were hollowed and the rail polished smooth by dozens of McGuiness hands.

Mr. McGuiness suffered from what Uncle John called, "the I'm gonna's." It was always "I'm gonna fix the fence," "I'm gonna paint the porch," "I'm gonna … I'm gonna …"

Their wire fence sagged from countless McGuiness boys clambering over it instead of using the gate, which hung between one hinge and a bent, metal clothes hanger. It was held shut with a loop of clothesline. The lawn was just clumps of wild crab grass here and there. The chopped-wood pile grew and shrunk as necessary. Despite the old man's, "I'm gonna stack that wood," the pile was burnt and replaced, used up again and again, but never truly stacked.

Along the front and back yards, between the fence and the sidewalk, were Ma McGuiness' irises. They filled every inch of the yard where other people had lawns. It was as if a tiny patch of sky had dropped down into the unkempt shabbiness of the McGuiness' yard. Huge flowers the size of coffee cups perfumed the air. Waves of blue-purple bobbing in the breeze dazzled the eyes of all. People walked blocks to feast their senses and to marvel that such beauty was capable of surviving the destructive ways of the McGuiness boys and wonder how Ma managed to protect them year after year.

She did it with a well-aimed broom and occasional curses. No one dared venture too close to her irises for fear of incurring her wrath. Her sons often bragged, "Bet Ma'd beat 'The Babe' himself if that was a bat instead of a broom!"

The children arrived at the fence. Mike lifted the clothesline loop and the gate sagged out.

"Wait here," he said.

His ma was hanging wash, her line strung from shed to apple tree to shed again, to the only remaining clothes pole, leaning uneasily, then back to the shed. Ma McGuiness always reminded Josie of a feather pillow, all soft and shapeless, even now with her clothespin apron tied around her middle. Her faded sack of a dress was patched and she was barefoot. Her gray-streaked hair hung over one shoulder in a loose braid. At the sight of Mike her face brightened and she started to reach as if to touch him, but pulled back.

"Frankie's finishing breakfast," she said turning to hang a wet undershirt.

"Okay, Ma."

Mike's Grandpa Cleary snoozed in an old rocker that was the same chipped and faded green as the back porch. In spite of the mild morning, he was bundled in a frayed sweater, and a piece of an old quilt was tucked around his legs. A battered fedora shaded his eyes from the sun's glare. Two McGuiness grandbabies scratched around in the dirt near his feet. At the bottom of the back stairs another brother, Kev, sat on an up-ended log, having his morning smoke.

Mike went up the stairs, Ma right behind him. Her laundry tub had been moved out on the porch for the summer so she could enjoy the fresh air and occasional breeze while she rubbed and scrubbed dirty McGuiness clothes. Sweat beaded up on her forehead and her flabby arms shook as she worked over the washboard. Frankie came out from the kitchen, eating a hard roll spread with thick slabs of butter. Ma turned and almost shyly put an arm around him, soap suds dripping off the ends of her fingers. He leaned against her soft body for a moment, then bounded down the stairs with Mike a few steps behind him.

"Be good, boys," Ma told them. "And stay together."

"Yeah, Ma."

Kev stuck a foot out and Frankie sprawled in the dirt, his roll landing a few feet away. "Clumsy little turd," Kev said.

Mike leapt from the steps onto Kev's back, punching wherever he could land a blow, but it was no match. Kev simply flipped him over a shoulder to the ground and straddled him, knees pressing into Mike's arms, pinning him down. Mike began a litany of swearing.

"Oh, big man!" Kev snarled around the cigarette dangling from stiff lips, his eyes narrow slits. Snake eyes.

Ma reacted at once. "You let them little guys be, ya lummox!"

"Shut yer hole, old bag!" he yelled back, raising an arm as Mike squirmed helplessly under his weight.

Ma picked up a pail of soapy, hot water and sloshed it on the pair. Kev, being on top, got the brunt of it. He forgot Mike and turned in rage to his mother, who threw the empty pail at him.

"Go! Go!" Ma urged her two youngest sons. "Go on! Now!"

Frankie scooped up his roll and scooted through the gate. Mike hesitated an instant, then, with one hand on a wobbly post, sailed gracefully over the fence to join the rest of them in the alley.

Ma, holding the brush end of her broom toward her, was ready for Kev, who was advancing up the steps.

"You old bag!" he screamed.

She poked him in the chest with the handle. "Come on," she taunted. "Come on! I ain't some little kid. I ain't scared of the likes of you!"

Kev tried to grab the broom, but Ma had played this game for too many years. She pulled back and, just as quickly, whacked him on the side of the head, bloodying his ear. Kev yowled in pain and rage like a cat whose tail just got stepped on.

Grandpa Cleary woke and stared about in confusion. "Sock 'em ... sock 'em a good one," he muttered, swinging useless old arms about. "Sock 'em ... sock 'em."

His voice trailed off. The two babies peered out from the protection of the rocker as *their* mother came out from the basement apartment to see what was going on. Frankie looked at Mike with wide, frightened eyes as the brawl escalated.

"She'll be okay. She can handle Kev," Mike said. "Besides ... Pa's home."

The back door was suddenly flung open and Mr. McGuiness roared out.

"What the God-damn hell! Can't a man have a bit of quiet in his own home!"

The children tore off down the alley, slowing only when they reached the rear of the church. Old Man McGuiness' voice could still be heard, bellowing through the morning air, rising higher and higher, overwhelming the other two.

"God-dammit! A man works all God-damn night and has to listen to all this God-damn noise! Ya's want a brou-ha-ha? I'll give ya's a brou-ha-ha!"

Mike took Frankie's roll and picked off the biggest pieces of dirt. "You can still eat it," he said. "Just keep picking the stuff off as you eat." He wiped his fingers on his jeans. "Be just as good as new."

"Yeah. Ya gotta eat a peck of dirt before ya die anyway," Danny told him as though it were a rule or a law of something.

Josie wondered if her mother had eaten a peck of dirt. Maybe if you didn't eat enough, you'd live and live until you finally finished your peck.

"So, you get to eat a lot of *yours* today!" Will added.

Why did he think that was so great? Maybe it meant Frankie would die sooner if he got filled up with his peck of dirt too soon.

Mike laughed and nudged Frankie on the arm. "Bet that's the first bath Kev's had all summer," he said. Frankie nodded and laughed obediently.

They started down the long alley, her brothers and Mike in front, and she and Frankie bringing up the rear the way they always did. Frankie was taking tiny bites, inspecting for dirt, and picking it off as he came to it.

Mike kept twitching and plucking at his wet shirt and Josie noticed tiny trickles of water had caused little clean streaks on his neck as they ran down from his hair. Suddenly he turned to walk backwards, staring at Frankie, his face so white the freckles the angels had scattered across his nose and cheeks seemed to pop out, and the few sprinkled in his eyes glinted gold against the cold blue irises. Frankie stared back, eyes wide and dark.

Mike turned his attention back to Danny and Will. "Hey," he said plucking once more at his tee shirt. "Ma usually waits 'til I take off my clothes 'fore she washes 'em." Pleased with his joke, Mike glanced over his shoulder to make sure Frankie appreciated it too. The two boys grinned at each other.

"Come on, let's get to the park," Mike continued. "Last year I found 24 cents."

Chapter Eleven
Trouble

Their purpose in the park was apparent. They were going to find loose change that had dropped from the pockets of people sprawled on the grass, watching the Fourth of July fireworks the day before.

"Yeah," Mike said. "They can't find all their stuff if it drops out in the dark. Last year I found 26 cents. Just laying there waiting for me."

Danny and Will exchanged glances, but said nothing. The last time Mike had told them about his luck, it had been 24 cents. Each time the amount got larger and larger.

Josie and Frankie trailed quietly behind their brothers, rarely speaking to each other. This morning Frankie was picking specks of dirt from his hard roll between bites. Josie thought hard rolls were wonderfully crunchy, spread with thick slabs of butter. Mrs. Lewendoski would occasionally treat them to one if they did some small job for her. But Daddy hated them as only Daddy could. If Aunt Becka brought any home, he would complain loudly.

"Only a Pollack would come up with such a dumb thing. So damn hard you could break a window with 'em!"

True, they were rock hard on the outside, but *inside* they were soft and fluffy as a cloud. It was so great to pull at the soft part, then munch the crust, its little pieces flaking off. She wished they had stayed to help Big Donny and Cas instead of going to the park today.

The cleaning crews, with loose-fitting white jackets over their regular clothes, were already busy by the time the children got to the park. Two men were stacking park benches along the pathway to be picked up and stored in the boathouse. Several others, armed with pointy sticks, were spearing paper cups and pushing them off again off with gloved hands into gunny sacks tied at their waists. The men moved slowly, as though they had all time in the world. Uncle John said that was why the letters D.P.W. were printed on their coats: "Darn Poor Workers."

The children spread out in a line to walk the slopes in search of coins, but the hunt was futile. Not a single penny was found hiding in the grass. When they flopped down to rest, Mike was very vocal about their disappointing luck.

"It's them damn crews," he fretted. "They get paid to do a job, but do they gotta take our money too?"

"We could go to the playground," Frankie suggested hopefully. This was an idea Josie felt was fine, but all he got was a "keep-out-of-it" look from Mike, who was determined to get some money, somewhere, somehow.

"I know!" he said. "Come on."

He led the way through the park to the Conservatory across from the sunken gardens: another "grownup" place, nice to visit on winter days, but one had to behave and not run ahead or chase around. It probably would be lots of fun to do so here where jungle plants and thick vines grew indoors like in a Tarzan movie.

There were beautiful flowers called "orchids" and everything smelled earthy, wild, and untamed. Occasionally a bird found its way in and fluttered around, adding to the realism. When you entered the main part of the building a stone walkway led to a waterfall and a make-believe stream. Two wings off this main area turned the building into a huge "T." These wings weren't very interesting, just long tables of potted plants with empty crates or piles of soil underneath, but you had to walk through them to reach the "wishing pond."

Today, with no Daddy or Aunt Becka to warn them, they hurried up the main walkway and down the side path, stopping on a stone bridge over-looking a pool under the waterfall. The water gushed out from gray rocks pleasantly, making the water restless and frothy on that end of the pool.

"See," Mike pointed to the coins lining the bottom of the pool, shining and glittering, enticing them. Each penny and nickel represented a wish.

"All them wishes," Mike laughed. "Guess what *I'm* wishing."

"Yeah. But we can't reach 'em," Danny said. "They're all under water."

"Maybe we could wade in," Will said.

"Nah," Mike answered. "Guard might see us. But the little kids ... they can duck under the bridge if we warn 'em."

Josie and Frankie eased themselves down the small slope to the water's edge, rolled up their jeans, and took off their shoes and socks. Josie pulled off her shoes without bothering to untie them, stuck in her socks, and placed them under a giant elephant ear, just the way an elf would do. She wondered if the elves were watching right now, ready to do some mischief because the children were stealing their coins. She looked around before stepping in the water.

It was surprisingly cold and the pond's bottom was slippery. This was not going to be as easy as they first thought, and somehow it didn't seem quite right. But it was too late now to ask questions. Josie picked up one penny, then another and another. Frankie was grabbing as many as he could, trying very hard not to fall in.

"Hey! What do you guys think you're doing?"

"Hide!" Mike hissed between clinched teeth. Both Josie and Frankie darted under the bridge. Josie pressed against the foundation as close as she could while Frankie hunched over, hands on his knees. His shadow was showing out on the pond.

The guard grabbed Will by the shirt collar. "You little s—. What do you think you're pulling here?"

Josie listened, afraid to breathe, her heart thumping loudly as she watched her brother get a good shaking through the watery reflections.

"Hey! We ain't doin' nothin'," Mike argued. "Just checkin' the falls is all."

"Don't give me no lip. I know what's going on here, ya little thieves."

With each word Will got shook again. The guard looked over the edge of the bridge.

"You down there! I see ya! Get up here."

Josie and Frankie exchanged glances but both were too terrified to move.

"I see ya hunched down there. Don't make me come getcha!"

Frankie gave a look of pure despair, then slowly, fearfully stepped out from his haven.

"Get your a— up here!"

Frankie picked up his shoes and climbed up to join the other boys.

"Empty them pockets."

"Leave him alone," Mike yelled. "He's just a little kid."

"Yeah. Well *you* ain't. Maybe I should just call the cops. See how ya like them apples."

Frankie stood quietly as the man went through his pockets, reclaiming the few pennies he'd managed to scoop up. Then he sat down to put on his shoes and socks. Josie remained still, safely back in the shadows, unseen by this scary giant guard. Perhaps the elves were looking after her.

"Now scram!" The guard shoved Mike to start him on his way. "If I see ya here again it'll be the cops."

The boys tore off down one of the wings, around to the main walk toward the door. The guard tossed Frankie's coins back in the pond. The unexpected tiny splashes caused Josie to gasp and the giant stood a moment listening, leaning over the rail suspiciously.

She waited, shivering for what seemed forever until he finally left. She quietly eased her way out of the water, retrieved her shoes, and scurried up to the bridge. Keeping low, she darted under one of the long plant tables, scrunched next to a bag of foul-smelling stuff and struggled to put on her shoes. She counted her loot. Two nickels and seven pennies. She stuck the nickels in her left shoe and the pennies went in a pocket. Now all she had to do was sneak out without being seen.

Two ladies came by, unaware she was hiding right below them. She waited until they had gone a short way, then crawled out and joined them, walking close enough that the giant might think she was with them as he made his rounds, glaring at her.

"What are those?" she asked the ladies politely.

They read the label to her: meaningless words, but she listened carefully. They were the slowest ladies Josie had ever seen. Each plant was discussed, each flower sniffed, and when the guard was on the other side, a plant or two was snipped.

"It's good to prune them back," they confided in her.

As soon as the door was in sight, Josie made a bee-line for it.

"Hey you! Hey boy! Get over here!"

Josie ran around the corner to the bathrooms. She darted into a stall, locked the door, then scooted down the row to another stall and stood on the toilet seat. She heard the door open and close as the two ladies came in. Then a knock and the now-familiar voice called in.

"Is there anyone else in there with you ladies?"

"No. No one."

"But one of the stalls is locked."

"Doesn't seem to be anyone in there. No feet."

"Can I come in?" he asked politely.

The giant came in and used a special key to unlock the stall, but of course no one was there. He checked the next stall and, on his way out, swung open a few more doors just to make sure.

"Them kids," was all he said as he left.

The two ladies "used the facilities," chatting while they did, as slow as ever!

When they left, Josie climbed down. She stepped out of the stall, trying to think of how she was going to get past the giant and out of the building. But he was searching for a boy.

She stuck Danny's hat under her shirt. Her hair stood on end, like a wild thing with a life all its own. She filled the sink with water and stuck her head in. Immediately her hair wilted. She took paper towels and dried it as best she could. It wasn't very good, but at least she looked like a girl now. She rolled her jeans up to between her ankles and knees so they appeared more girlish. Now to get out and find her brothers.

She opened the door cautiously, watchfully, and took a few timid steps to peek down the walkway of the main building. The giant was chatting with some grownups near the two wings of the "T." Josie made her break, scampering quickly to the door and safety. Once free, she'd worry about finding Danny and Will.

"Hey, stop!" the giant bellowed behind her, but Josie kept going, out the door and down the cement steps. Suddenly, she was grabbed from behind. She let out a scream.

"Josie. It's me," Will's voice in her ear calmed her and she turned to follow him into the dark safety of some bushes.

"Geez, what took ya so long?" Will asked. Without waiting for an answer, he continued, "Rest of 'em are looking for soda bottles in all the trash cans."

Josie and Will crawled through the bushes to a small clearing next to the fence where the others waited for them. They sat in a circle counting their loot. They had found two Nesbit's Orange bottles, both chipped, one so badly it was probably worthless.

"How much did you manage to get?" Mike asked her.

Josie pulled out the seven pennies.

"That's it? All that time and all ya got is seven lousy pennies?"

She had been about to take off her shoe and show off the nickels, but something made her stop. She'd risked being caught by that awful giant, had to hide and pretend to be with two strange old ladies, and now Mike was yelling at her that it hadn't been enough!

"It's more'n you got," Danny said quietly.

Mike raised one eyebrow and stared at Danny, then nodded.

"Yeah. You're right," he admitted.

Danny divided up the pennies. One for each.

"Josie gets an extra."

Mike didn't question or argue.

"The other one we'll buy something to share."

The children picked up the bottles and made their way through the park to a little store across from the sunken gardens. It catered mostly to the people visiting the park. Few of the neighborhood folks went there. In fact, Josie had never been in there before. It wasn't like Mr. Schick's at all; there were no potatoes or onions in the window, no meats in trays with bloody juices collecting around them.

There *was* a candy counter. The few items there had been moved to the edge of the shelves to appear to be more. It was a dusty, dejected place and the owner was equally uninviting. He was small and wiry, wearing an old, white shirt, now more gray than white. The collar was grimy around his neck where shaggy hair rubbed it. He took one look at the chipped soda bottles and, before they could say a word, he growled.

"Get outta here with 'em! You kids didn't buy 'em here! Don't try to get me to take your broken old junk!"

"Geez," Mike said. "Ya still will get the money from Nesbit's."

"Ya wanna buy somethin'? If not, get outta here! I ain't takin' no chipped old bottles offa yer hands."

"We got money," Danny said, heading to the candy counter.

Mike picked first. "Kits," he said. Then he began walking around the store, holding up an item every once in a while, and asking, "How much?" But the man ignored him. As soon as Frankie brought what he wanted, he joined Mike in asking this and that of the storekeeper until everyone was done and ready to leave.

As they were leaving the man said, "If ya wanna throw them bottles out ya can. There's the can."

"Yeah, yeah," Mike answered. "Then you can fish 'em out for yourself."

"Get outta here!" the man yelled. "Don't come back!"

Outside, Mike was furious. "Here!" he yelled. "Now ya can have 'em!"

He took the two bottles and smashed them on the walk right outside the door. The storekeeper ran out, screaming and yelling as the children tore off down the street.

"Call the cops!" echoed in Josie's ears, making him seem even more terrifying than the giant had been. But her brothers and Mike and Frankie seemed to think it was funny, so she began to giggle too. Her candy had never been so sweet. Mike reached in his shirt and pulled out two boxes of Cracker Jack.

"Looky what he donated. One for you guys and one for me and Frankie!"

Frankie smirked too. "Looky!" he said, holding up a small package of marshmallows.

"Hey! Awright!" Mike beamed at his brother. "Awright!"

They walked back to the park, this time heading where Frankie and Josie had wanted to go in the first place: the playground. There were a few older kids playing on the merry-go-round, standing up and walking around, trying to push each other off with lots of shouts and commotion. Some smaller kids were swinging and a group of boys sat along the edge of the sandbox talking and sharing a cigarette. Her brothers headed to join the bunch at the merry-go-round, but Mike yelled to Frankie, "Gimme the rest of them marshmallows."

Reluctantly, Frankie handed them over, then joined Josie at the swings. Mike sauntered over to the bunch at the sandbox. *He's probably hoping to snag a smoke using Frankie's marshmallows,* Josie thought. She was glad she hadn't shared her nickels. They were hers just as the marshmallows were Frankie's, but Mike seemed to think whatever he wanted was his.

Soon the swing had Josie hypnotized like it always did. The air blew through her hair. Her tummy dropped pleasantly with each swing. She felt herself flying like an airplane way up high, with clouds and birds below her.

"Hey," Frankie interrupted her dreams. "Hey, come on." He nudged her.

A policeman was talking to Mike. Danny and Will were still going 'round and 'round as though they were unaware. But every kid was watching. The rest of the bunch at the sandbox started drifting away like bad smells.

"Come on," Frankie pulled her into the bushes. They crawled along quietly to get closer so they could hear what the cop wanted from Mike.

" ...broke bottles," the cop said.

"Too bad ... wasn't me."

"Sounded like you ... Frankie ... two other boys ..."

"Just me ... Frankie's home."

"A little girl ..."

"Yeah, right ... I hang around with a little girl!"

The cop seemed to accept that. He looked around as if searching for someone else.

"I'm watching you. So, don't try no wise-guy stuff with me."

"Hey, I'm here. Been here all morning ... ask anybody." Only no one remained nearby to ask. Everyone had drifted off.

Josie pulled her cap out from under her shirt and stuffed her hair back under it. If they were looking for a little girl, she'd become a boy again. This was really very handy! As soon as the cop left, Frankie crawled out from hiding, with Josie right behind him. Danny and Will ran over.

"What's up?" they demanded.

"That jerk called 'em," Mike said, spitting. "Lousy jerk!"

"Maybe we'd better go before he comes back," Will suggested. And it seemed a good idea to the others, and even to Josie, who had no say anyway.

"Just wait 'til ya see what I got," Mike bragged. He poked Frankie. "with them marshmallows."

Josie thought he was going to pull out a cigarette, but instead it was some red things almost the size of a cigarette.

"Firecrackers! Wow!" Her brothers seemed pleased and Frankie seemed to think it was a great trade too.

They walked along, throwing firecrackers as they went. Big bangs and the sound of dogs barking followed them down the alley. Danny fished a can out of a trash box and they put a firecracker partly under it before lighting it. The can shot up in the air.

Every year Josie had heard the stories of children who lost eyes and fingers to firecrackers on the Fourth of July, but that only made this more exciting. The danger, the noise.

When they reached St. Matthews Mike and Frankie headed down their alley, and Josie and her brothers crossed the street to their house. Josie was suddenly aware of how hungry she was and couldn't wait to see Aunt Becka to tell her about the park and everything. She started to hurry, but Will grabbed her.

"Don't say nothin' about the store."

"Or the fags ..."

"Or the firecrackers ..."

She shook her head. Did they think she was a dumb baby?

Aunt Becka was furious when they came in. She scolded the boys mostly. How could they go off without telling her? How could they take Josie with her hair all messy? How could they worry her so?

She took Josie into the bathroom and started running water in the tub. "Just look at you ... what will people say? Get undressed while I get some hot water."

Josie took off the dirty tee shirt and jeans, and peeled her socks off. The two nickels dropped to the floor. How would she explain them to Aunt Becka? Josie knelt down and placed them, one on top of the other, behind the leg of the bathtub. She looked at her reflection in the mirror. A snarl-haired stranger stared back. No wonder Aunt Becka was upset!

Aunt Becka's anger was nothing compared to Daddy's. After he scolded them all, he took her brothers one at a time into the bathroom and paddled their bottoms. Each came out red-faced, trying not to cry, although a few tears did sneak out. Josie, who wasn't even spanked, cried out of sympathy for Danny and Will. But the worst punishment was yet to come.

"You will all stay in your own yard for the next two weeks, and no kids in to play, either! And you can't hang around with those trouble-making McGuiness boys anymore!"

Those two weeks dragged and Josie was at a loss at for what to do. She'd crawl under the porch and pretend Barbara was there with her playing house, but it wasn't much fun. Her brothers spent a lot of time sitting on the trash box, tossing a ball back and forth to whichever members of the gang were willing to stay in the alley and toss it back. Big Donny still came around. Daddy couldn't very well forbid his visits to his grandmother. Mike and Frankie were amazed that the children were punished at all.

"Jesus!" Mike said. "Who gives a darn if ya took off like that? It's not like they found out about the store or nothin'!"

It was while she was under the steps that Josie overheard a confusing bit of information. Aunt Becka came out on the porch and sat on the steps to wait for the mailman. Josie searched for a stick to poke through the crack to tease her. But before she could find one, Uncle John came home from a week of railroading. Aunt Becka started to tell him about Daddy's response to the children's absence.

"He was so angry. I mean, much more than he should have been."

"Drinking?" Uncle John asked.

"Afraid so. You know he has no sort of life. He really should get married again."

"I know."

"Maybe if I wasn't around, he'd have to ... you know, find someone. Not have me to depend on so much."

"That's no reason for you to rush into anything."

"Well, it's not like I'm exactly rushing, but—"

"But if you don't feel the way you should, you know it's not fair … not fair to either of you."

"I admit, it's not like with Del. But James is a good man. Catholic."

Josie listened carefully, not daring to move or let herself be noticed. Nothing seemed to upset grownups more than a kid sneaking around. She hadn't planned to eavesdrop; it had just happened. But sometimes grownups didn't give a chance to explain.

Aunt Becka continued talking. "I think it's for the best. I want a home of my own. Children. And if I'm not here … well, maybe Thomas will make more of an effort to meet someone."

"Sis, you're wrong. So wrong. He'll snap out of it when he's ready, and you marrying James or anyone else you don't love isn't going to change him."

"I care about James … really, I—"

At that point the mailman showed up. Uncle John stood up and reached for the mail.

"Good mornin'."

They both stood up and went inside. Josie remained quiet under the steps until she was sure they were gone. Then she crawled out to find her brothers.

Chapter Twelve
Aunt Becka Reads a Story

In the evenings after supper dishes were washed, Aunt Becka and Josie would join the "men-folk" in the living room. Daddy, if he was home and not at work, would sit in his corner of the saggy brown couch, listening to the radio droning quietly. The boys usually were sprawled on the floor, reading or doing their homework. If Uncle John was home, he'd read a book or pester the children into a game of Chinese Checkers. Josie loved to line up the colored marbles in designs, but to actually play the game seemed silly.

The best evenings were when Aunt Becka read stories. She'd read one for the boys: Tom Sawyer or a pirate story about lost treasure. Then she would take Josie on her lap and read a story to her. The rocker would creak pleasantly as Josie leaned back against the soft warmth of Aunt Becka and looked at the pictures. The words danced to the music of Aunt Becka's voice.

"The Owl and the Pussy-cat went to sea in a beautiful, pea-green boat …"

The words had a hypnotic effect on Josie.

"They took some honey and plenty of money wrapped in a five-pound note …"

Josie didn't understand the words but the rhyme and rhythm were soothing.

And when Aunt Becka got to the part, "What a beautiful Puss you are, you are. What a beautiful Puss you are," Aunt Becka would give

Josie a little squeeze and whisper in her ear, "What a beautiful Puss you are."

Josie knew Aunt Becka meant her. They were not just words from a story but special words, just for her. How lucky she was to have an Aunt Becka!

Josie would study the pictures while Aunt Becka's voice worked its magic.

"And hand-in-hand, on the edge of the sand, they danced by the light of the moon, the moon."

That picture was Josie's favorite, even though it meant the story was over. The Owl and the Pussy-cat hand-in-hand were so cute.

"Really they danced paw-in-wing," Aunt Becka would laugh. Then, pretending she were an owl, Aunt Becka would say, "May I hold your paw, my dear?"

Josie would giggle. "Let me hold your wing," she'd answer.

Aunt Becka would scoop her up and, paw-in-wing, they'd dance around the room, the room. They danced around the room.

And Uncle John and the boys would shake their heads and laugh at such silliness.

After the story Aunt Becka would help Josie brush her teeth, using a tiny rub of soap on her brush since there wasn't always money for tooth powder. Josie would wrinkle her face and spit and spit to get rid of the taste. Then Aunt Becka would help her into her nightie and tuck her in.

Together they said an "Our Father" and a "Hail Mary," and then Josie would bless them all.

"God bless Daddy," she'd say first because Daddy needed it the most. Then, "God bless Uncle John, Danny and Will. God bless Aunt Becka. God bless me, too. Is that okay?" Josie would ask.

Aunt Becka always nodded. Sometimes Josie would pretend to forget Aunt Becka. She'd say, "God bless Mr. Russell and Mrs. Russell," or "God bless Mrs. Lewendoski and Mrs. Schick." She'd peek at Aunt Becka.

"Who else?" Josie would tease. "Oh, yes! Mr. Leary's dog and his apple tree too!"

"Josie!" Aunt Becka would scold. "Now you're being silly. You shouldn't be silly when you're asking God for something."

Subdued, Josie would add, "God bless Aunt Becka."

Then Aunt Becka would cover her up and tuck the sides so she was "snug as a bug in a rug." Then she'd turn off the light and leave.

Josie would lay there and try to stay awake until Danny and Will came to bed. But instead, she'd wake up surprised to find it was the next morning.

Chapter Thirteen

Going to Grandmother's

One evening at supper Aunt Becka said something that made Josie stop worrying about what "nigger hair" meant.

"With all the problems with those hoodlums I'm sure glad the children are spending the rest of the summer with their grandparents."

Danny and Will nudged each other, delighted.

Around the time their mother had died, the children had gone back and forth between Daddy and their mother's family. Josie's recollections of those times seemed more like a vague dream than reality. The idea of leaving Aunt Becka was frightening. Then a new worry replaced all others. She simply could not remember what she called her grandmother.

The next day she sat quietly on the invisible stair, unseen, trying to remember. It was easy to just add "grand" to "daddy" to make "Granddaddy," but a grandmother was different. A mother could be called "Mama," so maybe she called her grandmother, "Grandmama." Josie whispered the word out loud. "Grandmama." It seemed too babyish.

Big Donny called Mrs. Lewendoski "Grandma," but that didn't fit either. Maybe she should just ask Danny and Will. But she worried they would think she was dumb, so she worried alone, keeping her fears to herself while trying to figure it out.

Two days later Grandmother arrived in a taxicab from the railroad station. The children ran out to greet her. "Grandmother!" Josie said, instinctively, as she was hugged. "Grandmother." She sighed in relief.

The next few days were busy and exciting as Aunt Becka and Grandmother packed all the things three children might need for the summer. New underwear and socks were purchased. Shorts and shirts. Shoes for playing. Shoes for church. Dresses for Josie. All went into the oversized suitcase until it couldn't hold another item. Then it was snapped shut, locked, and two leather belts tightened around it. Uncle John took it to be "railroad expressed" to Grandmother's house.

"Jo. Jo, Honey. Wake up!" Grandmother shook Josie into wakefulness.

"It's still nighttime," she whined, drowsily rolling over to face the room.

Danny and Will were already out of bed, stretching and yawning. Then it came to her. This was the day! The day they were to take the train all the way to Grandmother's house to stay for the rest of the summer.

Josie sat up, wide-awake, spiders of the night vanishing in anticipation of the day's adventure. Danny and Will grabbed their clothes and headed for the bathroom to dress, pushing and shoving each other good naturedly as they always did.

"Hurry now, Hon," Grandmother urged. "We have a train to catch and it won't wait for us!"

Josie dressed quickly, slipping into the red plaid dress Grandmother had chosen for her to wear on the trip. She picked up her shoes and hurried to the kitchen, aromas of breakfast beckoning. She held her shoes in front of her to show Aunt Becka, who sat at the table, watching the toaster. Aunt Becka shook her head slightly, so Josie crossed her arms, placing each shoe opposite from where it had first been.

Aunt Becka smiled and nodded approvingly. Josie sat down to put on her shoes, holding up each foot so Aunt Becka could tie them. Danny and Will were already seated, wiggling and squirming with excitement, unable to sit still.

"You're going to have your hands full with these two," Aunt Becka warned Grandmother.

Grandmother, covered with a flowered apron, stood at the stove, frying eggs. Her spoon made little clicking noises against the old cast-iron skillet as she basted a half dozen eggs with hot bacon fat until the whites were cooked and the yolks looked puffy and almost pinkish. Grandmother shook her head as she slid the eggs one by one onto a serving platter.

"They'll be fine once we're on our way."

She carried the plate to the table just as Aunt Becka removed the toast from the toaster and put in two fresh slices of bread. Grandmother dished out eggs to the children, took two for herself, and handed the plate to Aunt Becka. Aunt Becka buttered and cut both slices of toast and gave each one of the children a half.

"I should have used the oven to make the toast," Aunt Becka apologized. "This is going to take so long." She offered the remaining half to Grandmother whom just pushed it away.

"You take it. I don't mind waiting a bit."

It's real nice having breakfast served to me for a change," Aunt Becka smiled, taking the last egg. "Although I feel a bit guilty having company do the cooking."

"Nonsense!" Grandmother answered. "I'm family, not company."

They ate in silence. Josie glanced at her brothers as they wolfed down their breakfasts, not even bothering to play with their eggs. Danny usually popped the yolk with his fork, saying in a silly voice, "Oh help! Oh help!" as though the egg was speaking. Will loved to eat all the white, then pop the yolk into his mouth whole. Sometimes if no grownups were watching, he'd say, "Look, Josie!" then bite the yolk and let the yellowness ooze out the corners of his mouth and run down his chin. She would squeal, covering her eyes while Danny and Will laughed as though it was the greatest joke ever!

"When are you planning your trip?" Grandmother asked.

"Not until the end of August," Aunt Becka replied.

Josie listened carefully. She hadn't even thought about what Aunt Becka would be doing while they were gone. *Where would she be going?*

Josie waited for the grownups to give more information.

"That's when James has his vacation," Aunt Becka continued telling Grandmother. "He's coming up here for a few days, then we're both going back to Chicago."

Aunt Becka was going to Chicago with James! Josie had almost forgotten James and his quiet, disinterested, "That's nice."

"Are you taking a train too, Aunt Becka?" Josie asked, realizing at once that she shouldn't have spoken. For some reason grownups preferred to think kids didn't care or understand what they were discussing. And as soon as they became aware one was listening, they'd either be quiet or change the subject.

Grandmother and Aunt Becka exchanged a cautious look, confirming Josie's feelings.

"Little pitchers!" Grandmother said.

Aunt Becka just smiled at her. "No, Sweets. I'm taking a bus."

"Why are you going?"

"Oh," Aunt Becka hesitated. "Oh, just to see how I like Chicago."

How silly! Josie thought. Traveling all that way just to see if you like a place. And with "dull as dishwater" James!

Josie wondered why they said, "dishwater is dull" when it wasn't dull at all. It was fascinating! Filled with bubbles. It was fun to wash dishes, splashing the water around from cup to cup, making even more bubbles. Josie's thoughts rapidly turned to other things more interesting than a bus trip. Besides, Grandmother and Aunt Becka had changed the subject.

The back door opened and Daddy came in. "I called a cab," he told them. "Should be here in about ..." He pulled out his pocket watch. "In about 20 minutes."

The words had a remarkable effect on them all, causing a flurry of activity.

A cab! Josie's heart skipped with excitement. She could barely remember riding in a car, much less a cab! Danny and Will must have felt the same way because they both jumped up without asking to be excused. Grandmother stood up and removed her apron, then checked her purse, making certain the tickets were there.

Daddy set Grandmother's small grip next to the larger one that contained the children's necessaries: things they might need in case the suitcase Uncle John had shipped didn't get to Grandmother's right away. Aunt Becka stuffed some more things for the train into the old Schuster's shopping bag. Then she called Josie to come get her hair brushed.

Danny and Will ran to the bathroom in turns, to go one last time before they left.

Josie didn't know what to do with the flash of energy rushing through her, so she went to the front window and looked out into the darkness to watch for the cab. It didn't take long for the bright yellow-and-black car to pull up in front of the house.

"It's here! It's here!" she sang out, jumping up and down.

"Shh! Quiet down!" Daddy warned. "The Lewendoskis are still sleeping."

Subdued, Josie whispered loudly, "It's here! The cab's here!" just as the doorbell rang.

Danny and Will raced down the front steps, each trying to be the one to open the downstairs door for the cab driver. Daddy picked up the suitcase and followed the boys down.

"Quiet!" he ordered. But, of course, they were too excited to listen.

"See ya later, sis!" he called back to Aunt Becka, who stood by the upstairs door.

"I need kisses!" she said to the boys. "You can't leave until I get my kisses."

Danny and Will came tearing back up the steps and each gave her a quick peck on the cheek, then turned to race down again.

"Walk! Quiet!" Aunt Becka scolded them futilely.

Grandmother picked up her purse and the shopping bag, gave Aunt Becka a hug, then hurried down the steps.

Josie stood quietly, watching everyone, filled with unexpected sadness at leaving Aunt Becka. Suddenly she didn't want to go away to stay with Grandmother. She felt as though the tears might start to flow. The lump in her throat was awful.

"I need a kiss, Sweets," Aunt Becka knelt down so she was close to Josie's size. She seemed a little sad too. "You can't leave unless I get a kiss and a big, big hug from my Sweets. One that will last all summer!"

Josie threw her arms around Aunt Becka, clinging tightly.

"You'll be just fine, Sweets," Aunt Becka spoke soothingly to her. "Just fine."

She gently removed Josie's arms from around her neck.

"You'll have a wonderful vacation and I'll see you when you get back home."

Josie studied Aunt Becka's face carefully, embedding it firmly in her mind to last all summer. "Promise?" she asked.

Aunt Becka nodded, blinking back her own tears. "I promise," she said.

"Come on, Josie," Daddy called impatiently. "Come on!"

Josie stepped away from Aunt Becka and started down the steps, holding the rail cautiously. She turned to look back once more.

"Good-bye, Sweets. Have a good trip."

Josie continued down the steps.

"Have a good trip!" Aunt Becka called out again as Josie took Daddy's hand and walked to the cab.

The coolness of the night air surprised her, yet it seemed logical that the night would be cool, just as the shade was cooler than the sunshine. She shivered from the anticipation as well as the coolness.

Danny and Will were already in the back seat and Grandmother was climbing in as Josie approached with Daddy. The cab driver was putting the suitcases and shopping bag in the trunk. Josie crawled in next to Grandmother. The driver came around from the back and sat behind the wheel.

"All set?" Daddy asked as he opened the front door to sit next to the driver.

“Meter’s clicking!” The driver pointed to a little box in front of him with a clock on it.

They pulled away.

Josie stared out the window, fascinated by the familiar streets, now enveloped in shadows. The darkness gave them a strange, different look. Everything was quiet. Darkened store windows stared vacantly back at her. Few people were moving through the quiet, shadowy streets. Even the stop-and-go lights weren’t changing colors, but merely flashed red or yellow. The downtown streets, usually busy and bustling, were deserted.

As they approached the station, Josie could make out a small park across the street with trees and benches: a square park like the one near her home. A figure was lying on one of the benches. *Could someone be sleeping there,* she wondered. How fun! Sleeping outside like that! Like an Indian! Josie started to ask Daddy, but the cab stopped and everyone began climbing out.

The driver opened the trunk to retrieve their luggage. Grandmother started herding the children into the huge building. The sky was beginning to lighten, allowing Josie to really look at the station and take in every detail. It was the same red brick as St. Matthew’s church. It even had a steeple, only there was a clock on it instead of a cross. For a moment, a feeling of reverence swept through her as they walked up the wide cement stairs toward one of the half dozen doors.

A colored man in a blue uniform and red cap opened the door and took the larger suitcase from Daddy. He ushered them into the station.

In front of her, across the huge span of black-and-white mosaic floor tiles, was another door just as wide as the one they’d come in. An iron gate blocked the way through it. *That must be where the trains are,* Josie thought. To her left was a row of windows with bars over them, windows that opened, not to the outside, but to another room. Most of them were shut with shades pulled down. The two that were open showed men, dressed neatly in white shirts and ties, sitting on high stools. In back of the men were blackboards with writing and numbers

Josie didn't understand.

To her right was an immense room with benches, like pews in a church but with slating all around like a long oval, a continuous seat going around and around. Danny and Will raced for one of the benches and began sliding around, enjoying another of their spontaneous private games.

A few people sat quietly here and there, some snoozing, sleepy travelers like themselves, waiting for an early train. Grandmother walked over to sit between Danny and Will, ending their game. Daddy set the small grip down next to her and the Red Cap put the larger suitcase on the floor nearby.

"Thanks," Daddy said, handing him some coins.

"Thank you, sir," he answered, touching the brim of his cap.

"Why did you pay him?" Will asked loudly.

"Just to carry the suitcase?" Danny continued. "We would have helped."

"For nothing!"

"Hush!" Grandmother scolded. "Be still!"

"The man's got to make a living, doesn't he?" Daddy glared at them. "You'll have plenty of opportunity to carry it, I'm sure. Now settle down!"

The boys sat back, red-faced and quiet. Josie knew it was only for a little while.

"I'd better go check the timetable." Daddy glanced at his watch. He walked over to speak to one of the men behind an open window.

"Grandmother," Josie whispered. "I gotta go!"

"Didn't you do that at home?" Grandmother snapped.

Josie shook her head. "I forgot," she mumbled.

Grown-ups always seemed upset if a kid had to visit the bathroom. Yet they'd be even more upset if the kid wet himself. Grown-ups could be so confusing sometimes. Besides, they could go whenever they wanted, without needing to ask permission from anyone.

Grandmother's attitude softened, as though she realized Josie's feelings.

"That's okay, honey," she said. "I should go, myself." She took Josie's hand in hers to walk to the ladies' room.

When Josie had been a little girl, Daddy would take her into the men's room. She'd wait outside the door while he made sure everything was "okay" before allowing her to go directly into a stall. When she finished, he'd make her wait again until the coast was clear and everything was okay again. Josie tried to figure out what was wrong that had to become okay, but never could. When she asked Daddy, he said "because some men were using the facilities too." Whatever that meant! Daddy said it was necessary to do it that way, so they did. Still, it remained a puzzle. Whatever it was didn't happen in the ladies' room, because if she was with Aunt Becka or Grandmother, it was never necessary to wait.

This ladies' room was different from any other she had ever been in. There was a large waiting room with chairs and a couch that a lady was sleeping on, with a small boy hugging a stuffed doggie snuggled next to her. All the toilets were in a second room. A colored lady in a white dress sat dozing in a chair next to the row of sinks. Some of the stalls had boxes on the outside.

"We'll use this one, honey," Grandmother opened a different stall door. "Those are pay toilets. We don't need to use them."

"Why do you have to pay, Grandmother?" Josie asked.

"Well, if you're traveling a long way, it's nice to have a place to freshen up," Grandmother explained.

Freshen up? Josie wasn't sure what that meant. Probably just a polite way of saying "to go," she guessed.

When they returned to the others in the waiting room, Danny and Will were quietly reading comic books. "I needed the peace and quiet," Daddy answered Grandmother's unasked question. "Come on, Josie. You can pick out a couple too."

Grandmother chuckled, shaking her head as Daddy took Josie's hand and led her over to the little nook off the waiting room where magazines and candy and gum were sold.

A man's voice interrupted the silence. "Train leaving ... Chicago ... Now boarding ..." Josie didn't make it all out, but the waiting room erupted with noise as the slumbering occupants roused themselves and everyone, including Josie and her family, headed for the train. The crowd surged along, carrying Josie with it, through the now-open iron gate, down some stairs, and outside to a row of railroad coaches. Wisps of steam floated out from underneath them, alarming Josie until she realized there was no heat.

The train seemed a living thing, pulsating with controlled energy. The odors of hot metal, oil, and steam added to this illusion and Josie tingled with fear and wonder. All around her, unfamiliar grown-ups were rushing, moving her along with them. She spotted the Red Cap who had helped them, now carrying things for the lady who had been sleeping. She had the boy in her arms, now wide awake, but still clutching his stuffed doggie.

Grandmother and Daddy were walking briskly along ahead of her, causing a feeling of panic at being left behind. Then she became aware that Danny's hand held hers protectively and he was tugging her along.

The crowd thinned out as more and more people boarded the train. Finally, Grandmother and Daddy stopped at their coach and waited for the children to catch up.

Josie's heart was pounding. She was out of breath from the hurrying. Grandmother climbed up the high steps into the coach, then Danny and Will scrambled up. The conductor took Josie's hand, politely assisting her up, first to a sturdy metal stool that served as the bottom step, then two more steps into the coach. Daddy lifted both suitcases to the top of the step, then climbed up himself. *Was Daddy coming too?* Josie wondered.

"You got plenty of time," the Conductor told him, checking his gold watch.

Josie moved along, following the boys and being herded from behind by Daddy. The coach resembled a streetcar with two rows of double seats divided by an aisle. But these seats were nicer, higher and softer, like living room furniture with white, starched antimacassars attached where your head rested. At least, where a *grown-up's* head would rest. Josie loved that word, "Antimacassar." It sounded just like a name, as though someone might say to you, "I'd like you to meet my Auntie Macassar." She chuckled, pleased with the thought.

"Someone is glad to be going," Daddy said to Grandmother, tilting his head in Josie's direction.

Danny and Will pushed and shoved their way into a seat, arguing about who got to sit next to the window. As always, they settled it between themselves and Danny sat there, staring out the window at another train.

Josie and Grandmother moved into the seats across the aisle. Daddy put one suitcase on a high shelf above Danny and Will and the other above Josie and Grandmother. Then he hugged Josie.

"Good-bye, Sweetheart," he said softly.

She clung to him, feeling his embrace, the smell of him filling her. Cigarettes, sweat, the Sweetheart soap he washed with, all the things that combined to give that extraordinary aroma that made Daddy smell like Daddy.

He gave Grandmother a quick hug. "See you in September," he told her. Then he turned to the boys. "You two be good and help your Grandmother," he ordered sternly. "Don't give her any trouble!"

"We will," Will answered to the "be good" part of Daddy's command.

"We won't," said Danny responding to Daddy's second demand.

Daddy chuckled, shaking his head in amusement, and leaned over to kiss each one on top of the head. "Okay, good-bye."

"Bye, Daddy," both answered in unison.

Daddy started to leave, but instead he turned and touched Josie's head again. "I need another hug, Sweetheart," he said in a sad voice. "One to last all summer."

Josie's heart broke. How could she leave Daddy all alone in his sadness for a whole summer? Who would take the sadness away if she wasn't there?

She threw her arms around his neck, bumping Grandmother's purse to the floor. "Don't be sad, Daddy," she comforted him. "I can stay home with you, if you want."

"No, you'll have a fine time. I only needed one more hug, that's all," he reassured her. Then he turned and walked down the aisle, got off the train, and waved to them from the platform.

Josie picked up Grandmother's purse and tried to settle down for the unbearably long wait.

"How much longer?" Josie fidgeted.

Grandmother checked her watch. "Only a few more minutes."

"We're moving! We're moving!" Danny and Will announced, only to realize it was the train next to them moving forward, creating the illusion.

Their engine suddenly lurched forward, sending a shudder down through the whole train, coach by coach. Then another and another and another. Like a huge monster awakening from a nap, the train roused itself and began moving forward, faster and faster with each shuddering tremor.

They were on their way!

The gradual lightening of the sky allowed Josie to watch as other trains, then factories, houses and churches passed by outside her window. She had never seen a sunrise before. The beauty of the ever-brightening pinks and golds overwhelmed her. First, just a sliver of polished gold appeared on the horizon. Then, slowly, a brilliant ball of fire rose higher and higher, illuminating the sky. Josie stared, entranced. She had seen many sunsets in her life, but this very first sunrise held not only beauty, but also a wondrous expectation of a new day, as yet untouched. *That* she had never experienced before! It was magnificent!

She saw some tall buildings far off in the distance. Uncle John sometimes told her, "When I see the sun rise over the brewery, I know I'm almost home." Were those breweries? And what were breweries, anyway?

I'll ask Grandmother, Josie thought to herself, *but later, after all the glory in the sky is over.* Right now, she didn't want to miss even one magic moment of this splendid, brand-new morning.

"How long will it be ..." Danny asked, interrupting Josie's thoughts.

" ...before we get to Chicago?" continued Will.

"We just started!" Grandmother answered. "It will be at least an hour."

Josie didn't care how much longer it took. Everything outside her window was so wonderful, new and pretty and green. She couldn't remember ever seeing so much green. Miles and miles of green trees and green fields. Green! Green! Green! Green of every shade and shape. Green as far as the eye could see. The sky was like a huge blue bowl covering all the green. In the distance the green and the blue seemed to meet.

Does the sky really touch the ground? Does the blue meet the green in some marvelous, magical place where a little girl could stand on the green and reach up her arms to touch the blue with her fingers? Perhaps grab a puffy cloud to hug? *Oh, I wish I could,* she dreamed. She turned to ask if it was possible, but Grandmother had closed her eyes for a nap. Josie returned to the glorious panorama outside her window, the fields and trees, brooks and lakes, houses and barns. Small villages and crossroads with people waiting while the train rumbled by swept past Josie's view.

She was no longer riding on the train, curled on the seat next to her snoozing Grandmother. Josie had gone to that particular place where the blue touched the green. She stood on her tippy-toes to snatch a comfortable cloud and pull it down. After a few rather clumsy attempts, she managed to climb on top of it, being very careful not to fall through, of course. It floated upward, carrying her along. Now it sailed above the train, allowing her to see all the beauty there was along the way.

From the train she could see only one side of a barn, but from her cloud she could see the cows on the other side, and speak to them if she wished. From the train she could see people waiting to continue their journeys, some in cars, some on wagons, pulled by gray specked horses, some just standing. They'd wave as the train passed, but they never saw Josie's cloud. She could follow the wagon down the road and around the curve without ever being seen.

The scenery changed gradually as the train approached Chicago, and so did the cloud. More and more factories and buildings began appearing, and Josie's cloud began to dissolve. The train slowly came to a stop. Grandmother stood up to retrieve their luggage and the cloud vanished completely, leaving Josie back on board with the others. Everyone was scrambling to gather their belongings and be on their way.

Chapter Fourteen
Union Station

The conductor moved down the aisle of the coach, lifting down luggage for the ladies. He made his way to the rear and propped open the door leading to the area between coaches. Josie saw him pick up the sturdy little stool to use again as the bottom step. As everyone disembarked, he politely held out his hand to help those who needed it.

Meanwhile, Red Caps were swarming around, seeking people who might need assistance. The conductor waved one over and pointed to Grandmother's largest suitcase.

"This boy can help you, ma'am," he said.

The Red Cap gave them a warm, friendly smile.

"I need to take a Parmelee," Grandmother told him, "to make a connection in ..." She glanced at her watch, "in less than an hour."

"Follow me, ma'am." The Red Cap took off walking rapidly with both suitcases. Grandmother followed, holding her purse and the shopping bag in one hand, and Josie's hand in the other.

"Keep up, boys," she ordered in her no-nonsense voice. "There's no time to dawdle."

Josie could barely keep up, the pace was so fast. Her legs were moving as quickly as they could, yet Grandmother kept tugging her to move even faster. Danny and Will were half-running so they wouldn't be left behind.

The Red Cap led them to an outside cement platform.

"Wait right here, ma'am," he pointed to a sign. "One'll be along real soon to shuttle you to Union Station."

Grandmother checked her watch nervously. "Will it be long?" she asked, digging in her purse for some change.

"No, ma'am. They come regular," the Red Cap replied, tipping his hat as Grandmother paid him.

"The driver, he'll take care of your things here, and the Red Cap at the other end." Then he turned and hurried off.

At last Josie had a chance to look around. There were cars everywhere, more cars than she'd ever seen in her life at one time. And all seemed to be blowing their horns. The noise was deafening!

More and more people were joining them under the Parmelee sign, which Grandmother seemed to feel was a good thing. If other people needed to catch trains, then surely someone would be along to accommodate them.

Josie wasn't sure what a "Parmelee" was. She had never heard the word before. So, when the taxi car pulled up, it was a surprise. It was the longest car she'd ever seen. The driver jumped out almost before the car stopped, and raced to open the back door.

"Get in! Get in!" he ordered, while grabbing luggage and hurrying to open the trunk. Grandmother protested as he seized her shopping bag and crammed it into the trunk.

"No room, lady," the driver said. "Got your purse? Good! Get in, get in!"

Grandmother climbed in.

"Hold the little girl! Get in, get in!" He hustled Danny and Will into the car as well. "Sit there, sit there!" He pointed impatiently to a fold down seat behind the front seat.

He ran back to put more things in the trunk, then hurried back, ordering more people to "Get in! Get in!"

Josie sat squashed on Grandmother's lap while the boys perched uncomfortably across from them. A pretty young woman squeezed in next to Grandmother. She sat forward on the edge of the seat to make room for the two businessmen the driver insisted could fit. Another man, holding a briefcase, was put on the other fold-down seat.

"Let me put the case in the trunk," the driver urged, trying to tug it away, but the man refused.

"It stays with me," he said firmly.

The driver shrugged his shoulders. "Suit yourself, buddy," he said, and slammed the door.

He stuffed two more men in front, got behind the wheel, and away they went.

There was no possible way to prevent yourself from sliding and swaying back and forth as the car swerved through traffic. There was no way Josie could see outside either, and she noticed the only air came from a window in the roof.

When the pretty woman slid to the floor, the man with the briefcase reached instinctively to help her, only to have his case slide onto the other man's lap. Danny and Will couldn't fall because the girl was in the way, but their seat kept trying to fold back in spite of them sitting on it.

"Be there in three-and-a-half minutes!" the driver yelled out encouragingly.

Grandmother held Josie with her knees while trying to help the young woman back up to the edge of her seat. Finally, with help from the man next to her, she made it up, red-faced and embarrassed.

"Wow! What a ride!" Danny exclaimed happily.

"Yeah!" agreed Will. "Ain't it great!"

The man chuckled as his briefcase slid back to him. The young woman began giggling.

"Yeah," said one of the business men, "what a ride!" He started laughing too.

With that, everyone in the back seat exploded with laughter. The driver looked back, puzzled. One of the men stuffed in front tried to see what was going on, but couldn't move enough to do it.

"You all having a party back there?" he called out, causing them all to laugh even more as they slid around the next corner.

Finally, the Parmelee stopped. Grateful, everyone unfolded themselves and crawled out, brushing out the wrinkles and chuckling to themselves. The driver had already started unloading luggage and Red Caps were carrying them away. Grandmother herded the children together, grabbed the shopping bag and looked for a Red Cap. All were gone. The driver closed his trunk and disappeared in a puff of exhaust.

Grandmother checked her watch. "Come on, children!" she said. "We have a train to catch!"

She handed Josie the shopping bag, and Will, the shallow grip.

"Here, help me," she told Danny, and together they picked up the larger suitcase and started through the station.

Josie hurried behind Grandmother and Danny, and Will brought up the rear, puffing under his load. They made their way through the maze of benches and people to catch the next train. The place was enormous, people everywhere, yet no one looked familiar. *How many people were there?* Josie wondered. *Where were they all going? Were there so many places to go and see?* She would have asked Grandmother, but didn't know how to phrase such a complicated question. And Grandmother was moving so quickly it was difficult to keep up, and Josie feared being left behind. So, she simply absorbed all she could of the overwhelming surroundings.

Grandmother stopped at last near an iron gate. She set down her suitcase and the children quickly did the same. Danny swung his arm around, rubbing his shoulder. Grandmother checked her watch again.

"We made it," she reassured them, "in plenty of time."

Some people were already forming a line at the gate, but Grandmother remained on the side.

"They aren't going to let us on until they're ready, so we might as well be comfortable."

Josie became aware of the noise, a low roar created by so many people talking and bustling about, interrupted only by a man's voice over the loud speaker.

"Trains leaving ... Boarding gate ... phone call for Mr ..."

All the activity reminded Josie of the ants that ran up and down Mrs. Lewendoski's peonies, scurrying here and there, seemingly without purpose. Busy, busy, busy! A weary light-headedness seeped through her. Everything seemed unreal, so far away, as though in a dream.

"Jo!" Grandmother nudged her and popped a Life Saver into Josie's mouth. "We'll have lunch as soon as we get settled and on our way."

Josie's tongue rolled the candy around, savoring the orange, tangy flavor. Slowly she began to feel better.

"Trains leaving for ... gate 12 ..." the man announced, and the line began moving past the gate to the trains. Grandmother kept the children back until everyone else had pushed through. Then she led them out to catch the train that waited for them.

"Wow!" said Will, staring at the rows and rows of trains, more trains than Josie ever expected there could be in the world. And all in one place!

"Wow!" Danny agreed. Josie followed his gaze upward. All of it was covered by a huge roof. It didn't matter if the weather was rainy or snowy, the traveler would stay dry.

They moved down the platform. The children gasped in wonder at the vast number of trains. The conductor helped them on board and stowed their luggage in the overhead rack. This time they had four seats together. Danny and Will sat facing the rear toward Grandmother and Josie, everyone forming a neat little square. *Very cozy,* Josie thought. *Like a tiny living room!*

"As soon as they unlock the bathrooms we can wash up and have our lunch," Grandmother promised.

They waited impatiently for the train to move, this time because of hunger instead of excitement. Danny and Will began one of their games, taking turns pretending to push and pull the train forward. They tugged at the window frame, grimacing and groaning until the now-familiar convulsive shudder racked down from coach to coach. They sat back, grinning proudly at each other.

"Did they really make it move, Grandmother?" Josie asked, but there was no answer except Danny and Will laughing, and Josie felt foolish without understanding why. Grandmother shushed the boys and pointed toward the men's room at the back of the coach.

"Be sure to wash your hands," she told them.

Then she took Josie in the other direction, out the door into the area between coaches. The door they'd climbed through was shut, and on the other side was a similar door with only the bottom half closed. The top was fastened back somehow, and fresh air was rushing in. The floor was all gray metal with a raised design so you wouldn't slip. Josie could see the crack, marking where the two coaches came together.

She moved clumsily, the motion of the train affecting her stride. Carefully, she continued with Grandmother to the ladies' room in the next coach. There was a small waiting room with seats, and an adjoining smaller room with the toilet and sink. Josie went in first. It felt strange to go while rocking and swaying with the train.

"There's a pedal of the floor," Grandmother called to her. "And be sure to wash those hands."

Josie stepped on the pedal and the toilet flushed. *Was that the ground down there?* She wondered, watching the opening. Then she washed her hands, dried them carefully, and opened the door for Grandmother.

Josie walked back and forth around the waiting room, finding it easier and easier to maneuver. She tried jumping up to see if she would land in the same spot, but it was hard to tell for sure. She wished she had a ball along to toss in the air to see if it came back to her. I'll ask Grandmother, she decided. Grandmother came out and together they started back to their seats.

"Grandmother," Josie started to ask. "If I—" But Grandmother was too far ahead.

When Josie saw the crack, she knew how to tell. All she had to do was jump up and if she landed on the other side of the crack, she'd know for sure. But she landed right on the crack, too close from where she'd jumped to know for sure.

"Stop jumping!" Grandmother ordered. She pointed at the crack Josie was standing on.

"A boy lost his leg," Grandmother continued. "He was jumping and being noisy, and just as the train went around a curve, his leg went into the opening," Grandmother shook her head sadly, "and when the train straightened out again, it took his leg right off!"

Josie moved off the crack in horror. Was this true?

"He yelled and screamed, but no one came. He'd been naughty on the trip so everyone thought he was just fooling around some more."

Josie felt sick inside at the thought of that naughty boy, stuck there between coaches, screaming and screaming. She would *never* be naughty like that! Nor would she step on the crack!

"Step-on-a-crack! Break-your-daddy's-back!" ran through her mind. No! She'd never step on that crack again. The whole thought was terrifying.

"You'd better tell Danny and Will," Josie said to Grandmother, but as soon as they saw the boys the story was forgotten. Danny and Will were each sipping a cup of water, making Josie realize that she too was thirsty.

"Okay," Grandmother agreed, appointing Danny to take her. "And bring back an extra cup."

Danny led the way down the aisle to the water cooler. It had a little faucet and a holder above with small, cone-shaped cups. Josie pulled out a cup and Danny turned the water on for her. It was cold and tasted better than any water she'd ever had. There was a basket for the used cups built right into the bottom of the cooler, only they didn't throw their cups away. Instead they filled another one for Grandmother and made their way back.

It was impossible to try jumping while carrying a cup of water, but Josie was still curious. Would the train move along while she was temporarily suspended in air? If she jumped and jumped in one spot would she eventually end up at the back of the coach without even trying?

Grandmother started unpacking the lunch Aunt Becka had put in the shopping bag. There were cheese sandwiches with salad dressing, hard summer sausage on slices of rye bread, pickles, and hardboiled eggs, just like a picnic here in their little living room on the train. Aunt Becka had filled a thermos with juice and they drank it from the cone-shaped cups. Then they had Aunt Becka's oatmeal cookies for dessert.

Josie munched two cookies and, for a fleeting moment, missed Aunt Becka. She took a piece of wax paper, crumpled it into a ball, and tossed it up to see what would happen. Before she could figure it out, Grandmother poked her.

"We don't toss things around like that, Jo," she said.

"But, Grandmother," Josie tried to ask. "Will it come right back down or does the train move away from it?"

"Just stop it!" Grandmother ordered.

Subdued, Josie sat back, staring out the window, watching the scenery flash by and wishing she was back home with Aunt Becka where everything was known and familiar. The miles and miles of sameness was becoming boring, so she got out her comic book, but, unable to read, she soon became bored with that too.

Josie began to worry about being at Grandmother's for so long. Who would answer her questions? Where would she sleep? Would Grandmother fix her hair? She knew she'd been there before, but the memories eluded her. It was scary going off like this to a place and people you couldn't remember.

Did Grandmother think she was a naughty girl because of jumping and tossing the paper? Did Grandmother just scold or did she spank too? Aunt Becka never spanked and Daddy only seldom.

What would she call everyone? Did she call her mother's sisters and brothers "Aunt" and Uncle" like she called Aunt Becka and Uncle John, or just use their first names? She couldn't remember. She was sure she wouldn't call Uncle Andy "Uncle." After all, he was only a few years older than Danny and Will. Six years, to be exact. But what about the others?

Then she remembered how concerned she'd been about what to call Grandmother; but when she had arrived, it had all fallen into place. Maybe that would happen again.

A muffled, barely audible sound drew her attention. Turning, she saw Grandmother had taken off her shoes, propped her feet up on the edge of Danny's seat, and laid her head back, now snoring quietly. Her face looked young and relaxed, empty without her glasses. Will and Danny were sleeping too, curled together with their heads touching, shoes off, feet in opposite directions. Danny's glasses were tucked safely in his shirt pocket.

Josie was surprised to notice how much Danny resembled Grandmother. The same light hair framing a thin face. Glasses too, of course. It was really quite remarkable. She looked at her brothers, studying them thoughtfully. *How wonderful they are,* Josie told herself. So completely comfortable with one another. Neither remembered life without the other. They could almost read each other's mind, finish each other's sentences, work together without exchanging words. Two bodies, one mind is how Josie saw it. They were special.

She slipped off her shoes without untying them and placed them carefully on the floor in front of her, side by side as she'd taken them off. She wanted to remember for sure which one went on which foot. Aunt Becka wasn't there to help her and she wasn't sure yet about Grandmother.

She thought about her Grandmother, snoozing beside her. It was Grandmother for whom Josie was named. But her middle name was from Daddy's mother, "Delight." She loved the story of how Daddy's mother came to be named Delight. She'd been told about it so often it sometimes seemed she knew Daddy's mother better than Grandmother. She loved her daddy's mother even though she'd never met her, and was certain in some way, Mary Delight loved her too. If Mary Delight were the Grandmother next to her right now, Josie was sure she would be snuggling cozily against her, not feeling the uneasiness that kept trying to push out all the fun and excitement of this trip.

Josie wriggled her toes; the freedom of them felt good. She tucked her knees up under her chin and covered her legs with her skirt, brushing out any wrinkles. Then she wrapped her arms around her legs and leaned sideways. She stared out the window, allowing her mind to travel to a different time and place.

Mary Delight had been warm and loving, generous with hugs and stingy with scoldings and spankings. She fed stray cats and the hobos who came to her back door, although she did make them do work for her.

"The hobos, not the cats!" Uncle John would laugh. "Clean the sheds, weed the garden, things like that."

" ...so they can keep their pride," she'd explain. "There's naught shame in being poor of money, only in pride and spirit."

Mary Delight was the only daughter in a family filled with boys. In those days everyone wanted sons to carry on the family name, sons to help with the work, perhaps even a son to give to the church: a priest in the family was an honorable thing.

But Mary Delight's parents wanted a daughter after so many sons. They were grateful, of course, for their many healthy sons, but a daughter would be so special and sweet.

Daughters could be dressed in ribbons and pretty lace. Daughters would be a companion to their mothers, learning all the womanly arts of cooking and sewing and healing. Daughters were a comfort to their aging parents and could be counted on to say the prayers and light the candles after Death had come for them.

"Holy Mother," prayed Mary Delight's mother to another mother who'd never had a daughter and could feel empathy for her. "If I'm blessed with a daughter, she'll be named in your honor."

Sure enough, the next baby was a beautiful pink-and-golden girl with perfect little fingers and toes and soft curls and long eyelashes.

"What a delight she is," cooed her parents, "just a pure delight." Thus it was they chose her middle name.

Of course, the Old Priest was outraged at the idea. "Such a name!" he scolded.

"Not a proper Catholic name at all!"

"Mary's as proper a Catholic name as there is," reasoned her daddy.

The Old Priest continued to fuss, but Mary Delight's daddy remained firm.

The day was warm and the Old Priest was tired. His rocker beckoned from his shady porch.

"Mary Delight indeed!" he muttered. "Such a name! What are young people coming to these days!"

He shook his head, protested a bit more, and then relented. The baby was baptized "Mary Delight Fitzgibbon … in the name of The Father, The Son, and The Holy Ghost. Amen!"

To the outside world of priests, nuns, storekeepers, neighbors, and friends, she was "Mary." But to her adoring parents and brothers she remained always, "their Delight."

And it pleased Josie to carry her name.

Chapter Fifteen
The Train to Grandmother's

The train began slowing and the conductor came walking down the aisle calling, "Champaign! Next stop, Champaign!"

Was this their stop? Josie worried. Should she wake Grandmother, or would Grandmother become upset if she woke her unnecessarily? Then Josie noticed the conductor rousing some people so they wouldn't miss their stop, and decided to just let him wake Grandmother. But all he did was walk right past them, giving Josie a pleasant smile.

The train gradually slowed to a stop. What Josie could see of the depot was busy with people scurrying here and there, throwing kisses to departing travelers or greeting arrivals with hugs and handshakes.

Grandmother stirred a little as new passengers passed, carrying their luggage and taking the seats vacated by those departing. Danny sat up, rubbing his eyes sleepily.

"Where are we?" he asked, putting on his glasses to peer out the window.

"Champaign," Josie answered.

The train shuddered as it started up again, waking Will. He sat up, yawning.

"Champaign," Danny said, not waiting for Will's question.

Will stretched his legs out toward Josie's seat. He yawned again, raising his arms above his head and stretching so much his shirt pulled out from his pants.

"Wanna play cards?" he asked.

Josie shook her head. She didn't like cards very much. The numbers confused her. Not the hearts and diamonds, they were easy to keep straight. But she always called spades, "clubs" and called the clubs, "spades." It made her feel foolish to mix them up.

She turned back to the window and her thoughts. The trip was becoming very long and Josie's excitement was tempered by apprehension. She wished her memories of previous visits were clearer, or that she'd thought to ask Danny and Will more questions so she would know what to expect and what was expected of her. They seemed pleased to be going, so it had to be okay, didn't it?

The next thing Josie knew, she was waking up. Her head was on Grandmother's lap and Grandmother was stroking her cheek softly while saying, "Wake up, Jo … come on, honey. Wake up."

Josie blinked and sat up, feeling hot and sweaty. Grandmother adjusted herself, shaking out her skirt a little where Josie's sweat had caused it to stick to her leg.

"I'm sorry to wake you, honey," Grandmother apologized. "But my leg was falling asleep."

Josie nodded sleepily. She rubbed her tongue across her teeth to moisten her mouth.

"Put your shoes on, Jo. Then we'll go to the ladies' room," Grandmother said.

"I don't have to go," Josie muttered, leaning back against her seat, eyes closed, yawning loudly. She stretched out her legs and arms, enjoying the sensation as the blood flowed through her muscles. She flexed her ankles 'round and 'round, wiggling her toes, waking them up too.

"Put your shoes on, Jo," Grandmother repeated. "You'll have to go in a little while anyway, and I don't plan to spend the whole day running back and forth to the toilet."

Josie snapped awake at Grandmother's urgency. Grown-ups were so funny sometimes, assuming you should go just because they had to. She picked up one shoe, carefully lining it up with the correct foot. She began pulling it on without untying it.

"Jo!" Grandmother scolded. "Untie that shoe first. You're going to break down the back that way."

Josie felt her face redden as she undid the knot and loosened the laces. Didn't Grandmother know she couldn't retie them? She slipped her foot in the first one, then the second.

"I'll tie them for you Josie," Danny patted the seat in front of her.

"Can't you tie your own shoes?" Grandmother exclaimed.

Josie shook her head, putting up one shoe for Danny, watching his fingers swiftly weave the two laces into a firm, neat knot.

"You start school in the fall. You should know how to tie your own shoes before then!" Grandmother continued. Josie sat quietly, embarrassed, as Danny tied the other shoe.

"We'll just have to teach you over the summer, won't we?" Grandmother stood up.

Together they moved between the coaches to the ladies' room. It felt good to walk a bit. The hardest part of this trip was sitting still all the time. No walking or running. Josie's legs felt as though they wanted to run and run and run, but of course, that wasn't allowed on a train.

This time when they entered the ladies' room, two women were visiting in the outer room. The younger one held a baby close to her chest, its tiny head nestled into its mother's blouse.

Josie waited while Grandmother went in first. She rarely saw babies up close; no one she knew had a baby. Its tiny size surprised her, and so did the way its mother held it.

"Hi, Sugar!" the young woman greeted her. "What's your name?"

Josie felt the discomfort that always swept through her when an unfamiliar adult expected her to talk to them.

"Josie," she stammered shyly.

"You sure look cute," the woman continued. "All dressed so nice for your trip."

Josie hung her head at this un-accustomed friendliness.

"Where are you going?" asked the second, older lady.

"My Grandmother's," Josie replied politely.

"Your Grandmother's! How nice! Are you staying long?"

Josie nodded. "All summer, I guess." The thought of all summer there among the unknown, without Aunt Becka, filled her with apprehension.

"All summer! My goodness, such a long time! Is your mother going too?"

Josie shook her head. "No."

"No! All summer without your mama! I bet you'll miss her, won't you?"

Josie thought a moment. She felt many things about her mother, but "missing" her? To miss a person, you had to have known them. She still missed Barbara at times, and right now she missed Aunt Becka a lot. But her mother was more a vague, dream-like figure. Sometimes she felt an emptiness in her life as though something wasn't quite right, especially at moments like this when people talked about mothers and she couldn't really comprehend their intentions and feelings. Was that "missing" her? Josie wasn't sure.

"No," she answered, hesitantly. "I don't think so."

"I'll bet she'll miss you though," the lady persisted.

Did her mother miss her? Well, if she did, it was her own fault! Dying like she had! Josie pondered it a minute.

"No," she answered again.

"Oh, sure she will!" the young woman said, gently moving the baby out from her blouse.

Josie was shocked to see that the baby was sucking on the woman's—the woman's what? Chest?

How strange, she thought … and fascinating. She stared, wide-eyed, as the woman lay the baby on her lap, adjusted her blouse, and put the baby's head up on the other side. The baby made a quiet little sound and began sucking again on the other side.

The young woman looked down at her baby with such a love that for a moment Josie felt a pang of jealousy. Had her mother held her so close and with such protectiveness? She wondered.

"Do you like babies?" The older woman asked. Josie nodded.

"Maybe one day your mama will have another baby, and then you can help her," the younger woman smiled up at her.

Josie didn't respond. She just continued looking at the baby.

"Wouldn't that be nice?" the woman persisted. "If your mama had a baby?"

Josie didn't know what to say. Yes, it would be nice, but her mother would never have another baby, ever!

"She won't," Josie answered.

"You never know," laughed the older woman.

"No," Josie was positive. "She won't."

The two women chuckled. "My, you're certainly sure of yourself," the older one said.

"What makes you so sure?" asked the younger one, smiling at her.

Josie hesitated. At home no one ever openly talked about this. Mother was a forbidden subject most of the time. Conversations about her caused such sadness.

"Well," Josie began. "She's—"

Before she could finish the sentence, Grandmother opened the door.

"Jo," she called. "Come in here!"

Josie went in, expecting Grandmother to step outside, leaving her alone like before. Instead, she closed the door. It was crowded with the two of them squashed into the toilet area. Grandmother pointed to the toilet, so Josie sat down obediently. What was wrong? Why was Grandmother upset?

"What do you mean," Grandmother whispered harshly, "telling strangers family things?"

Josie was confused. What had she said? Grandmother had interrupted before she mentioned that her mother was dead. Yet that must be it. People mustn't know her mother was dead. Embarrassment and shame filled her. She'd almost told those two ladies the awful family secret. She knew never to talk about it when Daddy was around. But was it bad to mention it at all? To anyone?

"It's none of their business!" Grandmother told her. "They were just being nosy!"

Josie thought they'd been nice ladies, friendly, easy to talk to. And the baby! Well, it was so cute!

"You don't discuss private family things with strangers," Grandmother continued scolding. Josie got up. "Wash your hands," Grandmother ordered un-necessarily. Josie knew to always wash after going to the bathroom.

Josie pushed the soap lever, filling her hands with the greenish liquid. She rubbed the soap over her hands while Grandmother turned on the water for her. Josie rinsed her hands, letting the water run over and through her fingers, washing off the soap and the guilt of talking about her mother to strangers. She let the coolness wash away the bad feelings.

"That's enough!" Grandmother turned off the faucet and pointed to the towel roll.

Josie dried her hands carefully, reluctantly. The water had felt so soothing. Grandmother opened the door.

How was she going to face the two ladies, Josie wondered, now that she knew they weren't nice and friendly but "nosy" and knowing "family things." But the waiting room was empty. Gratefully, Josie followed Grandmother back to their seats.

She slid into her seat, moving as far over as possible. Her chest ached and there was a tight feeling in her throat. She wanted Aunt Becka and familiar ways. All she'd done today was aggravate Grandmother into scolding her about everything. Josie stared out the window. A whole summer! Her heart sank.

"Wanna play ..." Danny's voice penetrated her thoughts.

" ...cards?" Will finished.

Josie shook her head. She didn't really want to do anything but turn around and go home.

"Are you planning on sulking the rest of the trip?" Grandmother asked.

Josie shook her head. She hadn't been sulking. Merely worried. And she wanted to be left alone to sort out those worries. Of course, there was no way to explain that all to Grandmother.

"Okay," Josie said, turning her attention to the cards. "Only I can't play rummy."

"Sure, you can! You and I can play the same hand," Grandmother offered. "That way you'll learn how."

Josie moved closer to Grandmother as Will dealt out the cards. The last thing she wanted was to learn to play rummy, but there was no choice. At least she could snuggle next to Grandmother and enjoy warmth and comfort. Josie needed those things desperately from anyone, and at the moment only Grandmother was available.

Grandmother arranged the cards according to kinds. All the hearts together and the diamonds. Why did they call the black ones, "spades" and "clubs" when they looked more like trees and clovers?

Grandmother asked Josie which card to lay down. Should they pick up the pile? What about this or that? Whenever Danny or Will laid down all their cards, they'd be so pleased, and whenever Grandmother laid down their cards, she'd nudge Josie excitedly. Josie laughed or clapped her hands, but inside she thought, *who cares who wins? It's just a card game.*

It seemed forever before everyone else tired of the cards and they were put away. Grandmother read the comic books to Josie. They finished the last of Aunt Becka's cookies and went back and forth for water, just to move around and stretch their legs. Grandmother played "Simon Says" with them, putting the children through all sorts of silly antics: patting their heads while rubbing their tummies while tapping their feet. All at the same time!

Still the train ride seemed to go on and on and on forever!

Then the conductor came through. "Effingham," he announced. "Next stop, Effingham!"

Grandmother told the boys to pack the cards and comic books into the shopping bag while she pulled down the suitcases. She had them brush the cookie crumbs off the seats so they'd be clean for the next people.

The train slowed to a stop and the conductor helped them off.

"Been a pleasure," he commented as he set their luggage on the ground next to them. He touched the brim of his hat politely, picked up his little stool, and climbed back on board. He hung half-way out the door to wave an "all clear" to the Engineer. In a few minutes the train chugged out of sight.

Josie looked around and decided immediately that this was her favorite depot. It was not so big as the others she'd seen that day, but was definitely the cutest, with lots of flowers and red brick.

"You boys can handle the big one," Grandmother said, picking up the smaller grip. She handed the shopping bag to Josie. They made their way into the cool shadiness of the depot. Danny and Will, laughing and shoving as they always did, made a game out of half-carrying and half-dragging the suitcase. Grandmother left them while she went to talk to the man behind the ticket counter.

Josie glanced around the small waiting room. The only other person there was a custodian, slowly dry-mopping the wooden floors. The smell of polish permeated the air.

Grandmother rejoined them. "We'll have almost a two-hour layover," she told them, "so let's park our things and get something to eat." She had the boys lug the suitcase to the wall, then set the small grip next to it and the shopping bag on top.

"This okay?" she called out to the man.

"Just fine!" he answered. "I'll keep an eye on 'em for ya!"

Grandmother herded the children outside and led them across five sets of railroad tracks into a tiny restaurant. There was a long counter with stools where men wearing striped railroad caps sat, their I.D. buttons pinned on the sides.

Everyone turned to stare as Grandmother and the children walked in and sat at a corner table overlooking the tracks. When the waitress came over, Grandmother ordered four hamburgers without even looking at a menu or asking them what they wanted.

"And two chocolate malts, and a coffee for me, and bring an extra glass with the malts."

Josie had been in diners many times, usually with Uncle John. They all seemed alike somehow, with their long counters, napkins, and salt and pepper grouped together at intervals with the catsup bottles customers would politely pass to one another.

The waitress brought their food and Danny and Will began eating hungrily. Grandmother divided the malts between the three of them while the waitress went to fetch the coffee in a big, heavy mug. The creamer was in a tiny little milk bottle. *How cute,* thought Josie.

"Can we keep the little bottle?" she asked, thinking how fun it would be to have a tiny milk bottle with her toy dishes.

"Of course not!" Grandmother said, while tucking a napkin under Josie's chin to keep her dress clean. "What would you want it for, anyway? Now eat."

Josie took a bite of her hamburger and then tried her malt, but it was too thick for the straw. She picked up her spoon. What was it Uncle John called these kinds of restaurants? She stared at the spoon thoughtfully. Spoon something? Something spoon? Her mind searched for the word.

"These are really good," Grandmother said. "Not greasy at all."

That was it! A Greasy Spoon! Uncle John called some of these diners a "Greasy Spoon."

Josie studied the spoon, turning it over to check the other side. No, it wasn't greasy at all. This must be an okay place.

Suddenly she became aware that the spoon had the shape of a person's head. A lovely oval head. Of course, there was no body, just the spoon handle. But there was definitely a head. Josie imagined a beautiful face on the spoon with large eyes looking up at her. Josie smiled and spoke to the face, not out loud, of course, but the face heard her anyway.

"Want to walk around?" she asked the spoon. The spoon face nodded, so Josie walked it around her plate. The words, "the dish ran away with the spoon," flashed through her mind.

"I want to dance," the spoon face said, so Josie began to twirl it 'round and 'round. The spoon smiled gratefully. Dancing was more fun than shoveling food into a person's mouth, it told her.

Josie smiled, pleased that she could help the spoon enjoy itself. Perhaps the pretty spoon would like a dance partner. Josie picked up the fork, happily noticing that its tines were really a polished crown. The fork prince smiled as Josie introduced him to the spoon dancer. Slowly, with Josie's aid, they began to dance together, twirling 'round and 'round gracefully.

"Stop playing with your silverware!" Grandmother's words snapped Josie back to the diner and reality.

The fork and spoon returned to being just a fork and spoon, and everyone else was almost finished eating. Josie hurried to catch up. They walked back across the tracks to the depot where Grandmother settled herself comfortably on a shady bench.

"You can play a while," she told the children. "But stay clean. Don't get yourselves messed!"

It felt so good to move around outdoors after a whole day of sitting. First, they explored the area around the depot. They played tag around the empty baggage wagon and "follow-the-leader" through all the nooks and crannies, balancing carefully around the raised flower beds.

Josie admired the flowers, enjoying their scent as the breeze helped them nod at her. She wanted to pick one to show Grandmother and ask her what they were called, but she knew it wasn't allowed. "You can't pick the flowers," Daddy always told her. "They don't belong to you. Besides, others want to enjoy them too." If Mr. Russell was here, he could tell her what they were.

A moment of homesickness swept through her. Danny and Will were pretending to be airplanes by holding their arms out to form the wings and making engine noises. Josie joined them, buzzing around.

"Children!" Grandmother called, interrupting their flying. "Danny! Will! Come on, now! Jo! Time to get ready!"

They returned obediently, and the boys were sent to the men's room to wash up. Grandmother took Josie to the ladies' room and inspected her carefully.

"Your dress is wrinkled," Grandmother fussed while brushing at the skirt. Josie looked down. Of course it was; dresses wrinkle easily. There was no way to avoid it!

"Well, can't be helped, I suppose," Grandmother checked Josie's face and hair. "Here, wash your hands."

Grandmother turned on the water and dampened a corner of her hankie to wipe an unseen spot off Josie's mouth. Then she pulled a brush from her purse and organized Josie's curls.

"There," she said, finally satisfied. "You look just fine for someone traveling so far."

Danny and Will were already waiting for them. Grandmother proceeded to give them the "once-over" too. She sent Will back to scrub his hands. Danny's cowlick was dampened with some spit, in an effort to make it behave.

"Tuck in your shirt."

"Brush off your slacks."

"Wipe that dust off your shoes."

"Stand up straight. Let me look at you."

"I want to be proud of you all when we get home," she explained, attacking a smudge on Will's forehead with her dampened hankie. "Here," Grandmother held out the hankie. "Spit on it," she commanded Will, who had no choice but obey.

"Stop wiggling!" The cleaning continued.

Will's face was scrunched up and red with embarrassment.

"Turn your head," Grandmother rubbed some more. "Guess it's just a shadow," she said, folding the hankie into her purse.

Danny and Will grinned at each other, one rubbing his cowlick, the other rubbing his forehead, sharing one of their private thoughts. They helped Grandmother collect their things and went outside to wait for the train and the last leg of their journey.

"Which direction will it come from?" Danny asked. He and Will fidgeted, looking up and down the track.

Grandmother pointed. The three of them stood watching, leaning forward over the tracks, trying to be the first to spot it.

Then, there it was: a tiny black speck in the distance, barely visible except for the smoke rising upward from its stack. Josie stared, hypnotized, as the locomotive grew larger and larger. The ground vibrated under her as it chugged toward them. The noise grew louder and louder. Black and shiny! Fascinating! Powerful and scary! Closer and closer! The smell of it filled her nostrils. Still, she didn't move. It held her there, mesmerized.

Grandmother tugged her shoulder. "Don't stand so close! Those things can suck you right under!"

Josie snapped out of her spell and stepped back as the engine roared by followed by the coal car, baggage cars, and a few passenger cars. She felt the airflow increase around her, lifting her skirt gently and tickling her legs.

The brakes squealed their protest as the engine stopped, sending convulsive shudders back along the full length of the train. The conductor opened the door before it had even stopped, and jumped down with his sturdy step-stool for them to use.

"Evenin,' Mrs. Witt," he greeted Grandmother.

"Good evening, Mr. Albright," she replied as the children climbed up.

"These Celia's youngsters?" he asked, looking them over.

Grandmother nodded. Mr. Albright lifted the suitcases up.

"I'll bring 'em along directly," he said. "Y'all go sit down."

The boys hurried to find seats. Soon they would be home at Grandmother's and their excitement was obvious. Grandmother's was too. Only Josie remained uncertain. The unknown was so scary. If only she could remember what it had been like during previous visits.

What was expected of her? Where was the bathroom? What if she wet the bed?

The train seemed to stop at every little town and crossroads along the way, causing Danny and Will to fidget impatiently. They grew more excited at each of these whistle stops, while Josie grew more and more apprehensive.

Would Grandmother scold about things that Aunt Becka didn't mind? What was Granddaddy like? Did he spank? What did she call her aunt and uncles? Were they nice? Would they love her as much as Uncle John and Aunt Becka? Worry, worry, worry!

"Next stop is ours," Grandmother announced cheerfully.

Danny and Will almost wiggled off their seats in excitement. And in spite of her worries, Josie found herself caught up in their enthusiasm.

Chapter Sixteen
Arriving at Grandmother's

The train squeaked to a stop and Mr. Albright helped them off.

"Enjoy your visit, children," Mr. Albright smiled and tipped his hat. "Mrs. Witt."

Josie looked around at the gravel platform and tiny yellow depot. They were the only ones getting off. Grandmother went to talk to the ticket seller at an outside window.

"Your Granddaddy isn't here yet," she said when she returned to the children. "We might as well start walking."

She moved the two suitcases out of the way.

"He'll pick these up later," she said. "They'll be fine here."

Danny and Will knew the way, but everything was new to Josie. There were houses with big front porches and large yards. No flats at all. Everyone said, "Good Evening" or "Hello" as they passed. The air was so warm and sweet, everything clean and tidy. There were even empty lots without any buildings at all. It was so different, yet familiar too. Josie knew they were only a few blocks from Grandmother's house.

How could she know that without really remembering? She knew that on the corner of this block was a church, a white, wooden church with a square steeple but no cross on top. And kitty-corner from the church was a vacant lot, and next to the lot was Grandmother's house: a big white house with gingerbread trim and two porch swings that Danny and Will would pretend were two stage coaches.

Suddenly a car pulled up next to them and Granddaddy got out.

"Hey there!" he yelled. "You folks need a ride?"

The children rushed to hug him. Josie buried her face in his shirt, the smell rejuvenating her memories. Uncle Andy climbed out from the front seat and hugged Grandmother.

"Come on," Granddaddy said. "Let's get on home."

Granddaddy opened the back door and Danny and Will climbed in. He motioned for Andy to get in.

"I was in the front seat," Andy said.

"You're in the back seat now," Granddaddy answered.

"It's not fair," whined Andy. "Why should I sit in back?"

"I could sit in back," suggested Grandmother.

"No!" Granddaddy insisted. "Get in back, Andy. Now!"

Andy's face was red and angry, but Josie couldn't understand why. Even Danny and Will looked puzzled. Andy climbed in next to Danny, and Granddaddy helped Josie and Grandmother into the front.

"Special little precious baby sits in front," Andy grumbled.

Does he mean me? Josie wondered.

"Oh, be quiet!" Granddaddy said. "You know there's not enough room up here for you." ♡

Chapter Seventeen

Josie at the Fabric Counter

Josie was fascinated by that special connection between babies and mothers. Had she shared a special connection with her own mother? Had her mother held her protectively, stroked her tenderly as she snuggled close? Had she buried her face against the warm, sweet safety, feeling and smelling the very essence of her mother? It was comforting to believe so, even though she had no way of knowing. She yearned for just one tiny little memory.

Whenever Josie watched a baby and mother, she hoped a memory would stir and fill her. And if not, she could pretend she had one. So, it was natural that the only people Josie noticed that day near the fabric counter were a baby and its mother.

When it was her turn to be waited on, the mother moved to the counter and set the baby on the edge carefully, with one hand across the baby's chest, fingers wrapped gently around its tiny shoulder.

Josie moved closer, elbows on the counter, chin cupped in her hands, to admire the baby. She was a lovely, golden-brown-and-pink baby with dimples at her elbows. Her toes wriggled playfully. It would have been delightful to tickle those chubby little toes and play "this-little-piggy," but, knowing such familiarity was inappropriate, Josie contented herself by just smiling and making faces as the baby peeped shyly around her mother's arm. Two tiny pearly teeth glistened on the bottom of her mouth whenever the baby giggled. Her mother had braided the baby's hair into eight tiny pigtails, each tied with pink yarn that matched the little pink sun-suit. How cool and comfortable it must feel to have braids like that, Josie thought. Her own head itched with sweat under her frizzy curls.

The mother's arm was brown with a reddish tinge, as though sunburned just a little. She wore a cotton housedress with blue flowers and a starched white collar like most ladies did when out and about. Her hair was pulled up tightly in a knot, similar to Grandmother's. Except for tiny beads of sweat forming on her upper lip, she seemed cool and comfortable in spite of the heat.

"Yard of this please," the mother said politely, pointing to the bolt of yellow gingham. She looked down at Josie and gave her a fleeting, almost imperceptible smile. Josie's attention returned to the baby, who had stopped chewing her fingers and was now sucking on her mother's arm and making baby noises.

"A fine thing!" A woman's voice interrupted the moment. "A fine thing indeed, when white folks gotta wait while a nigger gets taken care of first!"

Josie felt her face grow hot and redden as embarrassment swept through her. She hadn't heard that awful word since coming to Grandmother's, and now someone was calling attention to her right here in front of everyone. Now Grandmother would be aware that she was that awful thing. Josie glanced to see Grandmother's face and saw her stern lips tighten together in obvious disapproval. She felt Grandmother was only waiting until they were alone to scold Josie.

"Josie, you must stop being a nigger or I won't take you along anymore!"

Yet how could she stop when she had no idea what she was doing to upset people so much? No one else had noticed, not even Grandmother, until this one woman found her so awful, so terrible she had to call everyone's attention to it. Even the mother reacted, stiffening slightly, fingers closing around her baby as though to protect it from Josie's awfulness.

The lady waiting on the mother seemed embarrassed too. She

suddenly was very nervous and distracted, so much so that another saleslady appeared.

"I'll finish up here," she said. "You take care of her." She nodded in the direction of the disruptive woman who now had a smug, self-righteous look on her face.

"Nigger," she muttered again with a self-satisfied sniff in Josie's direction as she went on to tell the saleslady what she wanted.

"Do you want anything else?" The second saleslady snapped at the mother as though it were all her fault.

"Just these buttons," the mother answered quietly, removing her pocket book from a cloth shopping bag.

This second saleslady was so upset she dropped the change next to the purchases and hurried away, leaving the mother to pack her own things. Josie noticed that the mother's fingers trembled slightly as she picked up the coins. Did she fear for her baby? Did she think Josie's awfulness would be contagious? Perhaps it was something she might catch just because Josie had stood too close. Sometime in the future would her baby be a nigger too?

The mother slid the handles of the shopping bag over her arm and picked up her baby to leave. The baby laid her head on her mother's shoulder and giggled as they wove their way between other customers, disappearing in the direction of the stairs. Grandmother moved up to make her purchases, barely glancing at Josie or the other woman who was being waited on.

Later, on the way home, Josie stared out the window at the unfamiliar streets of this unfamiliar city. The wind blew through her hair, cooling her scalp. Grandmother hadn't said a word about the incident at the store, but Josie could tell she was upset as they left.

After meeting Granddaddy and the boys, however, Grandmother seemed to have forgotten all about it. It was almost too much to hope for. Josie leaned back sleepily. As she closed her eyes, she became aware of the conversation between her Grandparents.

"Creating such a fuss! *I* was the one who was next in line. *I* should have been upset, not that trashy woman!" Grandmother was angry, all right. But not with Josie. She was furious at the woman who had made the comment!

"White trash!" Grandmother fussed again. "She was so smug, so proud of herself. Just plain white trash!"

"Of course," she continued. "It *was* odd to wait for a Negro to be waited on first."

"Why?" Granddaddy asked. "Wasn't it her turn? If it was her turn, then it was her turn!"

Grandmother chuckled in agreement. "I know."

"Never did make sense to me," Granddaddy said. "The idea that it's rude to wait on a Negro while white folks stand in line. In some stores the Negroes would have to wait all day, maybe come back in the morning, hoping no white folks were there. Starve to death just waiting to be waited on!"

Grandmother nodded. She wasn't going to scold Josie after all. Josie's heart was in her throat, but she had to ask. Had to find out why people called her that awful name. Maybe it was dumb to draw more attention to the fact, but now was the time to finally know just what a nigger was and how she could stop being one.

Josie took a deep breath and sighed. "What does nigger mean?" she asked.

Grandmother turned to face her. "There! Do you see what that trashy woman's gone and done!" She fussed.

"It's a nasty name," she said finally, turning back in her seat.

Josie knew that!

"It's a nasty name for colored people," Granddaddy explained.

For colored people? Josie couldn't believe it!

"What?" she questioned. "Why?"

"Well, it's a low term for a Negro," Granddaddy added. "And it's a word we don't use."

Josie sat back in amazement, her thoughts racing. Then she heard Grandmother saying, "I know she doesn't see many colored people up there, but I must tell her it isn't polite to stare so. It was the cutest little baby, though. Her mama had her so neat and clean, polished like a door-knob."

Chapter Eighteen

The summer had ended; the long train ride back home was over. As soon as Daddy unlocked the front door, Will and Danny bolted past him and tore up the front steps.

"We're home! We're home!" they shouted.

Josie hurried up as fast as she could. She was anxious to see Aunt Becka and tell her all about the summer at Grandmother's. Daddy laughed as she scrambled upward and patted her gently on the bottom as they went up. A "love tap" he always called it when he patted her like that.

Aunt Becka was hugging the boys at the top. Josie wiggled and shoved her way in to get her share of the hugs and kisses. Everyone was talking at once.

"We went to the railroad …" Danny started.

" …roundhouse!" Will finished. "And to a farm …"

" …with Uncle Parnell."

"I had a kitten!" Josie pushed in. "I had a kitten!"

"Really? How wonderful!" Aunt Becka laughed, greeting each of them with tears and kisses. "I missed you all!"

Daddy came into the room. "Hey, hey, hey!" he said. "One at a time. There's plenty of time to tell everything."

"That's right," Aunt Becka agreed. "Right now, there's someone I want you to meet."

The children became aware that another person was standing in the doorway, watching them. She was a rather plump older woman with gray hair and wire spectacles. She seemed quiet and grim.

"Hello, children," she said, smiling at them with one of those smiles that grown-ups use when trying to appear friendly and polite to children. Suddenly they were quiet, unable to think of anything to say. Josie's hidden senses told her something was up. It was strange how she could tell when grown-ups were up to something and not telling her. But she knew.

"This is Miss Tooley," Aunt Becka said. "She's going to take care of you."

Josie could tell that Danny's and Will's senses must have clicked in too because they quietly looked over Miss Tooley, then looked at Aunt Becka, and back into the living room at Daddy. Josie stood there, sizing her up. *I don't like her,* Josie's mind was telling her. But, of course, one could never say that to a grown-up.

"Say hello," Daddy ordered. "Forget your manners?"

"Hello," the three said in unison, still scrutinizing Miss Tooley carefully.

"Hello, children," she repeated, pasting on her smile again for them. "Welcome home."

"How come she's here?"

"How long?"

"Why?"

"Where are you going?"

Danny's and Will's questions came pouring out, saving Josie the necessity of asking them herself.

"Hey, hey. Slow down," Daddy said.

"She's going to be taking care of you from now on," Aunt Becka explained, "because James and I are married and I'm moving to Chicago with him."

It was as though a black void had enveloped Josie. She was stunned. Aunt Becka leave? Live in Chicago with dull, old James? Even Danny and Will looked shocked.

"Married in the priest's home a few weeks ago," Aunt Becka was saying.

"When?" Danny forced out the question. "When are you leaving?"

"Not for a week or so," Aunt Becka's voice sounded strange. "Just long enough to get Miss Tooley acquainted with the house and you all." She seemed to choke a little.

All the while, Miss Tooley stood there, watching them. Daddy walked past her into the kitchen. Josie stood dumbly, wondering what to do next, what to say.

Aunt Becka couldn't leave. It was impossible to imagine life without her. How could they possibly get along without her? Who would care for them, or love them, if she was gone? Surely not this fat, ugly old woman with the pasted-on smile.

Somehow, they all ended up in the kitchen where Aunt Becka had cookies and lemonade for them. They ate and drank automatically without tasting.

"Tell me about your summer," Aunt Becka coaxed.

Slowly the children began to talk, telling of their adventures without enthusiasm. Miss Tooley sat there, listening to every word they said.

Nosy, ugly, old, fat woman!

In the weeks following Aunt Becka's departure Josie moped around the house, lost and forlorn. There were times she wished she had said good-bye, given her one last kiss. She wished she had smelled her sweet clean scent just one last time so she'd be able to remember it now. Her plan had been a dumb one. Aunt Becka had left anyway. Kiss or no, she had left.

Once Josie was in the kitchen when Daddy came in. She hadn't heard all the words, just " …Aunt Becka is here."

Joyfully, Josie ran to greet her. But there was only Daddy and her brothers.

"Where is she?" Josie asked, confused.

"Not Aunt Becka," Danny said.

"Just a letter from her," finished Will.

Daddy tore open the envelope and began reading.

"Dear all," he began. Then it was just words about her new house and the color of the rugs and furniture. *Who cares?* Josie thought to herself, and went back to the kitchen.

Daddy called out to her, "Aunt Becka writes that she misses you!"

Josie just drank her coffee-milk. If she misses me, it's her own fault for leaving, Josie thought. If she missed me, she'd come back home.

Later, Josie went in the dining room. She moved a chair over to the knick-knack shelf and took down the tiny winged horse that had been Aunt Becka's favorite.

"I'll leave this for you to remember me by," she had told Josie.

Josie looked at the horse, rolling it around in her fingers. It wasn't glass, so if she dropped it, it wouldn't break. Slowly, carefully, Josie took hold of a tiny wing. Snap! The wing came off easily. Josie put the horse back on the shelf. It was easy to find the exact spot because Miss Tooley hadn't dusted in so long.

She climbed off the chair and pushed it back to the table, still clutching the tiny wing in her fist. She walked to the radiator and dropped it down, down into the furnace, she thought. Destroyed forever. Gone forever like the lost marbles that Danny and Will had dropped down there so long ago. Gone forever, and she didn't care one bit.

It was weeks before anyone discovered the horse was missing a wing.

"Perhaps it only had one wing," Miss Tooley said.

Daddy was just puzzled. "I don't think so," he replied.

Grown-ups were so dumb sometimes, Josie thought.

Chapter Nineteen
Daddy Reads A Story

Josie wandered into the living room, clutching her storybook. *If only Aunt Becka was here,* she thought. No one ever read to her anymore, at least not as well as Aunt Becka used to, making the pictures come alive, weaving the story together as her voice rose and fell, paused or went faster. No, no one read to her like Aunt Becka had done.

Certainly not Miss. Tooley, who spent the evenings in her room listening to her own radio, munching cookies. *No wonder she's so fat!* Josie thought unkindly. Miss. Tooley had taken over Aunt Becka's room. It no longer welcomed her on scary nights, no longer smelled sweet and pleasant. Now it smelled of Old Fat Woman, not Aunt Becka.

Josie curled up in the big chair to look at the pictures and try to remember the words as Aunt Becka's voice would say them.

"The Owl and the Pussy-cat went to sea in a beautiful, pea-green boat. They sailed away for a year and a day—" That much she remembered. "They took some money and plenty of honey, wrapped in a ..." In a what? Josie searched her mind, trying to remember

She glanced over at her brothers sitting at the dining room table, busy with their school work: Will's dark head almost touching Danny's lighter one as they bent over their papers. Perhaps if she begged them, they would read to her. But they always hurried through it, mispronounced words, and argued when she told them it should be "wonderful puss," not "beautiful puss." Besides, it was forbidden to bother them when they were doing their important school papers.

She looked at the book again, tracing the pictures with her finger.

"And they danced by the light of the moon," she said out loud, remembering how Aunt Becka laughed and then they'd dance together, to everyone else's amusement.

Daddy came into the living room and sat down on his corner of the couch. He put his bottle of beer next to the radio, reached into his shirt pocket for a cigarette, and lit it. The match made a little scratchy noise and the odor filled Josie's nostrils. He leaned back wearily, inhaled deeply and sighed.

Josie climbed out of her chair and crawled up beside him, snuggling comfortably. Daddy put his arm around her and pulled her close. His finger found her earlobe and he began rubbing it gently between his thumb and fingers, making little circular motions. Josie loved this tenderness. How wonderful Daddy was. How she loved him! He almost made her loneliness for Aunt Becka disappear.

She lay still, hugging her book, almost afraid to move, afraid to break the spell.

"What'cha got there, Sweetheart?" Daddy asked. "Should I read it to you?"

Josie sat up, elated. Except for the boys blundering versions she hadn't heard it since Aunt Becka left. Daddy would read it. Then she'd be able to remember all the forgotten words. She handed Daddy the book and leaned against him so she could see the pictures as he read.

"The Owl and the Pussy-cat went to sea," The words flowed as Daddy began. "Wrapped in a five-pound note," he continued.

"Too long have we tarried ..." He sounded strange.

"They sailed away for a year and a day— What the h— kinda book is this?" he asked angrily.

"The Owl and the Pussy-cat, Daddy," Josie explained worriedly. What was wrong with her book?

"Getting married? By a turkey?" Daddy complained. "It's a mockery!"

"It's just a story," Josie tried telling him. "Aunt Becka ..." Her voice trailed off.

"A five-pound note! That figures! Written by a G—d-mn Englishman!" Daddy was getting louder and madder.

"It's okay, Daddy," Josie pleaded. "You can read a different one." Why was Daddy so mad? What was wrong with the story? Why had Aunt Becka read it to her if it was bad?

Josie felt so awful, guilty because she enjoyed this story so much and now she'd gone and made Daddy so irritated. She reached to remove the offensive book from Daddy's sight, hoping to calm him, and have him quiet again.

The noise had distracted the boys from their homework.

"It's just a nursery—" Danny started to say.

"Get back to your work!" Daddy snapped.

Dutifully her brothers bent over their work, ignoring what was happening. Josie tugged at the nasty book. She had to get it out of Daddy's sight, remove it, restore peace again. Why had she even tried to let him read this terrible story?

She was so dumb, so awful to cause Daddy such annoyance!

Daddy stood up, jerking away from her grasp. He took the book and ripped it half.

Josie gasped, dumb-founded. *Oh, God!* She thought. Why had she done such a terrible, terrible thing, enjoyed such a terrible story? Why hadn't Aunt Becka warned her that it was a bad story instead of reading it to her? Didn't Aunt Becka know it was written by a G—d-mn Englishman?

Daddy tossed the two halves of the ripped book on the floor and sat down.

"Get another book, Sweetheart," he said calmly, his anger gone as suddenly as it had flared.

Josie didn't want to hear a different story. She didn't deserve to hear a story; she'd made poor Daddy so upset over "The Owl and the Pussycat." She shouldn't have asked him to read it. Still, she dared not risk making Daddy angry again. Reluctantly she went to pick out a different story. Which One?

Not *The Three Little Kittens*. If *one* Pussy-cat made Daddy upset, what would three of them do? Besides she liked that one. What if Daddy tore it up too? *Winkin, Blinkin, and Nod?* That one rhymed too much, like *The Owl and The Pussy-cat*. Maybe it too had been written by a G—d-mn Englishman. Was that what Daddy thought was wrong?

The solution came to her in a flash! She picked a book she really didn't care for very much, her least favorite. If Daddy tore it up it wouldn't matter to her.

"Here, Daddy," she smiled, handing him the book.

"Once upon a time ..." Daddy began reading pleasantly.

The next day when Danny and Will took out the trash, they rescued her ripped book.

"Here, Josie," Will said. "You can still look at the pictures ..."

" ...if you hold the torn parts together," continued Danny. "Only you'll have to hide it ..."

" ...so Daddy won't find it." Will added.

Josie took the ripped book and crawled under the front porch. It was the only place she could think of where there was no chance of Daddy finding it. She knelt in front of the flat rock and spread the torn halves on top where the sunlight filtered through the cracks. She lined up the pictures to determine what damage Daddy had done.

The pea-green boat was barely damaged; only its very bottom was torn away. However, the dancing Owl and Pussy-cat were completely ruined. Their heads were on the top half, while their legs twirled 'round and 'round on the bottom half. No matter how she tried, they just looked ragged and forlorn.

She felt so guilty that she'd enjoyed the story, guilty because she'd caused Daddy so much anger and pain, guilty because Danny and Will risked punishment by saving the wicked book, and guilty because she had accepted it and was now hiding it. She felt guilty even because poor Owl and Pussy-cat could no longer dance happily together "by the light of the moon," and it was all her fault.

How could she make Daddy happy when she was such a dumb, bad girl?

Still, she was happy to have this torn, ripped shred of Aunt Becka. She turned the pages carefully one last time, embedding them in her mind. Then, wrapping her arms across her chest, she hugged herself, her right hand gently stroking the top of her left arm, petting herself, rocking herself in the dust and the shadows until she was comforted.

She took the top half and laid it on the bottom half so the pea-green boat was showing. Then she crawled as far under the stairs as she could and, lying on her tummy, pushed the book under the bottom step. Only she would know it was there. She could sit out there on that step anytime she felt like it and peek through the cracks to see the pictures and remember …

… even if it was a bad story and she was a dumb, bad girl.

Chapter Twenty
First Day of School

The long summer was over. Now, the most exciting day was about to begin for Josie: the first day of school. She had looked forward to this day and there were so many things she had to learn before she could go. Danny and Will had taught her how to print her name, not just "Josie," but her whole name: "Josephine." And they helped her memorize her address too. She had also spent a great deal of time practicing tying her shoes. Sometimes she did it backwards so the laces didn't lay back and forth, but lay sideways and looked funny. But mostly she did okay.

Then the day came, the day she had been preparing for! (Danny and Will had started back to school a few days earlier.) She wore her red plaid dress with the white collar and red socks. She tied her own shoes, the ones that just a week ago had been her Sunday shoes.

"Take them off when you get home from school," Daddy told her. "They are just for school and not for playing in."

Josie nodded. Shoes were very expensive so they each had "play shoes" and "Sunday best." And now she had "school shoes" too. How grown-up she felt!

After breakfast, Daddy curled her hair carefully and tied a huge red bow on top of her head. Josie approved of herself in the mirror. Then Daddy took her hand and off they went. It was so special that they even used the front steps.

They crossed the street to St. Matthew's playground, but instead of going into the school they kept walking toward the alley.

"Aren't we going to school?" Josie worried.

"St. Matt's doesn't have a kindergarten," Daddy explained. "We're going to the public school. Next year you'll be at St. Matthew's."

"Oh," Josie accepted his answer. She wasn't even sure what a "public school" was.

They walked down the alley. If Josie had been alone or with the other kids and not all dressed up, she would have scrambled up the cement wall next to the alley and balanced along the narrow top, high above Daddy's head. Instead, they crossed the street and passed the old people's home.

It used to frighten Josie to pass by there. The old men and women would stare at her, eyes blank in withered faces, spooky and scary, like wispy ghosts. Then one day a bunch of the kids were walking that way together. Josie's fright must have been obvious, at least to Mike McGuiness.

"Whatcha scared of, Josie?" he asked. "Them old people? H—, they can't hurt ya! They can't even hardly walk! Watch!" Mike smiled up at the windows and the blank faces. He raised his hands and waved.

A remarkable thing happened. The old faces lit up! The eyes came alive and all the wrinkles formed a smile back at them. One old woman shyly waved back.

Mike grinned at her. "See? Makes 'em feel good," he said. "Who else can ya give such a good feeling to just by smiling and waving?"

After that she was never afraid and always smiled and waved too.

Josie had walked this way many times and knew where P.S. 21 was, only she hadn't realized she would be going there. It was a huge, gray brick building, not cozy and cute like St. Matthew's, which was small and square and made of red brick. The playground was huge too, with a fence around it and games painted on the surface. At St. Matthew's the girls had to draw their own games on the sidewalk because the playground was gravel and the big boys sometimes blocked off the street to play in the road.

As they walked up the steps and entered the building, Josie

suddenly felt apprehensive. The halls echoed under their footsteps and everything smelled like varnish and polish. Josie clung to Daddy's hand. She looked at the other children, equally frightened, clutching their mother or older brother or sister.

Daddy led her to a bright, colorful room with a big circle painted in black on the floor. An old, skinny woman greeted everyone pleasantly.

"Hello, children," she said, or, "Hello, John. Is this your little brother?" or, "Why, Mrs. Thompson. How nice to see you again."

Everyone seemed very glad to see her.

"Hello, dear," she greeted Josie. "How special you look today."

Josie smiled shyly.

"Just take a seat in the circle while your Daddy fills out some papers," the old woman said.

Josie turned to Daddy and wanted to cling to him as some other children were doing to their mothers, cling to him for safety and comfort. But she knew such behavior would not be tolerated.

"I'll see you after school, Sweetheart," Daddy said. "Have a good time."

The old woman smiled down at Josie. "Go have a seat by the other children," she said. The old woman's smile was sweet and delightful and Josie decided at that moment that she really liked her.

Josie walked to the circle and sat down a little bit away from the other kids. Many seemed to know each other. Then someone plopped right next to her. She turned to see the chunkiest boy she'd ever laid eyes on.

He was wearing shorts and a striped polo shirt that stretched over his tummy. One knee had a band-aid that covered an injury while the other knee had a scab. His face was sprinkled with freckles and his hair was carefully combed in place, although a cowlick was doing its best to escape a Vaseline prison. Above his polished shoes, Josie noticed his socks didn't match. But he had a marvelous grin, the biggest grin she'd ever seen.

"Hi!" he said. "I'm Daniel. What's your name?"

"Hi," Josie said quietly. "I'm Josie."

"You've got the biggest bow I've ever seen!" he beamed.

"I do?" Josie could feel the redness creep over her face.

"Yeah. It's really great!" he said, settling himself comfortably.

Josie smiled. More kids were arranging themselves in the circle and Daniel seemed to know most of them.

"That's Joe and that's Keith and that's Darlene," he told Josie as he pointed to them. ♡

Chapter Twenty-One
Daddy Fights

The doorbell woke Josie. She lay quietly, wondering if she had really heard it or not, waiting. Would it ring again? She listened for any movement from her brothers. All she heard was their soft, regular breathing. Maybe she'd dreamt it? Then it came again, a funny sort of *buzz, buzz,* as if someone wasn't quite pushing it hard enough.

She sat up. *We never have company,* she thought. *No one ever rings our bell, even during the day. Who could be ringing it at night?* It was a real puzzle.

Josie slipped out of bed and tip-toed through the dark room to the door. Danny and Will hadn't even moved. They were still breathing that soft regular way people do when asleep.

There it was again! A half-hearted *buzz, buzz*.

She heard Uncle John's bed creak as he got up, and the funny step-scuff, step-scuff as he passed her bedroom, heading to answer the front door. Curiously, she opened her bedroom door just a crack to see what was going on. Who could be ringing the bell so late at night?

It was good Uncle John was here to answer the door. He wasn't always here, only on layovers from his railroad job. If he'd been gone, it would be really scary!

Now she could hear muffled noises, like someone stumbling or scuffing their feet. Uncle John's voice was low, so low she couldn't make out the words. The other voice sounded a little like Daddy's. She couldn't be sure. Oh, that was silly! Why would Daddy ring the bell when he has a key?

Josie opened the door wider. *Yes, it is Daddy!* She thought. *What's wrong? Something must be wrong!* Every muscle in her body was tense, waiting, listening, focused. Josie was very good at knowing when something was wrong.

Then she saw Uncle John helping Daddy walk through the dining room. The sight of Daddy shocked her so, it never occurred to Josie to duck back into the shadows so she couldn't be seen.

Uncle John was holding Daddy under the arms so he wouldn't fall. Daddy was wobbling. His hat was pushed crookedly on the back of his head. And his face! *Oh, God!* She thought. His face was a mess of blood. Blood was running down over his nose. It was dripping onto the front of his shirt. Even his tie, the one she had picked out for him last Christmas, had blood on it. He put a hand to his face and that was all bloody too.

He kept muttering something. "Dirty S.O.B. hit me … bar." Mumble … mumble.

Uncle John was trying to quiet him. "Shh," he was saying. "You'll wake everyone."

Daddy just muttered louder. "S.O.B. hit me!"

Uncle John maneuvered Daddy into the bathroom and got him to sit on the toilet seat.

"Shh," he was saying. "Let's get you taken care of. Shh."

Josie had never been so scared. Her heart was pounding. Who could have hurt Daddy so terribly? Poor Daddy. He kept muttering about "S.O.B." Who was that? She'd never heard of anyone like that. Maybe she should wake her brothers. They would know what to do. She stood there, shivering, trying to sort it all out. Slowly, almost as if there was nothing she could do to stop herself, she walked out to the dining room where she could see into the bathroom.

Uncle John had taken Daddy's jacket and hat off and was wiping some of the blood off his face. Daddy's bloodied right hand was soaking in the sink.

"My God!" Uncle John was saying. "How did this happen?"

“You sanctimonious …” Daddy mumbled. “Think you’re so …” Mumble … mumble.

“Shh!” Uncle John whispered. “You want to your kids to wake up, see you like this?”

“Son o’bi—, Son o’bi—!” Daddy was saying over and over. “Son o’bi—!”

Daddy was being nasty to Uncle John. Josie couldn’t move. It scared her when Daddy was like this. “Drunk again,” Danny and Will would put it. She’d never seen anyone bleeding so much. How much could someone bleed before they died? What if Daddy died? What if he bled to death right there in front of her? Who would take of them? Where would they live? Danny was so smart and Will so funny, someone would want them. But she was just there; would someone want her?

She felt something sticky on her bare foot and looked down. She had stepped on a drop of blood, Daddy’s blood. There were drops of Daddy’s blood leading to the bathroom. She must have moved or made some noise because suddenly Daddy said loudly, “Who’s there?”

Before she could answer, Uncle John turned to her.

“What’s the little brat want?” Daddy snarled.

Uncle John put the wash cloth down and told Daddy to be quiet. He came over to Josie and squatted down in front of her.

“Go back to bed, Josie,” he said quietly.

Josie looked past his shoulder at Daddy, then back at Uncle John. He seemed to know what was worrying her.

“He’ll be okay,” he promised. “It looks a lot worse than it is.”

He stood up, took her shoulders, and turned her around to head back to her bedroom.

“Go back to bed. I’ll take care of him.”

Josie walked back to her room. She turned a minute to look back. Uncle John motioned her to keep going. She crawled into her bed, her warm, soft, bed, and pulled the covers up over her head, hiding.

When morning came, Josie stretched as wakefulness came over her. Her brothers were up already, teasing and punching each other. The events of the night before were forgotten, only the feeling of something wrong was left. Something terribly wrong. What? What was wrong? Josie felt this way so often. Guilty, worried, scared for no reason. Just this awful feeling of something wrong.

Then she remembered. Had that really happened? Had Daddy really come home all hurt and bloody? Maybe it had been a bad dream. She turned to her brothers.

"Did you hear anything last night? Like the doorbell ringing?" she asked.

"Nah," answered Danny. "Who'd ring our door bell? Especially at night?"

"You must have dreamt it," Will laughed.

Yes. That must have been it. It had just been an awful, bad dream. Relief flooded over her. Yes. A bad dream. That's all it was.

She sat up in bed and swung her legs over the edge of the bed. A bad dream. Sure, that's all it had been. She stood up. She had to get dressed and forget about that silly old bad dream, she told herself.

Only … only there was something sticky on the bottom of her foot.

Chapter Twenty-Two
Peace on Earth

Thoughts of Christmas settled around Josie the way snowflakes settled around the yard, drifting to fill nooks and crannies, swirling around porches and between buildings in graceful, soft piles of icy white. Ice coated each branch with sparkling dust to transform the ordinary into a magical fairy land.

Everything around Josie reminded her that Christmas was coming. The fragrance of Mrs. Lewendoski's baking filled the back hall with the smell of Christmas. Each day, coming and going through the hall was such a delight that Josie wanted to knock on the door and beg for a taste; but of course, such conduct was unthinkable.

Each evening before supper, Josie hunched near the radio to listen to "Billie the Brownie" and his friend Larry read letters from other kids and tell how many more days were left before Santa himself arrived in Milwaukee for a special parade on National Avenue. Josie had never written Santa; it was greedy and impolite to ask people for things. Besides, you were going to get whatever you were going to get, no matter what you asked for. But how fun it would have been to hear her name announced on the radio and have everyone else hear what she had written!

At school, the sister was teaching them a new carol. Each day, the students would go over the words and sing "Hark! The Harold Angels Sing." This new song was wonderful, even though the words made very little sense to Josie. Why were they singing "Hark, hark?" The word sounded so harsh.

She had always thought the angels must have sung something sweet and soft. "Hark!" was neither sweet nor soft. "Peace on earth and mercy mild; God and sinners reconciled." That sounded pleasing - puzzling, but pleasing. "Angelic host proclaim ..." Were they singing about the communion wafers in the middle of a Christmas song? Host? Host, what? Pro ... pro ...? It must have something to do with candy canes, although why that was in a song about angels was confusing. Still, the music and most of the words just sounded so wonderful that those minutes of song became the best part of the school day.

All around the neighborhood, front windows glowed with candles, announcing that the baby Jesus was welcome in those homes. Miss Tooley told Josie why it was so important to put candles in the window. Baby Jesus roamed the world on Christmas Eve, searching for a place to stay, and the light in the window showed that He was welcomed there. It would be nice if their house was chosen some Christmas Eve, if the doorbell rang and there stood the baby Jesus looking for a place to spend the night. Only Miss Tooley would no doubt scold Him for tracking in snow, and feed Him something awful like oatmeal.

Almost overnight, Christmas trees began appearing on front porches or leaning near back doors. Mrs. Lewendoski's tree was in the front window where everyone could see the delicate straw ornaments her mother had made many years ago. Mr. and Mrs. Russell had set up their tiny feather-tree with real little white candles clipped on that were only lit on Christmas Eve. Each morning when the Sister asked, "Who has their tree up?" more and more children raised their hands. But Josie's hand never went up. This, the most important and wonderful ingredient of Christmas, hadn't even been bought yet. Christmas wouldn't—couldn't—arrive until the tree was up!

At night in the darkness of her room, she'd ponder the magic that was Christmas. What would they do if the baby Jesus really *did* appear at their front door, requesting a place to stay? Were barn animals really given the power to speak on Christmas Eve, and if so, what did they have to say? Were there really elves watching to see if she'd been naughty or nice?

Her dreams floated through a cookie-scented forest of Christmas trees where elves and angels sang and danced and welcomed her, as though she too were a magical creature no different from them. Each morning she awoke, knowing Christmas was one day closer, and that they needed to buy their tree before all the good ones were gone and only the ugly ones remained!

Josie could see in her mind the exact tree that she wanted: a perfect little triangle of a tree, a tree she could allow her paper dolls to climb on and play in among the branches, a cuddly little tree she could just about hug that wasn't too tall, just tall enough so a smiling daddy could lift a little girl up to place the angel on top. Her attempts at conversation during supper always pointed out that they'd better get going!

"The Lewendoski's got their tree already. You can see it through the window," and "Isn't Mr. Russell's tree funny-looking? He's already put it up again!"

But all Daddy did was stare straight ahead as usual, chewing his food, with little interest in what he ate or what she said.

Danny and Will seemed unaware too. They fooled around, wiggling and pushing each other, despite Miss Tooley's ineffective, "Settle down, boys." Her brothers never seemed affected by anything or anyone other than themselves. *Such closeness must be nice,* she thought, not that she was ever jealous; that was simply how they were. Josie envied only one thing about her brothers: they were able to remember her mother, *really* remember her.

Josie's memories were vague: someone soft and sweet-smelling rocking her, humming a tune that always eluded her. But Danny and Will could remember all sorts of things. They could remember a picnic at a beach when Mother and Daddy laughed together. Such a remarkable memory! Daddy so seldom laughed now. Oh, he'd smile occasionally; at least, on the outside there was a smile, but his eyes seemed as sad as ever. She couldn't remember the last time she'd seen him laugh.

Danny and Will remembered when Daddy laughed all the time, starting with easy little smiles that burst suddenly into laughter as he danced 'round and 'round the kitchen table with her mother in his arms. The boys could close their eyes and see their mother, feel her touch, even remember her smell. Sometimes, Josie would sniff at an object she knew her mother had touched, and breathe deeply to see if any part remained behind. But of course, there was no guarantee that what she smelled was really her mother's essence.

Miss Tooley didn't seem to care about memories or Christmas either. Fat, old women probably didn't even know how important the Christmas tree was. Fat, old women didn't seem to know how important *many* things were. If it had nothing to do with neatness or school or going to church, Miss Tooley didn't seem to think it was important.

"They're selling trees at that lot on National Avenue," Josie would say to deaf ears.

No matter how often she brought up the subject, no one else seemed to care a bit.

Then one Saturday during lunch, while Josie was daydreaming of elves and where and how they might stay warm when the snow buried Elftown, and while Danny and Will were spelling out names with their alphabet soup and eating all the names of the kids they didn't like, and while Miss Tooley was pleading her litany of "Settle down, boys," and "Stop it now, boys," and "Eat your lunch, boys," Daddy leaned over the table and asked, "Whadd'ya say we get our tree this afternoon?"

Josie's heart soared as she gulped her soup. Her brothers stopped their game to finish eating.

"Better bundle up. It's nippy outside," Miss Tooley warned.

Resentfully, Josie struggled into her snow pants while everyone else stood and waited for her. Her brothers just grabbed their jackets and were ready to go, but she had to wear snow pants too: bulky old snow pants like a little kid.

The boys scampered ahead, leaping down the stairs two at a time past Josie, who walked carefully, holding the rail.

"I'll go grab the sled," Danny said, heading for the basement.

Daddy stared blankly and said, "Sled? Forget the sled! We're going for a tree, not sledding!"

"But last year we used—" Will stammered, his voice trailing off as Daddy kept walking out the back door and down the brick walk to the alley. The boys exchanged puzzled looks and followed Daddy. Josie ran to slip her hand into his. Danny and Will chased each other over mountains of snow the plow had left behind, throwing snowballs at imaginary foes. Daddy set the pace, staring straight ahead, ignoring her bothers' antics. They turned at the end of the alley, walked another block to National Avenue, then three more blocks to the lot.

The vacant lot had been transformed into a forest of pine, like something from a storybook. Danny and Will ran off to have snowball battles with one another in the make-believe wilderness. Entranced, Josie sniffed the piney air and began tiptoeing slowly between the trees, searching for elves. They must surely live in a magical place like this. She pretended to be a little girl who lived in some woodsy place where people had to cut their own trees. She followed a rabbit track, certain it was a trail meant just for her.

Then she spotted it! The perfect tree was right there in front of her, waiting for her, a perfect little triangle of a tree. The rabbit had been right, and she was so smart to follow it.

"Here! Here! This is the one!" Josie danced from one foot to the other, clapping her hands in excitement. "Here! It's perfect! Let's get this one!"

Daddy came to see and the boys ran from wherever they'd been hiding to take a look.

"It's too small," Danny and Will said together.

But Daddy walked around it and said, "When we put it in a stand, it'll be taller."

They were joined by a skinny man bundled in a raggedy overcoat held closed by a huge, rusty safety pin. Each time he moved, the coat flapped open, exposing his dirty sweatshirt. His knit cap had a hole where a tuft of greasy, brown hair poked out. His face was covered with whiskers that were not much cleaner than his hair.

"How much?" Daddy asked.

The man blew on his cold fingers. He had gloves, but the thumb and first two fingers stuck out of holes.

"Six-fifty. All these trees is six-fifty," the man sniffed.

"Too much!" Daddy exclaimed. "Way too much!"

"Hey, I just work here, Mack! That's the price," the man shrugged and wiped his nose on the sleeve of his coat.

"Tell ya what," Daddy said, "I'll flip ya for it. Double or nothing."

"Can't do it, Mack. I just work here. What would I tell my boss when he sees this here tree gone, but no six dollars and fifty cents for it?" He held one grimy finger to a nostril and blew hard. The snot flew out across the snow. Danny and Will snickered appreciatively, but Josie stared in horror as he proceeded to do the other side, too.

"Well, maybe you'd have his six-fifty *and* six-fifty in your pocket, too," Daddy said loudly, his eyes glinting strangely.

"Can't do it, Mack. Sorry." He took deep breaths, in and out, as though it were a wonderful thing he could do now. In and out. In and out.

"You chicken or what? Cluck, cluck!" Daddy shouted.

Josie's tummy did a little flip and her face grew hot. She'd never seen Daddy behave like this, at least, not in front of everyone.

"Hey, Mack, I don't need this crap. Ya want the tree, pay six-fifty! Ya don't want it, don't buy it!"

"Call me 'Mack' one more time—"

Other customers were gathering, watching and wondering what all the commotion was about. Josie stepped back, hoping to blend into the gathering crowd, knowing the redness of her face now spread to cover every inch of her. For a moment, she feared she might throw up vegetable soup all over this pretty place. Why did Daddy have to be so loud and angry in front of everyone?

"Get outta here!" the man screamed. "I don't need no drunk giving me no grief! Scram! I wouldn't sell ya a tree if ya begged me!"

"I wouldn't take one of your dried-out old trees for nothing!" Daddy shouted back.

Josie's tummy did another little flip and her mouth filled with a sourness she managed to swallow. It burned all the way down. Danny and Will looked at the gathering crowd

"Come on, Dad," Will said.

"Let's go." Danny took Daddy's arm to lead him away.

Daddy jerked unsteadily, swearing under his breath.

"There's another place a few blocks down," Will said.

"Let's go there," Josie pleaded. She was willing to do anything to get away from all these people staring at them, snickering, shaking their heads, staring at her and her brothers as though they were something odd, something to be pitied or despised.

They formed a straggly parade down National Avenue. Daddy led the way, muttering curses under his breath. Josie followed a few steps behind, her tummy gradually quieting itself. Her throat slowly stopped stinging as she rubbed her tongue against her teeth and swallowed over and over again. Her brothers, subdued for a change, brought up the rear.

What had happened? What had gone wrong? What had she done? Maybe if she hadn't wanted a tree so much, or if she'd picked out a different tree, one that Daddy would have been glad to pay for— There must have been something wrong with her tree. That must have been it. He would have paid the man and they would be heading home with their tree right now if there hadn't been something wrong with it.

Daddy was wonderful, so wonderful! Everything about him was wonderful. Oh, there were times he could become unpleasant, unpredictable, but he was still her wonderful Daddy. Even if he smelled sour and behaved strangely, it was only because one of them had caused it, even if they hadn't meant to. One of them would say something and Daddy would be off in a fury or just sit and cry quietly to himself.

Poor Daddy, so sad, yet often suddenly loud and angry, shouting just like that with no warning, just yelling and upset. Maybe it was his smell that made him so mad and loud. Was that possible? Did his sourness bother him and make him angry? No one else she knew smelled so differently when they were angry. Why did he change like that in front of everyone, turning from her wonderful Daddy into an angry, scary stranger?

The worse thing of all, the most shameful, was that she had backed away from Daddy: backed away, hoping people would not know that they were all together, backed away, pretending she wasn't with him. Denying him. Like Judas had denied Christ. Daddy was so wonderful, and she was a betraying Judas. Her face reddened as disgust for herself seeped into her soul and filled her with shame. Her daddy was buying her the Christmas tree she'd been wanting for so long, and she had tried to pretend she wasn't even with him.

Josie ran to catch up with him and slip her hand once more into his, to show everyone she *was* with him. She would not deny him again. In her heart, she begged his forgiveness for whatever it was she might have done to hurt him so much.

The next lot was not the magical forest the first place had been. There were no elves here. All the trees were $7.50 and not one suited Daddy, so they walked a few more blocks to another lot. Josie was colder than she could ever remember being. Her feet were numb and she had to go to the bathroom, but it wouldn't do to bring up the subject and risk making Daddy mad. Her brothers were themselves again, throwing snowballs and chasing each other, laughing and pushing each other into the snow banks as though nothing had happened.

At the third lot, Daddy found a tree he liked: not a soft, sweet, huggy little tree, but a hard, ugly tree, too tall with branches that were almost all the same length from the bottom to the top. But Daddy thought it was nice, and of course, he knew best. Certainly, *she* hadn't done such a great job of picking the first one.

"How's this one, sweetheart?" he asked.

Josie nodded, taking care not to rile him again.

"How much?" Daddy asked.

"Seven bucks," said the man minding that lot.

"Whadd'ya say, fella? Wanna flip?" Daddy offered. "Double or nothing."

The man hesitated before answering. "Sure, buddy, why not?"

Daddy fished a quarter from his pocket. "Call it, sweetheart. Heads or tails?"

"What?" Josie asked, tummy tightening again at this unknown, potentially dangerous responsibility that she knew required caution.

"Heads or tails. Heads or tails! Call it, da— it!"

Josie's mind raced to sort out the danger. Her throat tightened.

"Heads or tails?" Daddy demanded impatiently.

"Heads, I guess," Josie said in a strange little voice she barely recognized.

Daddy flipped the coin, caught it mid-air, and slammed it down on the back of his left hand. He raised his right hand so both he and the tree man could see.

"Tails!" the man crowed. "Thanks, buddy! Ya made my day! I'll have a shot on you after I'm done here today!"

Daddy pulled out his wallet and paid for the tree. "Bring the sled here," he called to the boys.

"But, Dad, you said—" one started.

"—not to bring it," the other finished.

"What do you mean? How the h— will we get this tree home without a sled?" Daddy's eyes glazed over with a wild glare and he swung his hand, cuffing Danny on the back of the head. "Stupid kids!" he mumbled. "Can't make a g—d-mn call, can't remember a stupid sled."

Danny straightened his cap, trying not to let Daddy see him rub his head or the blink back the tears that threatened to spill out of his eyes. But Daddy did notice.

"Cry-baby," Daddy scoffed.

"We can carry it, Daddy," Josie said, drawing Daddy's attention away from Danny. "We can all carry it."

"Guess we'll have to, won't we? I just paid fourteen bucks for the dumb tree! I'm sure as h— not leaving it here!" His words were like a slap across her face.

Daddy picked up the stump of the tree. Will grabbed the top and motioned Danny to take the other side. Josie rushed to reach between the prickly needles to do her part.

It wasn't long before her arm began to feel like it was going to drop off at the shoulder. Her jacket sleeve had pushed up and the exposed part of her arm was cold. The tree needles were scratching her skin raw, but she dared not let go and cause Daddy more work. Cold seeped into her, filled every inch of her body. Her nose began to tickle and run, but she didn't dare let go long enough to wipe it. The disgusting vision of the man at the first lot blowing his nose came to her. There was no way she would allow herself to do something like that, so she rubbed her mitten across her nose to stop the annoying drip, drip.

The mild need to "go" had turned into an urgency. To wet herself was unthinkable and would surely cause Daddy to change into the scary stranger. She walked along, keeping up as best she could, not caring about anything except getting home and getting warm and going to the toilet. She sunk into a world of her own, a world of cold and fatigue and aching bladder. Her feet moved without her willing them. Just step—step—step. She began counting them. One step. Two steps. One step. Two steps. Then through the haze of cold and pain, she became aware of her brothers whispering to each other.

"He's plastered!" Danny said.

"Yeah, drunk as a skunk!" Will answered. "Drunk as a skunk."

Danny started to giggle. "How drunk is a skunk? How drunk can a skunk get?"

Will started to giggle too, sharing one of their private little jokes. "Stinkin' drunk!"

Danny nodded. "He's drunk as a … a monkey! Yeah, he's hanging one on. Get it? Monkey … hanging?"

Will shook his head and pretended to be disgusted, then started to giggle.

The first man had called Daddy that too: a "drunk." Josie twisted around to talk to them over her shoulder. "What does that mean? Dru—"

"You kids getting tired?" Daddy asked, interrupting Josie's question and, without waiting for an answer, dropped his end of the tree. "You can rest here a while. I'm going in." He headed for the door of *Arnie's Tap*.

"Can I go to the bathroom?" Josie asked.

Daddy stared at her, blinking as though he hadn't realized she was still along with them. "Of course," he said kindly, like her regular Daddy. "You two—" he glared at the boys, "you two watch the tree."

He opened the door with a polite little bow and pointed the way to the ladies' room, then turned to Arnie, the owner. "Give me a Corby's."

In the ladies' room, Josie took off her jacket and pulled down the straps of her snow pants. She carefully laid toilet paper over the seat, the way Aunt Becka had always insisted. It felt so good to sit for a minute, even on a toilet seat. She pulled a wad of paper and blew her nose. Then she struggled once more into her snow pants. She ran hot water over her hands to warm them, then sat on the floor and leaned against the radiator.

How nice it would be to just sit here forever, so nice to just sit and rest a while, to warm up, to nod off here in this cozy place. Her eyes felt heavy and she began to float pleasantly away. But suppose Daddy wanted to leave and she wasn't waiting with her brothers by the tree? He'd be mad again and who could blame him? She'd already caused enough problems for him today. Rousing herself, Josie bundled up and went outside to join her brothers.

"Is he coming soon?" asked Danny.

Josie shrugged. "He was talking to some man."

They sat together on the bottom step. No one said a word. Josie felt a lot warmer since she'd been inside, and sitting squashed between her brothers helped keep the cold away.

"Hey, guys! Whadd'ya doin'?" Bobby Dobrowski and his cousin, Butch, were crossing the street, heading toward them, looking for trouble the way they always were.

"Why ya sittin' out here for?" asked Bobby.

"Your old man in there hangin' one on? Ain't it so?" Butch added his two cents' worth, staggering and pretending to grab the side of the building to keep from falling. "Oh, I'm so dizzy!"

Bobby hiccupped loudly. "Oh my! Better gimme a drink."

Danny jumped up. "Shut your face before—"

"—we knock your brains out!" Will leaped up.

"If ya had a brain," Danny finished.

Bobby and Butch kicked the Christmas tree as they ran past, laughing and hiccupping. "Yer old man's a drunk!" they yelled back.

Danny heaved a snowball that hit Butch in the back, but he just kept running, laughing and shouting, "Yer old man's a drunk!" over and over until they were halfway down the block and could barely be heard.

"What's a drunk?" Josie asked.

Danny and Will exchanged the look they always had whenever she asked what they considered a dumb question. It was the same look as when she had asked what those words meant that were scrawled on the back wall of St. Matthew's school.

"Really. What does it mean?" she asked again.

Danny sat down beside her. "Well, he drinks too much."

"Beer, whiskey, that stuff," Will continued, plopping himself next to Danny. "That's why he acts funny. The way he does."

"Funny?" Josie was puzzled.

"The way he was today. Ya gotta have noticed."

"So mean and … funny. Not 'ha-ha funny,' but you know. *Funny*." Danny said.

"Why does he? Drink that stuff, I mean, if it makes him so mad?" Josie questioned. "Why would he do it? Maybe he doesn't know he gets like that."

"Maybe," Danny shrugged. "I don't know."

Will stood up, scooped up some snow, and threw a snowball at nothing special.

Josie thought a moment, then asked, "Will he ever be like he was before?"

"I guess," Will answered, "if he stops drinking that stuff."

"Yeah," Danny, always the wisest one, added, "they say booze is like poison to some people."

Josie leaned forward, her chin on her hands. "Maybe if we told him how, how funny he is, maybe he'd stop." Her voice caught as a sudden sadness washed over her. "Maybe …"

Danny put his arm around her in an unexpected display of tenderness. "I know," he said. "I felt the same way when I found out."

"How? How did you find out?"

Danny started the story. "We were buying candy at Schick's and some ladies were talking to Mrs. Schick, and one of them said how sad it was that Mr. Walker was drinking so much. Another of them said, 'Yes, he's becoming as big a drunk as Mr. McGuiness.'"

Mike McGuiness' dad was always wrinkled and messy-looking. He stumbled a lot and everyone snickered when he walked by. He'd beat up on Mike, too. "The old man give it to me," Mike seemed to brag whenever he had a black eye or a bruise someplace, as though he were proud of it or something. Then he'd add, "I'll be givin' it back to him one of these days!" Mike's eyes would look so cold and faraway, as if he could really see that day in his mind. He'd slam his fist into his palm and laugh, but it was a cold, scary laugh that it made Josie shiver.

"But Daddy's not at all like Mr. McGuiness," Josie protested. "He doesn't look like him. Mr. McGuiness looks so … so dirty and so mean."

"Well, yeah, he's different, but still, he's a drunk," Danny sighed. He leaned back against the wall. "He's a drunk."

Josie leaned back against the wall too, quietly trying to understand it all.

Suddenly Will announced, "I gotta use the can." And he left.

Jody snuggled close to Danny, soaking up warmth and comfort. "Does he know it?" she asked. "Does Daddy know?"

"Know what?" Danny shifted to ease her off his arm.

"Know he's a drunk?"

"I don't know. Maybe when you're a drunk, you don't know it."

"Maybe if he knew, he wouldn't do it anymore," Jody said.

"Maybe," Danny shrugged. "Maybe."

Will joined them again. "He's really hangin' one on. Shooting some craps with some old guy."

"It'll be a while then. Better let me up," Danny said. "It's my turn now."

He went into the bar, returning a few minutes later.

"Boy, he really got sore when he saw me. Said he didn't need me around. Said he'd be right out."

They settled down again, but didn't have long to wait. Daddy came out, tripping over the mat and catching his coat on the door. His eyes were glassy as he stared at them huddled on the step, the tree by their feet.

"Come on. Let's go home. Why h— are you sitting out here in the dark?"

They picked up the tree and started for home again. Daddy put the tree on the stair in the back hall. "We'll get it upstairs tomorrow," he told them.

The kitchen was bright and warm. Miss Tooley had supper waiting for them. "My goodness, you took a long time! Get washed up right away and come and get it."

They hurried to shed jackets, and Jody peeled off her snow pants and headed to wash her hands. Her brothers were already waiting at the table by the time she got there.

"Did you find a nice tree?" Miss Tooley asked as she dished up a brackish stew. The potatoes were gray and unappetizing, the carrots over-cooked and mushy.

"Sure. It's real nice," Danny answered, lowering his eyes to inspect his plate.

Will glanced at Danny, then agreed with a little laugh, "It's great!"

Miss Tooley looked at Jody. "Well, what do *you* have to say about it?"

Josie stared at her plate. She felt empty. The magic was gone. The tree and the lights and everything else no longer mattered. All the elves were gone, dead and gone. There was nothing and she didn't really care. She felt the slow warming of her feet and toes, but deep inside her, down, down under her heart where her soul dwelled, there was only ice. And that ice was spreading throughout her body, down her arms and legs, spreading out and dripping off her, making the whole room cold. The whole world was cold, cold and dead as the elves.

Josie looked across the table at her brothers eating supper as though it might really taste good. Daddy, at his place at the head of the table, was staring straight ahead, sadly chewing his food without tasting it.

She thought of all that had happened that day and how empty she felt. But it wasn't really poor, sad Daddy's fault. It was only the stuff that he drank. She couldn't spoil everything with how she really felt. It would only cause more sadness, and Daddy was already sad enough. Who was she to add to that sadness? Besides, Daddy might get angry again and act like Mike McGuiness' dad, and it would be all her fault—hers and the stuff he drank.

Maybe, maybe this was like when you're scared of something or a bully at school threatened you. You just pretended you weren't really afraid, just pretended everything was okay. Then pretty soon, it *was* okay. Maybe that was the secret. Maybe that was what her brothers already knew.

Pretend. Just pretend.

"Oh yes, Miss Tooley!" she bubbled as she mashed her potatoes. "It's the best tree ever! I can't wait 'til we get it up!"

Chapter Twenty-Three

Daddy's Room

Josie woke up. No, not really woke up, but *became aware,* aware that she was cold, colder than she'd ever been in her life. And afraid. The words, "watch out … watch out" floated through her mind. She was crouched on the edge of Daddy's bed, her back against the wall, and cold, so cold.

Daddy was muttering something in his sleep. It sounded like he was dreaming of fighting Japs. "Little yellow rats!" he yelled. "Watch out, here they come."

"Watch out." That must be it. *Daddy wants me to watch out for Japs. But they're not here, only in his dreams,* Josie reasoned. *Why am I here?* She thought. I haven't crawled in bed with Daddy for years. When she was little and nightmares overcame her, she'd creep through the dark house and crawl in with Daddy.

"Spiders again?" Daddy would ask.

Josie would nod and she could snuggle in. It was safe and warm and wonderful there next to Daddy. No spiders in the night.

As she grew older, Daddy would send her back to her own bed. She'd lie there, terrified to fall asleep, terrified to move, lest the spiders came again, perhaps for real this time.

Daddy had changed too, no longer warm and safe, but sour-smelling and strange. She would never have come in here to Daddy's room for comfort. Why was she here? How did she get here?

Daddy will be angry if he finds me here, Josie worried. The warm safety of her bed beckoned her. She had to get back, back to her own room, her own bed. Safety!

Slowly she inched her way down to the foot of Daddy's bed. Daddy tossed and yelled out, "Stop 'em! Stop 'em!" She froze, waiting in the darkness until he was quiet again. Then slowly she climbed over the foot board to the floor. She crawled quietly to the door and opened it carefully. Daddy thrashed around, muttering again about Japs.

She went through the door, closing it softly, and raced through the dining room to the safety of her own room. She opened the door and leaped into her own little bed. She was so cold and afraid as she hid under the covers, but the warmth of her own bed and comforting sound of Danny's and Will's soft breathing soon put her to sleep.

The next morning when Josie woke, everything seemed the same as always. And the strangeness of the night before faded from her memory.

A week went by or maybe two or more. Children lose track of such things, so Josie wasn't really sure when it all happened again.

Again she "woke up" after not really being asleep. She was again crouched on Daddy's bed and cold, so cold and afraid. He was again tossing and muttering in his sleep.

How did she get here? She sat, shivering in the darkness, wondering how this had happened again. A vague memory came to her.

Daddy had come home and woken her up. He wanted her to come with him. He was sour and smelly, not her regular Daddy but the stranger he was becoming more and more often. She fought waking up and protested against the intrusion into her sleep. He'd shushed her, directing her back to his room. Well, she figured, maybe it will be like before, warm and cozy, and I'll just go back to sleep there.

When they got to Daddy's room she'd crawled into his bed, moving way over, as far away from him as she could. He smelled so awful, it wasn't pleasant to snuggle close like it used to be. But Daddy had insisted she lay close to him. He put his arms under her head "for a pillow," he'd said. Then he took his hand and put it—.

"Please, Daddy!" she'd cried. "Please, Daddy. Don't!"

The next thing she was aware of was the cold.

What had happened? Josie couldn't remember. All she knew was she had to return to her own room, her own bed.

Slowly she inched to the foot of the bed. This time though, as she tried to climb over the foot board, the bed sort of squeaked and swayed a little. Daddy suddenly became quiet, no tossing, no muttering.

"What? Who's there? What do you want?" he demanded.

Oh, God! Josie prayed.

He was awake! Quickly she scurried across the foot of the bed as Daddy kicked at her.

"What are you doing here?" he hissed at her. "Get back to your own bed."

He kicked her as she climbed out of the bed, causing her to stumble. She half-fell, half-ran to the door and opened it. As she hurried through the kitchen, Miss Tooley called out, "What's wrong?" but she just kept going until she was safely in her own bed.

Again, she lay in the darkness, trying to sort it all out. What had happened? It was all so confusing. After a while sleep came, restless sleep, filled with spiders.

Again, in the morning the memories of the night before had faded. When Miss Tooley asked if she'd had a nightmare, she answered, "yes." It was the truth. She'd had a nightmare all right.

Later, after school Aunt Becka came over. She was talking with Miss Tooley. Josie knew as soon as she walked in something was being discussed. Quickly her guard was up.

"Josie," Aunt Becka called. "Come in here."

Josie went in cautiously. It felt like one of those times one had to be very careful.

"Josie," Miss Tooley asked. "Why were you in your daddy's room last night?"

Josie felt her heart leap inside, but outside she remained calm. One had to be careful, careful because one never knew what grown-ups might do.

"Daddy wanted me there," she answered.

"But why?" asked Aunt Becka. "Why did he want you there?"

Thoughts flashed through Josie's mind. She knew what they were concerned about. But how could she tell them? Besides, Daddy had stopped when she begged him to. Hadn't he? If she told them, even if she'd known how, everyone would be upset with her. There would be yelling and it would be all her fault. Besides, how could she tell them? And anyway, Daddy hadn't really done anything. Had he? He'd stopped when she cried. Hadn't he? *Hadn't he?*

"Well," Josie replied, as calmly as possible, because when things were most dangerous one had to be very, very calm. "He wanted me to watch out for Japs."

"Japs!" Aunt Becka looked puzzled.

"He was dreaming, I guess," Josie continued, "about Japs and I was to watch out for them."

"Japs?" Aunt Becka repeated.

"There weren't any, of course. They were just nightmares, I guess."

Aunt Becka and Miss Tooley looked at Josie. They weren't sure what to make of her story. She'd made Daddy look foolish to them, all that stuff about Japs. She didn't want to make Daddy look foolish. Poor, sad Daddy.

"Well if anything ever happens, tell us," Aunt Becka said.

Josie felt almost grown-up. She knew exactly what Aunt Becka meant, yet how could she ever tell her? Besides, Daddy had stopped. Hadn't he? Told her to forgive him. Hadn't he? Told her to forget about it.

So, she did.

Chapter Twenty-Four
Things That Go "Bump" in the Night

Josie woke cautiously. Experience had taught her it was best to remain quiet, as though still sleeping, taking a moment or two to figure out what was happening before letting others know she was awake. This way she had at least some idea of what to expect when everyone else became aware that she had rejoined them.

She listened carefully. Something had caused her to wake up. But what? Her brothers were breathing quietly in their sleep. She matched her breathing to theirs just in case someone was listening. If she could tell by a person's breathing if they were awake or not, others could too.

In … out … in … out. She focused on any sound that might give a hint as to what had awakened her.

Miss. Tooley's snoring came from Aunt Becka's old room. That strange, grinding noise had frightened her when Miss. Tooley first became their housekeeper, working its way into her dreams like the raspy voice of the devil himself. But now it was comforting in its familiarity.

There was the gentle hum of the refrigerator and the wheezing and sighing of the house as it settled itself, like an old woman settling into a creaky rocking chair. There was muffled music and talking from the radio. Daddy must have come home from his nightly walk and turned the radio on. That must have been what woke her. Daddy was home and had turned on the radio. That was all. Just the radio.

She was about to relax her vigilance when she heard the bedroom door being shut. Daddy had been looking in, checking on them and now, satisfied that they were asleep, he closed the door. Josie shuddered. She'd almost moved and given herself away, let Daddy know she was awake. Lord only knew what would have happened then.

She never knew what to expect from Daddy these days. One minute he'd be her regular Daddy or even poor, sad Daddy, and the next minute he'd be scary Daddy with the wild, strange eyes and sour smell. So, it was best not to deal with him at all unless it was absolutely necessary.

Josie stretched out and opened her eyes. The room was dark, but she wasn't afraid. She found the dark soft and comforting. It surrounded you, hid you, made you invisible. It was so dark you "couldn't see your hand in front of your face." Where had she heard that expression? The thought fascinated her. She held her hand up in the darkness and waved it gracefully back and forth, but of course she couldn't see it.

Perhaps she really wasn't moving it. Perhaps she just *thought* she was moving it. How could she be sure her hand was waving there in front of her if she didn't see it? She put both hands together and moved one. The other followed dutifully along.

Was this what being blind was like? Never being sure if you were doing what you wanted to do because you couldn't see and know for sure? Just blackness all the time, never to see sunshine, never to be able to climb to the highest top of a tree, never to see the dance of sunlight and the shadow below? How awful!

Now that she was fully awake, Josie realized she had to go to the bathroom. *Maybe that's why I woke up,* she thought. *Maybe it wasn't Daddy at all, just that I have to go.* But that meant she had to walk through the dining room and down the hall to the bathroom, and Daddy was in the living room with a clear view of everything. *Maybe I'm better off wetting the bed,* she thought.

It wouldn't be the first time ... probably not the last either. All three of them wet the bed at times. Danny most of all.

"That's why I sleep on top," Will would laugh as he scrambled to the top bunk.

The room always had a faint, almost sweetish smell of urine, unpleasant at first but after a few minutes hardly noticeable at all.

Josie thought about it. Wetting the bed was uncomfortable, cold and damp. She preferred going to the bathroom. However, her problem was still the trip through the dining room and down the hall where Daddy might see her. And that led to … to what? Josie wasn't sure and uncertainty made her cautious. She pondered her options. There were just the two. Either get up and risk the trip to the bathroom or stay and wet the bed and be uncomfortable the rest of the night.

She slipped out of bed and crept to the door. She opened it a crack and peeked out, trying to see if Daddy was awake or asleep. She could see the living room light was on and could hear the radio clearer now: voices saying recognizable words. "Boston Blackie" was talking to a woman. "Don't worry about it," Blackie said, but the woman just kept sobbing and sobbing. Josie couldn't see Daddy, so she opened the door wider and stepped out into the shadows of the dining room.

Daddy was sitting in his corner of the couch, his right arm up, cradling his head. A cigarette smoldered in the ashtray, sending up a narrow ribbon of blue-gray that swirled gracefully with each tiny draft and drifted through the lampshade. A bottle of beer sat next to the ashtray.

Josie squatted, hugging her knees to her chest, and studied Daddy.

He seemed to be sleeping. It was hard to tell for sure. He didn't move. He was breathing quietly, the way people did when they were asleep.

She decided to risk it.

She closed her bedroom door, then hurried through the dining room, down the hall, and into the bathroom. She didn't turn on the light. She went as fast and as quietly as she could manage. She didn't use any telltale paper that might give her away later. Besides, Daddy always yelled about how much paper was used. She didn't dare flush. The noise would wake him for sure.

Now she had to get back to her room.

She peeked around the bathroom door. Daddy had picked up his cigarette and smoke clouds wafted around his head and filled his corner, creating eerie shadows. Music from the radio added to the almost dream-like scene. Josie leaned back against the wall to wait.

She peeked around again, anxious to get back to bed. Daddy put out the cigarette and picked up the bottle of beer. He stared at it a minute, swirling the liquid 'round and 'round. Then he set it down again, leaned his head back against the couch, and sighed as though falling asleep again.

Josie felt the tension building. The night coolness penetrated her thin pajamas, causing a wave of uncontrollable shivering.

Oh, God, she prayed. *Let him fall asleep. Let me get back to bed!*

She looked again. Daddy was walking straight toward her, holding the beer bottle. Her heart leaped to her throat. She forced herself to melt into the shadows and held her breath, not daring to move, not daring to breathe.

Oh, God. I never should have gotten up, she thought.

As he passed the bathroom door, Josie closed her eyes. There were times when she could sense someone looking at her, so she dared not risk a look at him. He might feel her stares and discover her lurking in the bathroom. What would happen then? What would he do? How could she explain why she wasn't asleep like she was supposed to be?

She was certain he'd hear her heart pounding, but he just passed by to go to the kitchen. She heard him put the beer bottle in a case in the pantry. Josie's mind raced with each possibility. If he went from the pantry to the refrigerator for another beer, he wouldn't be able to see her. If he stayed up, maybe he'd stop to use the bathroom. If he went to bed, he'd come in the bathroom for sure.

She had to move, move now. Now was the time to get back to her room and the safety of her bed: her warm, cozy and safe bed. She could make it to her room while he was in the pantry. Now!

Josie scurried down the hall, through the dining room to her bedroom door.

"Who's there?" Daddy called. "Who's up?"

Josie opened her door, slipped through, quickly closing it behind her, and jumped into bed. She pulled the blanket up and closed her eyes as Daddy yanked the door open.

She listened as he walked into the room. Her breathing! She must control her breathing! She fought to breathe quietly like her brothers. In … out … in … out. Her heart was racing, but her breathing was controlled.

Daddy leaned over her bed. His smell, sour and unpleasant, seeped through her blanket. She heard him cross the room to the boys' bunks. Josie opened her eyes just enough to watch through her eyelashes. Daddy swayed unsteadily, staring at the boys. Suddenly his fist flew out as though on an invisible spring and whacked Will.

"When I ask who's there, answer me, da— it!"

Will jumped and began to cry and rub his shoulder where Daddy's blow had landed.

"What's wrong? I didn't do nothin'."

"'Didn't do nothing," Daddy mimicked. "Never do nothing!"

As he turned, he stumbled, awkwardly banging against her bed, swearing and mumbling under his breath.

"G—d-mn kids … fooling around …"

Danny sat up and rubbed his eyes, confused by the ruckus. "What? What's going on?" Josie lay quietly controlling her breathing. In … out … in … out.

"Get to sleep! Stop fooling around!" Daddy snarled, "or I'll be back!"

He leaned against the doorway and stared at Josie, who was still pretending to be asleep.

"Good God!" he said. "That girl could sleep through a war!"

He slammed the door, leaving them in the darkness. Josie opened her eyes. Across the room Will buried his sobs under his pillow and she heard Danny stand up to comfort him. She debated if she should go to him too, confess that it was really her fault.

But what if Daddy heard her? She might get them in trouble again, so she just stared into the soft, safe, comforting darkness until she finally fell asleep.

But the spiders of the night invaded her dreams again, tormenting and terrorizing her until morning when Miss. Tooley opened the door and barked, "Time to get up!"

Josie opened her eyes and stretched. As soon as she moved, she felt the wet, from the middle of her back to almost her knees. Her pajamas clung, cold and clammy with the wet as she crawled out of bed. She pulled her blanket back to allow the mattress to dry before bedtime tonight.

Then she gathered her clothes and walked through the dining room and down the hall to the bathroom to wash and dress and get ready for school.

Chapter Twenty-Five
Spider Dreams

Everything was dark. Josie was filled with a dreadful, overwhelming terror, fear so awful she was aware of nothing else. A light attracted her gaze. She looked up at it and saw the spider hanging there above her head, its web stretching downward, almost touching her.

She ducked to avoid it, only to be face-to-face with another spider, hanging in its web, a strange, blue spider with black legs. Something brushed her neck. A large, yellow-and-orange spider was dangling there.

What is it? Josie wondered. *What is happening here?*

Oh, God! Spiders! She gasped. *Spiders everywhere! Not again! Oh, God, not again!*

Josie felt something moving on her arm. A fuzzy black spider was crawling up her arm! Quickly, she brushed it away. Something was on her leg. Another fuzzy black spider!

Brush it off! Brush it off! Ordered her mind.

Josie obeyed, brushing quickly before it moved any higher. Then another and another. She brushed spiders off frantically. The first spider suddenly became huge, filling up all the space. It was red! No, orange! No, yellow!

Run, Josie, run! She thought.

Yes*! Yes!* She responded.

Her legs couldn't move. Couldn't move! What was wrong with her legs?

Run, Josie! Her mind urged her.

I'm trying! I'm trying! She replied.

Oh, God! said her mind. *It's so big and the colors don't stay! Run!*

I can't, can't, can't. My legs won't move, move, move!

Run, Josie! Why won't you run? Her mind scolded.

Josie looked down at her feet. They were so heavy. What was wrong with them? Why wouldn't they move?

They were gone! They had vanished beneath a swarming mass of spiders. A fuzzy, black, moving mass of spiders crawled over and under one another up her legs! Fuzzy black spiders.

Higher and higher they crept, too many to brush away. Up to her knees! Too many to shake off. Up to her waist! Higher and higher.

Pull yourself out! Pleaded her mind.

How? Josie cried frantically. *How?*

She reached up to grab something, anything, to pull herself out of the living quicksand of spiders. Her hand touched something.

It was the web of the huge, red, orange, yellow, orange, red spider. It hung there, changing colors so rapidly Josie couldn't focus on anything else. Its black eyes shined on her, watching her, waiting to do its death dance for her.

Do something! screamed her mind. *Do something!*

What? Josie screamed back. *What should I do?*

Wake up! Wake up! Wake up! answered her mind. *It's only a dream, dream, dream!*

Josie's eyes opened to the darkness of her bedroom. She lay there, shaking in terror, skin crawling from sweat, heart beating so loud. Had she really screamed? Had her scream wakened her?

Fear stuck in her throat like a lump of cold oatmeal.

Dare she move? Were spiders here in her bedroom now? On her bed? Under the blankets? For real? What did she feel on her leg, a spider?

No, only sweat.

She listened. Do spiders make noise? No. It had only been a dream.

She heard her brothers breathing softly in their sleep. No spiders for real this time.

Just a dream, that's all. She was awake now. It had been only a dream.

Only a dream.

Chapter Twenty-Six
Miss Eileen and Sister

Josie sat on the iron railing that led up the stairs of St. Matthew's church, right next to St. Matthew's playground and the school Josie attended. She loved to sit on the rail, watching the other kids running and playing together. Even though she had no special friends, it made her feel like one of them just watching.

Mostly she loved to twirl over and hang upside down to see all the kids running while on their heads. The sight of everything upside down fascinated her. At home she'd lie on the couch and look at all the furniture appearing to be suspended from the ceiling. In her imagination she'd be walking across the ceiling, stepping carefully around the light fixtures. Her brothers agreed it was neat, but they didn't seem to find it as wonderful as she did.

Josie was thinking about all the changes that had taken place lately in her life.

Uncle John had moved out to one of the boarding houses near the railroad yard. She seldom saw him anymore, not that she had when he'd stayed with them. But it had been nice just knowing he had been around. Miss Tooley had left too. She had never fussed over Josie and wasn't really a very good cook. But she'd always been there. She could be grumpy sometimes. Will and Danny would make jokes and laugh about when Miss Tooley was grumpy - never when she could hear, of course. That would have brought trouble because they were expected to show respect for grown-ups. Yes, Miss Tooley could get grumpy, but she'd always been there.

One day when they all came home from school, Daddy introduced them to a new lady. She was younger than Miss Tooley. Josie could never remember her name. Finally, it was decided they should call her Miss Eileen. Miss Eileen was okay when Daddy was home, but as soon as Daddy went to work, what a change!

She had so many rules, Josie couldn't remember them all. One was "no children in the living room." The first time they learned that rule was when Daddy went to work and they were listening to Jack Armstrong. Miss Eileen came into the living room with a broom and started to "sweep" them out.

At first, they thought it was a joke, but the force of her "sweeping" changed that idea in a hurry. Even when they'd tried to tell her Jack Armstrong was on, she'd kept whacking at them with the broom. Danny pointed out that at least it had been the bristles. If she had used the handle, it would have really hurt.

Now they spent their evenings in the kitchen when Daddy was at work. Miss Eileen would sit in the living room, listening to the radio. Sometimes they'd sit near the door, trying to hear the stories too. But the radio was too low, and besides, there was a hall and the dining room in between. Usually they sat at their little table and colored or talked or did homework.

Lights weren't permitted, another rule. As soon as it was dark enough to put on a light, it was bedtime. They would pull the curtains back, trying to get whatever extra light they could to extend their time up. Josie wondered what would happen when winter came and it was dark almost after school. How would they get their homework done if they had to go to bed right after supper? Maybe the rule would change.

Rules changed each day and Miss Eileen kept getting madder and madder when one was broken. She'd get so mad sometimes that she'd put one fist in her mouth and pull your hair or hit you with the other fist. The first time it happened, she'd gotten mad at Danny. No one knew what rule he'd broken, but suddenly there she was, biting her fist and hitting Danny with the other. Will started to giggle; it looked so strange. But they quickly realized Danny wasn't laughing. He was crying. She was really hurting him.

After that, it seemed every evening at least one of them caught it. Her head was still sore after two days. Miss Eileen liked to pull Josie's hair while biting her fist.

At night, the three of them would cuddle together in Josie's bed, often discussing what to do. Tell Daddy? No, Daddy wouldn't believe it anyway. Miss Eileen had complained that they didn't get up when she called them and Daddy believed her. Now Daddy never called them, he just came in the room and dumped them on the floor.

"That's the way they do it in the Army," he'd shout as he tipped them, mattress, blankets and all, onto the floor. It had gotten so that Josie woke up as soon as anyone walked into the room. If anyone touched her, she'd be on her feet right away, even before she was awake.

Josie's head was starting to ache from hanging upside down, so, in one swift motion, she twisted upright. She thought it was really clever the way she could twirl like that. No one else ever seemed to notice how she could do it. The other kids were running and playing with one another and never noticed her. Some of the girls were jumping rope, but they never included her unless she'd just swing the rope. She wasn't allowed to jump. It was true she wasn't very good at it, but neither were some of the other girls and *they* weren't made to just swing the rope. So, Josie preferred to twirl on the rail instead of suffering the humiliation of being just a swinger and not a jumper.

This year she had a new sister for a teacher too. She could never remember the sister's name. They all had strange sounding names, after different saints, she knew that, but saints had lived so long ago that their names weren't heard anymore. Names like "Philnuna" or "Clemistiria." This sister's name was really strange and always eluded Josie. She'd try so hard to get it right but seldom did. Maybe that's why the sister didn't like her. She couldn't remember Sister's name.

Sister complained constantly to Josie about everything: how she couldn't learn arithmetic, how she couldn't spell, how she didn't "act like a lady." That puzzled Josie. How did ladies act?

Josie tried to be nice to everyone because that's what she thought being a lady meant. She never scratched in public because Uncle John told her "ladies never scratch in public." Josie thought that was unfair. Men could scratch whenever they had too, but ladies had to stay itchy. Unfair! But if that's what being a lady meant, well, Josie would have to stay itchy. Still, the sister would complain she wasn't acting like a lady!

Today it had been the "walking like a boy" thing again. Josie couldn't figure that one out either. Boys and girls walked alike, one foot in front of the other! What was Sister talking about? It had been really humiliating today; she had made a big deal of it.

After everyone had gotten settled in their seats, Sister said, "Josie, stand up!"

All the kids turned to stare as Josie stood up. She felt so funny, she'd only half-stood, one knee still resting on the seat of her desk. The rest of her slumped over her desk.

"Stand up!" Sister shouted. "Stand up straight! You know what "stand up" means, don't you?"

Josie knew her face was turning red and she felt funny as all the other kids started to giggle.

"I was just shocked when you came into church today," she started. "You showed no respect! Stomping up the aisle like a boy! Shame on you! Entering the house of God with no respect!"

Josie was puzzled. What did she mean? Josie walked like everyone else. Did that mean that God didn't like the boys in church either? After all, if walking like a boy meant disrespect, what chance did boys have?

"Josie! Do you hear me? What do you have to say for yourself?"

Josie just stood there, remaining silent. *What does she mean,* Josie thought. I'm nice. I'm a lady as much as I know how to be. I never swear or talk sassy to grown-ups. I never shoplift like May and Karen do, and Sister doesn't say *they* aren't ladies.

"If you don't start behaving like a lady, I'll make you use the boys cloak room until you learn," Sister continued.

Josie looked around the room. Most of the girls were still giggling, but most of the boys had stopped. Some were showing sympathy. Sister usually singled out boys for this sort of embarrassment. In fact, she was the only girl made to suffer like this. *If I share the cloak room with the boys,* she thought, *I'll be okay. Most of them I can lick in a fight and, from the noises that come from there, they have more fun anyway.*

"Well, what do you think about that?" Sister was demanding.

Josie stood by her desk. "I don't care," she replied.

Sister glared at her. "Don't care, huh? Well, just march yourself into the cloak room and think about it a while! And for heaven's sake, try to walk like a lady!"

Josie crept out to the long, narrow room where coats and hats were hung. She hoped she was walking like a lady, however that might be.

She could hear Sister's voice going on and on, but didn't pay attention to what was said. She looked at the coats hanging. Some of the girls had really pretty ones, so clean and nice. Cute hats too. *Oh God,* she thought. *I hope no one misses anything today or Sister will say I stole it!*

After a while Sister allowed her to come back and take her seat for religion class.

But now it was recess, a few minutes of just enjoying free time, twirling on the rail. Josie swung back to hang upside down when two girls, Mary and Ellen, approached her.

"Why do you do that?" Ellen asked.

"Aren't you afraid you'll fall on your head?" asked Mary.

Josie swung upright again. No one ever came over to talk to her. She felt very flattered. She explained how neat everything looked upside down, so different from how it usually looked. And no, she wasn't afraid of falling. She hung on tight and, if she felt herself tiring, she had only to swing upright again.

"But what about your dress flying up?" Mary wanted to know.

Josie explained how she'd tuck her skirt tightly under her to keep it in place. After all, if she didn't, it would fall over her face and she wouldn't be able to see how neat everything looked. Mary and Ellen seemed interested. Mary hung her head down, trying to see how things looked upside down.

"It really is much better to hang," Josie said.

Mary came up to sit by Josie. Josie's heart was filled with joy. Someone wanted to do something with her. Someone was interested in what she enjoyed. Maybe she'd even become a friend! How wonderful! A friend! Maybe *two* friends! Josie was elated. Mary was worried that she might fall, but Josie reassured her. "You'll know when your arms and legs get tired. Besides it's only a little way to the ground. You can just lower yourself down."

Mary was ready to try it. Her dress was tucked under her just right when Patti came over.

"What are you doing?" she asked Mary, giving Josie a dirty look.

Mary explained what she was going to do.

"You remember what Sister said," Patti continued.

"I know," said Mary. "But I'm having fun!"

Josie felt so glad. Mary was having fun with her.

"But Sister said you shouldn't play with *someone*." Patti emphasized that last word.

Josie was puzzled. Who could be so awful that Sister didn't want you to play with them? She didn't know anyone so naughty you couldn't play with them. Even Mike McGuiness had friends and he was the naughtiest person Josie knew.

"Who is it?" Josie asked. "Who aren't we suppose to play with?"

Patti ignored Josie's question.

"Come on," she said to the others. "Come on before Sister sees us."

"But *who*?" Josie insisted. "Who is it?"

Patti gave Josie a smug look. "You."

Josie felt her face get hot. Mary and Ellen started to walk away with Patti. Mary looked back at Josie as if to say something, but Patti grabbed her coat and pulled her along. Josie felt like crying, but swung upside down instead. She wouldn't let anyone make her cry. Crying meant they'd hurt you, touched you, made you care what they'd done to you. Josie was never defeated, never, even if the other person was bigger and stronger. Josie would never let anyone be a victor over her! Never!

She hung there a long time until she heard the bell ring. Then she swung up again and stepped in line to go back into the school.

"You shouldn't hang upside down so long," one of the older boys said as she walked by. "Your face is all red."

Chapter Twenty-Seven
Shopping with Daddy

Josie sat, staring out the window as the old streetcar clinked along. That's how streetcars sounded ... *clinka* ... *clinka* ... *clinka*. If she allowed herself to drift away, they sounded like the trains Josie took to her grandmother's house. Streetcars were sort of make-believe railroad trains.

It was so pleasant sitting here, listening to the *clinka, clinka,* watching the houses and stores slip past her window. Daddy was taking her downtown to buy some clothes for school. Most kids had gotten new things way back when school started. Here it was almost Halloween and Daddy was taking her for school clothes.

All her dresses were too short and tight. They cut under her arms, making red welts. Sister had complained how short the skirts were. If the skirts seemed too short to Sister, she made you kneel down and if the skirt didn't touch the floor, she would have a fit! Then she'd make you sew pieces of rags onto the bottom so it would be long enough, or "modest and ladylike," as Sister put it.

If you were lucky, another girl or two would "catch it" too so you could help one another with the sewing. It was funny though, some girls never "caught it," even when their skirts were too short. They could do just about anything and Sister never scolded. Sometimes Josie wondered if Sister really thought that all Josie had to do was get in the street car, go downtown, and buy her own dresses, and not have to wait for Daddy to take her.

Personally, Josie thought, *I wish I could wear cords and shirts like Danny and Will.* Boys clothes were so comfortable. They hung loose with no bows or buckles, no buttons down the back. You could run and jump, twirl on the railing, climb trees, all that neat stuff, and not have to worry about getting dirty, tearing your dress, or having your panties show. Sister seemed to feel that having your panties show was worse than murdering someone!

Josie chuckled to herself as an image of a little girl (who looked a lot like Josie) entered her mind. The little girl was being led down the corridor to the electric chair, like that movie James Cagney was in. The priest was mumbling prayers and the warden was very serious as he told the little girl, "This is what happens when your panties show!"

"What's so funny?" Daddy asked, smiling down at her.

Josie's daydream vanished. "Oh, nothing. I just thought of something funny."

Daddy put his arm around her and pulled her close to him. She snuggled against him, soaking in the warmth and the tenderness. He was her regular Daddy today. No sour-smelling, angry stranger, just wonderful, warm Daddy.

Thursday morning, he had come home from work just as they were having breakfast. Miss Eileen never bothered much at breakfast, just toast and coffee-milk.

"You brats just pick anyway!" she'd grumble. So, when Daddy walked in with a box of sweet rolls, they were delighted. Daddy laughed as she and Danny and Will dug into the box, picking out their favorites.

It was wonderful seeing Daddy in the morning. Usually they were in school before Daddy got home. At lunchtime he'd be sleeping, so they only saw him from after school until he left for work. He was working a lot recently, it seemed. Daddy said it was because there was a lot of overtime, whatever that was. Josie had such mixed feelings. She missed her Daddy, but at the same time she was afraid of him. It just depended on which Daddy it was. One never knew ahead of time which Daddy you would see. Sometimes she thought she had her regular Daddy, but suddenly something would cause him to be so angry and she knew then it was really the sour-smelling Daddy.

As she had reached for a jelly-filled donut Uncle John called a "bismark," Daddy looked over at her.

"You look as though you could use some new school dresses. I bet you've grown a foot."

Then he laughed and made her stand up and turn around.

"Yes, by golly. You certainly do need some new dresses. Whaddya say, Saturday we'll go downtown and pick out a few?"

Josie was delighted. New dresses, and no more rags to be sewn on the too-short ones. At last!

It was scary though. What if Daddy was drunk? It was embarrassing to go out with him when he was drunk. And it was scary too, because he would get so angry at people, yelling and shouting.

Once he'd gotten in a fight with a bus driver. Josie thought the bus driver was going to hit him, but all he'd done was stop the bus and told them to get off. Daddy swore and tried to sock the driver, but the bus driver just gave Daddy the fare back and said, "Get going, jerk. Go plague someone else!" Everyone had stared as she and Daddy got off, looking out the windows at them as the bus drove away.

Daddy had swayed back and forth and then started to walk home. He had fallen once, but she'd helped him up. He kept muttering and swearing under his breath until a taxi came by and they flagged it down.

"We'll go home in style," he'd told her, "not on any g—d-mn bus!"

Josie always tried to be very careful and good when Daddy was like that. Somehow, she knew if she was very, very good, Daddy wouldn't get so upset and angry.

At school on Thursday, Josie hadn't even minded when Sister pointed out her too-short shirt and got out the rags. She would have all new ones next week anyway. Daddy had promised.

But the terrible thought kept nagging at her. What if Saturday morning came and Daddy was drunk and she had to go downtown with him? Usually mornings were okay. She comforted herself with that thought.

Saturday morning Daddy had come into her room. He shook her gently enough, but she'd sprung out of bed, terrified. Daddy seemed surprised.

"Gosh. You must have been having a bad dream. I'm sorry if I scared you," It was her regular Daddy. Josie shook with relief.

"Are you okay?" Daddy seemed concerned.

Josie nodded. How could she explain that *he* had caused her terror? That his dumping them on the floor, yelling and swearing, so many mornings had trained her to jump awake at the slightest touch to her bed? She had to always be careful not to do or say anything that would upset Daddy. He could change into her different Daddy so quickly. As long as he was her regular Daddy, it made no sense to risk telling him the truth.

She dressed quickly, pulling on one of the too-tight dresses. Daddy buttoned up the back for her, forcing the button and button holes together.

"You are getting to be a real young lady," he said.

I wish you'd tell Sister that, Josie thought. It would have been so comforting to tell him how Sister said she wasn't a lady. Maybe Daddy could tell her how ladies behaved, and then Sister would be satisfied with her. But it was best not to say anything. Daddy might be angry at her for disappointing Sister.

Daddy was so wonderful this morning. She felt so special being alone with him. Miss Eileen and the boys were still asleep. It made sense to shop without them because she and Daddy would be looking at little girl things.

Daddy fixed her hair, forming the curls gently around his fingers. "Your hair is so much like your mother's," he said sadly.

Josie worried he'd get too sad. Sometimes when Daddy would get that sad, far-away look, she'd feel so sorry for him and be sad too.

She hated her curls, even if they were like her mother's. What she really wanted was pigtails. Curls were such a bother, but with pigtails your hair stayed where you wanted it, no bouncing around. Besides, some of the kids called her "Jigg-a-boo-Josie." She wasn't sure what that meant, but knew they meant it to be mean. Even Danny who was so smart wasn't sure. "I think it's a mean name for negroes," he said. Josie was still puzzled. Why would anyone call someone a name just because they were negroes? If God didn't want negroes, he wouldn't have made them. It was all very confusing.

"Josie," Daddy straightened up, moving her gently away from him. "Why don't you ring the bell so we can get off at the next stop?"

Josie roused herself from her thoughts and pushed the button between the windows, letting the driver know someone wanted to get off. Several other people were getting off at this stop too, but Josie had been the first one to push the button. It made her feel very important. Inside she was bubbling with such good, warm feelings. *Why couldn't it be this way all the time?* she wondered. This must be how other kids feel, the ones who have mothers and daddies who aren't sad.

She skipped down the street, holding Daddy's hand. He was so wonderful, young and so good-looking, she thought, certainly younger and better-looking than all the other daddies she knew. And when he was like this, he was wonderful. Her heart burst with love for Daddy.

He squeezed her hand as if to tell her how much he loved her too. What a wonderful, wonderful day this was. A fleeting thought of what was probably going on at home with her brothers and Miss Eileen intruded into her feelings. She refused to let it and continued to just soak in and enjoy this special morning with Daddy.

When they arrived at the store there were people waiting to get in. The store wouldn't open for a few minutes. Josie hopped impatiently, thinking of the dresses waiting inside for her and Miss Arlene, the special lady who always helped her pick out clothes. Daddy came to this store because Miss Arlene was so helpful and Josie liked her so much. Sometimes Josie fantasized that he might fall in love and maybe marry Miss Arlene. Then she'd be there to help Josie all the time.

Sister would never complain again if Miss Arlene was there to pick out Josie's clothes every morning.

Josie had asked enough questions of Miss Arlene to know she wasn't now married but had been once. It was very mysterious. Her husband hadn't died like her mother had, but still, she wasn't married now. Miss Arlene had no children and yes, she would have loved them, especially a little girl like Josie. She'd even given Josie a hug when she had answered that question. Josie wondered why Daddy couldn't see what a marvelous mother Miss Arlene would make. Miss Arlene couldn't ask Daddy out. Everyone knew the boy had to do the asking. And Daddy! What was the matter with him anyway?

Miss Arlene greeted Josie warmly.

"I thought perhaps you had come in when I wasn't working," she said. "There isn't a big selection anymore, but we still have some pretty dresses in your size."

Josie knew exactly what she liked: nothing with too many ruffles, nothing too fussy, but red; Josie loved red dresses. Miss Arlene took Josie into the dressing room to try on the dresses. If Josie liked one then she'd walk out to show it to Daddy. He always liked it too. He never tried to force her to buy any dress she didn't feel comfortable in. It made her feel so grown up to pick out her own dresses this way.

Sometimes Miss Arlene would bring a dress that was too, *too* cute, the kind some of the other girls wore. Those were not for her. She always chose the simplest ones, without bows and ruffles. She picked out three dresses. One was red plaid with white sleeves and collar and yoke. It looked like a "jumper," as Miss Arlene called it. Another one was just like it only in blue-and-green plaid.

"Are you sure you want two dresses so much alike?" Miss Arlene asked her.

Josie nodded. "They aren't the same. The colors are different."

The third dress was her favorite. A red plaid skirt and white top with a little red jacket that could be worn or not, as you wished. Daddy laughed with her as she chose each one, sharing her happiness and excitement. Miss Arlene picked out socks, undershirts, and panties for Josie. Daddy bought her a red sweater with buttons down the front.

It would have been nice to hug Miss Arlene good-bye. Hugging people you liked felt so good, but somehow Josie felt that it wouldn't be right, not "appropriate behavior" as Grandmother says. So, all she did was smile and say "thank you." As they left, Josie turned to take one last look at Miss Arlene, whom she loved so much. Miss Arlene smiled and waved before turning to wait on another customer.

On the streetcar going home, Josie became aware of just how hungry she was. Daddy hardly ever stopped to eat anywhere, so she didn't bother to say anything. It never seemed to make much sense to ask for or expect something when you already knew the answer would be "no." Then as if Daddy had read her mind he asked, "Want to stop for a hamburger?"

Josie grinned up at Daddy and nodded.

Instead of riding to their regular stop, they got off a few blocks further down and headed for *The Coffee Pot*, which had "the best burgers in the world!"

Josie sat, eating and thinking what a wonderful day it had been. Why couldn't it be this way forever? Why did Mother have to die and leave everyone so sad and alone?

When they were ready to leave, Daddy ordered some food to take home for Miss Eileen and the boys.

Josie's beautiful day was starting to fade away. Poor Danny and Will had been home all day with awful Miss Eileen and Josie felt a little guilty. She'd had such a wonderful day with her wonderful, regular Daddy. She wanted to enjoy every minute she had left of this day, so she refused the guilty intrusion and slipped her hand into Daddy's. He picked up the bag of burgers and Josie clutched her new dresses, folded neatly in their bag. And hand-in-hand, they walked home.

Chapter Twenty-Eight
Boys Fight Back

As soon as she walked into the house, Josie knew something was up. Danny and Will were lying on the floor in the living room, playing checkers and listening to the radio. Miss Eileen was in the kitchen, banging dishes and pots angrily. Yes, something was up. She was so taken back by the sight, that she almost blurted out, "What's going on? How come you're in here?" But Danny caught her eye and she knew to be quiet. Will mouthed "later," without making a sound.

"Later?" Josie could hardly wait. What could possibly have happened that allowed Danny and Will to be in the living room while she and Daddy were gone? Miss Eileen would never stand for that. It was one of her rules, enforced with the broom.

"Later," after everyone had eaten and Daddy went to get some sleep before work, they told her what had happened. It was unbelievable.

"After you left," began Will. "Miss Eileen came in as always."

"But," said Danny, "this time, it was gonna be different!"

It seemed she'd started in on Danny to "sweep" him out like she always did.

"I just got mad," Danny explained, "and took the broom away and swept *her* out instead!"

Incredible!

"At one point," Will was laughing. "She tried to get it back, but Danny held her away. He just shoved the broom in her stomach and held her back!"

Josie was amazed at her brother's bravery. To fight back against Miss Eileen! Wow!

"She'll tell Daddy!" Josie warned.

No, she can't," Danny said.

"We thought it out," said Will. "If we can't tell Daddy she hits us because we break her rules …"

" …she sure can't tell," continued Danny, "that we hit her back!"

It made sense. How could Miss Eileen explain getting hit with the broom?

"She'll get you back," and Josie worried that when she did it would be awful.

Danny and Will nodded.

"Right, We'll just have to be ready."

Nothing happened during the weekend. They listened to the radio. An uneasy peace lay over the house. Miss Eileen didn't make a move until Daddy was at work on Monday evening.

They were all sitting around the dining room table, doing homework, when Miss Eileen grabbed Danny by the hair and yanked him out of his chair. She threw him to the floor and dragged him to the bedroom door. Danny was screaming and scratching at her hands, but Miss Eileen wouldn't let go. She pulled Danny up to his feet, shaking his head back and forth by his hair. Will sprang up, his chair flew over, and he leapt on Miss Eileen's back like a monkey. He wrapped one arm around her neck, hitting her with his other fist, yelling, "let my brother go!" over and over.

Miss Eileen pushed Danny away as hard as she could. He flew across the bedroom and landed on Josie's bed. Almost at the same time, she swung around, ramming Will into the door as hard as possible, knocking him to the floor. She put one hand in her mouth, muttering sounds of rage. The other hand became a fist. She headed for Danny, who was lying across Josie's bed, dazed, glasses gone. He pulled his legs up as if to protect his body from her blows. She descended upon him, swinging wildly, blows falling on his legs. Suddenly, Danny pushed both legs out as hard and as fast as he could, right into Miss Eileen's middle. She flew backwards, hitting the bunk beds with full force. A funny noise came out of her. Fists dropped, her face went white. She turned and ran into the bathroom.

Josie, who had sat in shock while all this was going on, finally could move. She picked up Danny's glasses and walked to the bedroom door. Will sat rubbing his shoulder and Danny sat on her bed, rubbing his head. They exchanged looks.

Danny grinned at Will, then both boys grinned at Josie. Victory!

For a few days, things were peaceful. Miss Eileen left them alone. They moved around the house as they wished, listening to the radio, sitting in whichever chair they wanted to, breaking all the rules that Miss Eileen had made up. She did nothing to stop them. For a while they worried about when the next attack would come. Then it seemed maybe there wouldn't be any more fighting. They'd won and maybe Miss Eileen wouldn't try again. She still pulled Josie's hair each morning while fixing it. She'd still jerk the boys by their hair, but there were no real beatings anymore. Miss Eileen seemed to be controlling herself. Still, Josie worried. Miss Eileen would find an opportunity to get her revenge.

It came one Saturday morning.

Daddy had taken the boys for haircuts, leaving Josie curled up on the couch listening to "Let's Pretend." Josie was so involved in the fairy tale, thinking how wonderful it would be if fairy tales were true, because then she and her brothers could be rescued by a fairy godmother and Miss Eileen would be turned into a toad or something equally slimy. But Josie knew such things didn't happen in real life.

Suddenly, Miss Eileen grabbed her hair and was dragging her out of the living room.

"Get in the kitchen, brat! No children in the living room! Remember, brat?" Miss Eileen was yelling, jerking Josie's head back and forth to make it hurt worse. Josie was shocked. Even for Miss Eileen, this was a vicious attack. She had to fight back. Her brothers would expect it of her. They'd fought so hard! Could she do less!

Josie reached back and grabbed Miss Eileen's thumb and pulled it back as far as she could. Miss Eileen gasped and turned Josie's hair loose. Quickly Josie was on her feet, facing an enraged Miss Eileen.

"No!" Josie yelled. "No! Leave me alone!"

Miss Eileen didn't seem to hear her. One hand went into her mouth; the other became a fist. She charged at Josie, battering away wherever the fist fell. Josie felt dazed as the blows beat down on her. She pushed out at Miss Eileen to keep her away. A sudden stabbing pain rushed through Josie's right hand. Between blows, she saw that Miss Eileen's brooch had come open and was sticking into her hand below her little finger and ring finger. There was no getting loose. Josie was panicked. Miss Eileen just kept pounding her while the brooch held her there.

If I pass out, Josie thought, *she'll kill me!*

With one tremendous jerk, she pulled her hand free. The pain shot up her arm, but she was able to get away from the terrible blows. Miss Eileen kept coming at Josie, flinging her arm up and down, beating her with one fist. Drool was running down around the other fist that she was biting.

Josie kept backing away and was now up against the wall, the wall near the bathroom door. She knew she couldn't take much more; her arm was numb with pain. She felt herself getting dizzy. *I can't pass out. I can't,* she told herself, while inching down the wall towards the bathroom. As soon as she felt the doorway, Josie bolted quickly into the bathroom and, before Miss Eileen could react, locked the door. Miss Eileen pounded on the door a few minutes and then gave up.

Josie sank to the floor, safe. She was unaware of how long she had sat there before she realized that it was quiet and she was really hurting. Her scalp ached. Her shoulders, where most of the blows had landed, ached, but most of all her hand was a fire of pain. She looked at it. There was hardly any blood, but the puncture was an angry red swelling. Slowly, Josie picked herself up and went to the sink. She turned on the cold water and held her hand under it to stop the burning pain.

She was shocked at the sight of herself in the mirror. Her hair was a tangled mess. Her face was so white! Suddenly she felt sick, quickly leaning over the toilet just in time. Afterwards, she sat on the toilet seat, holding her hand in the cold water. She reached up and took a washcloth with the other hand and wet it to wipe her face. Slowly, she came around. Her aches were still there, but only her hand concerned her. She'd never had anything hurt so badly before. Even a sprained ankle hadn't hurt like this.

There was a banging at the bathroom door. Josie jumped, alert.

"Get outta there, brat! Other people gotta go!" Miss Eileen yelled through the door.

Josie ignored her. Instead, she leaned her head on the cool toilet tank, still soaking her injured hand. Miss Eileen pounded a few more times and then gave up again.

Josie looked at her hand. It was still throbbing terribly. She opened the medicine cabinet and took out the Mercurochrome. She knew she should use iodine, but that stung, and Josie just couldn't handle any more pain. She dabbed the red Mercurochrome on the puncture and stuck her hand back in the water.

She was so tired it was hard to sit there, so she wrapped her hand in a towel and sat on the floor, leaning back against the door. She could hear Miss Eileen moving about, but in here Josie knew she was safe. There was no way in. The bathroom lock worked only from the inside. There was no key that Miss Eileen could use. And if she called for help to get Josie out, she'd have to explain why Josie had locked herself in. So, Josie was safe in here until Daddy and the boys came home. Safe. Safe. Josie dozed off. Her brothers' voices woke her. How long she had slept, she had no way of knowing. She hung up the towel, flushed the toilet and opened the door.

Danny and Will took one look at her and knew she'd gotten it. Daddy wasn't with them; he'd stopped off at *Arnie's*. Miss Eileen glared, but didn't try to touch her. Will grabbed Josie's jacket and handed it to her. The three of them went outside. They sat on the front porch while Josie told her brothers what had happened.

"We'll have to give in or she'll take it out on Josie!" Will said.

"No!" Danny argued. "If we give in it will be worse than ever."

"Maybe we should get her?" said Will.

"And let her know it's because she hurt Josie," continued Danny.

Josie shook her head. "If you attack first, then she can tell Daddy."

"That's true," Danny and Will both agreed.

"What can we do?" said Danny.

"I'll just have to fight back myself," Josie said. "If she hits me while you're there then get into it, but otherwise ..." The sentence trailed off.

Danny took Josie's hand. It looked terrible. "You could tell Daddy. Show him this."

"No. Daddy would only take her side, say I shouldn't misbehave." Grown-ups always believed other grown-ups, Josie reasoned. Besides, where was Daddy now?

"By the time I see Daddy this will be healed up."

Danny and Will nodded. It was no use telling Daddy. And there wasn't anyone else to turn to. They'd have to wait until Miss Eileen hit Josie while they were there. Meanwhile, Josie would have to defend herself as best she could.

A week later, Josie's hand was still sore. In fact, it was worse. It was swollen and where the puncture was it was all purple. She could hardly write. Sister, who usually complained about Josie's penmanship, complained even more this week. But how could Josie explain her sore hand without telling how it had happened? And Sister wouldn't care. If she *did* believe Miss Eileen's brooch caused it, she would believe Josie deserved the beating too. It was impossible to tell Sister, so Josie just listened to Sister's complaints with her head down, hoping she would let her sit down soon if she thought Josie was sorry enough.

Daddy was gone a lot, so he didn't even notice that Josie's hand was so swollen and hurting. Danny and Will checked it each day. They put iodine on it and Danny told her to soak it in warm water as often as possible. Josie soaked it whenever she went to the bathroom, but cold water felt so much better. Only, her hand wasn't getting any better.

Chapter Twenty-Nine
Josie Fights Back

It was Saturday again. Daddy had brought home sweet rolls for a treat. As Josie reached to grab one, Daddy noticed her hand. He grabbed it and Josie jumped with pain.

"What happened?" Daddy asked. "It looks terrible."

Josie wanted to tell about how Miss Eileen had beaten her so badly and how the brooch flew open, jabbing her hand. But you couldn't trust grown-ups. If you complained about one to another, then you really were in trouble. Besides, Daddy never would believe her and there was Miss Eileen, looking at her over Daddy's shoulder. If Daddy *did* believe her and fired Miss Eileen, fine. But what if he didn't fire her, or worse, thought Josie was lying. That would be awful. They'd be at Miss Eileen's mercy, worse off than ever.

Josie glanced at her brothers, knowing they were thinking the same thing. Should she tell Daddy the truth? Risk it or not?

"I jabbed myself sewing," Josie told Daddy.

"You don't sew," Daddy persisted.

"I know, that's how come I jabbed myself."

"But, Josie. It's in your right hand. How could you jab yourself in your right hand when you hold the *needle* in your right hand?"

Josie was stumped. It was true. She never could have jabbed herself like that sewing. Maybe she should just tell Daddy the truth. Only now that she'd lied, Daddy would be angry because she'd tried to lie. It was hopeless. There was no going back to the truth; Daddy would be upset.

No going ahead with the lie; Daddy would know.

"I don't know how it happened," she sighed in desperation.

Daddy was so concerned that he took her in the bathroom and took out his pocket knife. Using the small blade that he kept razor sharp, he opened up the scab covering the puncture and gently squeezed the swollen area. Pus came oozing out. Lots of pus. Then he had her soak it in warm water.

"Always warm water, sweetheart," he told her.

He seemed so concerned that Josie began to wish she had told him the truth. Maybe he would have believed her, understood, taken her side. No, this was best. Someone at least knew her hand was sore and would care for it. As for the rest, well, Danny and Will and she had handled it so far. They could trust one another, but to trust Daddy was uncertain. Right now, he was gentle and caring. But that could change too, quickly. This was best, safest for them all.

"If you notice little fine lines coming out of the purple area, tell me. Even if you must wake me up," Daddy was saying. "If I'm at work, go tell Mr. Schick at the grocery and have him call me right away. Promise?"

Josie nodded. It was so wonderful when Daddy was like this, so concerned, so loving and kind. If only Daddy was like this always, she would tell him about Miss Eileen. He'd make her stop. If only he was like this always, if only. "If only the moon was really green cheese and came to Earth, no one would ever go hungry," Grandmother used to say. Well, the moon wasn't green cheese and wouldn't come to Earth and there were lots of starving people here and Daddy wasn't always like this. So, forget the "if onlys."

Daddy put some iodine on her hand and put a band-aid over the puncture. Her hand felt better already.

As the days passed, Josie's hand began to heal. But the three of them worried, waiting for Miss Eileen to make her next move. She still jabbed at them when she walked past, or punched them while they sat doing their homework. But nothing really bad. She pulled Josie's hair harder and harder each morning while brushing it. They knew it was coming soon. And the longer between attacks, the more vicious it was going to be when it did come. And Josie would be the target. They all knew that. Miss Eileen didn't dare take on both boys; Josie would be the target for sure.

An uneasiness lay over them, even as they moved around the house, enjoying their hard-won freedom. Sometimes they would stay in the kitchen like before if they sensed Miss Eileen was ready to erupt. In some ways, the waiting was worse.

The boys had left for school early because of a paper drive and Miss Eileen was fixing Josie's hair. As always, she was jerking and pulling with unnecessary roughness. Josie's involuntary cry of, "Ouch!" made Miss Eileen furious. Josie had learned not to complain; it only made Miss Eileen meaner.

"Ouch! Ouch! Ouch!" Miss Eileen mimicked Josie, jerking her hair with each "ouch." Then, taking hold of hair on both sides of Josie's head, she began to sing. She jerked Josie's head this way and that in time to her singing.

Josie felt the fury building up in her. How much of this was she supposed to take? Anger overwhelmed her. Filled with rage such as she never experienced before, Josie reached up and grabbed Miss Eileen's hair in both fists.

"Stop it!" she screamed in a voice she barely recognized. "Stop it! Stop it! Stop it!"

She pulled herself up off the chair by Miss Eileen's hair. Miss Eileen let go of Josie's hair, but Josie was completely out of control. She continued to hang onto Miss Eileen's hair, hanging there off the chair, screaming, "Stop it!" as loud as she could. Miss Eileen was screaming now too, trying to make Josie let go. Josie suddenly became aware of what was happening and let go.

Miss Eileen ran into her bedroom. Josie sat there, her hands full of Miss Eileen's hair. Slowly, she stood up, revolted at the sight. She threw the hair down, brushing her hands together to clean them. She picked up her hair brush and went into the bathroom. Her own hair was a mess, but she fixed it as best she could. She washed her face and hands, grabbed her jacket and books, and left for school. She'd beaten Miss Eileen on her own. There wouldn't be another one-on-one between them, Josie knew.

She smiled to herself as she walked off to school. *Just wait until I tell Danny and Will,* she thought with a grin.

Chapter Thirty

Walking to the Movies

They moved down the walk, heading for the Majestic, Danny and Will up ahead, Josie in the rear. At school Sister had read a story where the character did a "hop, skip, and a jump," getting to the destination very quickly. So Josie was "hopping, skipping, and jumping." It wasn't very fast at all, in fact, if there was a difference between the "hop" and "jump," Josie couldn't see it.

Maybe I'm not jumping right, she thought. So, she tried another method for the jump. No better, in fact, rather awkward. Maybe the story person hadn't worn a heavy jacket and snow pants. It was hard to move any way at all in snow pants!

"Hey! Hurry up!" Danny called.

"We'll be late!" Will added.

Late! That wouldn't do. The best seats would be taken or you'd have to sit next to some kid who stunk or something. Or worst of all, you'd have to sit under the balcony where your head was a target for everything from popcorn to spit!

Josie hurried to catch up, the coins Daddy had given her rattling in her mitten. Daddy hated it when she put her money in her mitten.

"Put it in your pocket for God's sake!" he'd grumble. "It's not going to fall out!"

But as soon as she was out of his sight, the money was transferred to her mitten. It felt good to hear it jingle, like tiny bells, or to stretch out her fingers and feel the coolness, and then hold the coins tight until they were warm. She could tell if she was holding a penny or a dime by just touching it, as though her fingers had eyes on them. Most of all, they were just easier to get to in your mitten. When they were in your pocket sometimes a dime would catch down in the lining and you had to fumble around, trying to dig it out while all the kids in back of you complained about the wait.

"Come on, come on!" they'd yell, or, "Hey, Stupid! Forget your money?" It could really be embarrassing!

As Josie caught up, Will glanced at the watch on his wrist. "Maybe we ought to run awhile."

Danny looked over at it too. "So we won't be late."

Danny and Will had received matching watches from Uncle John. Will had lost his. Daddy didn't know yet. Danny had Will wear his sometimes so Daddy wouldn't notice one was missing. So far, so good.

What had really happened to the watch was a real mystery. Will had left it on the dresser and when he came back it was gone. At first, he accused Danny of hiding it, then Josie. Of course, neither of them had done it.

"Miss Eileen," Josie said. "She was in here."

She must have taken it, they'd decided, to get Will in trouble or perhaps to give it to her own son. Josie remembered how surprised they were to hear that Miss Eileen had two sons who lived with their grandmother.

"They get to live with their grandmother," Will had complained. "While we get stuck with *her*!"

It wasn't fair, Josie felt. "Why can't we live with our grandmother and give Miss Eileen back to her sons?"

Every summer for as long as she could remember they'd gone to their grandmother's to stay. Grandmother would come and pack their clothes, shaking her head over the sad condition of Josie's underwear and socks.

"We'll have to get you some new things," she'd tell Josie.

Josie would feel so guilty. How could she stop wearing out her underwear? Shoes, well, you could stop kicking rocks and cans and stuff or not drag your feet. Jeans, you could not crawl or play too rough. But underwear? How could you not wear out underwear?

Grandmother would send the huge "grip," as she called it, ahead by "Railroad Express." And by the time they arrived at Grandmother's house, the suitcase would be there. It was sort of neat, Josie thought, only why did one thing take so long to get there when the four of them could get there in a day?

Summer at Grandmother's was so pleasant. They could go in and out at will, from room to room without fear. The bedwetting, while not stopping completely, was better. Grandmother would get them up at night and give them clean sheets the next day if they had wet.

At home it was the same sheets for weeks on end until you'd see all the brown stains overlapping each other. It was awful when you first went in the room, but after a few minutes it didn't seem so bad. Some of the kids at school would hold their noses as she or Danny or Will walked by, saying "P.U." Only they didn't stink. They'd sniff each other and couldn't smell a thing. The kids were probably just saying something to be mean.

Josie would worry each spring. What if Grandmother didn't want them? What did she call Grandmother? Was it Granny or Grandma? What if her aunts and uncles didn't want her there? Oh, the boys were welcome. Anyone could see how wonderful they were! And everyone was happy to see them. But what about *her*? She worried. What if they really only take me along because of Danny and Will? What did she call all her aunts and uncles? What if she called them the wrong name and they all laughed at her?

Worry! Worry! Worry! Josie would worry for weeks.

Everything fell into place, of course, as she saw everyone, but the following spring she'd start to worry all over again.

Danny and Will started to run.

"I can't run so fast," Josie complained. "I've got these darn old snow pants on!" Danny and Will slowed down to a trot to accommodate her.

"It's okay," said Will.

"We'll still make good time and not get so winded and tired," Danny added.

They trotted along for a couple of blocks, then slowed to a walk to catch their breaths. They would do that a lot if they were walking a long distance: trot a block, walk a block. They could really go a long way like that without getting too tired.

Josie felt sweat building up. She hated the snow pants. They were so heavy and made her work so hard just to move around. Besides, the boys didn't have to wear them! Why did she? It wasn't fair!

"We're in time!" Will said, pointing ahead where all the kids were waiting outside the theater.

Matinees were such fun. There were kids from all over. Some you only saw there. You would never meet them at the park or another show, only here. They went to different schools. It was neat to meet kids who greeted you with smiles and waves, friendly, not caring about anything about you except that you were friendly and fun too.

The three of them joined the line of kids waiting outside for the theater to open. Kids were pushing and shoving, laughing and greeting each other. Most had bought their tickets already.

Chapter Thirty-One

Saturday

Josie lay in bed stretching herself. Her bed was dry; that was good. She stretched her legs out, feeling her blood move down to her feet as she wiggled her toes. It was Saturday. No school, no need to get up early, dress and be at church at eight o'clock. No school with Sister, Sister who embarrassed her, humiliated her, pointed out all her shortcomings to the other kids.

Not that she didn't have shortcomings, she was boyish and funny looking. She didn't understand all the subtleties of girlhood, but she wasn't so naughty as Sister seemed to think. When she went to confession she'd tell the priest how disrespectful she was in church. She'd even confessed how her hat got knocked off, by accident of course, but Josie knew girls had to cover their heads in church to show their respect. And there she had been, her hat lying on the floor, her head disrespectfully uncovered. Luckily Sister hadn't seen it, but God had. So, Josie dutifully confessed her sin, begging forgiveness.

It was really difficult being good and ladylike, especially when one had no idea of what was expected to make one good and ladylike.

Josie quickly closed her eyes, breathing carefully as she heard a noise outside her door. Josie was always cautious about letting people know when she was awake. It was safer that way, she'd found. It was like being invisible, pretending to be asleep. People moved around talking as though you weren't even there. Invisible!

It was Miss Eileen at the door!

"Get up!" she yelled as she opened the door. "You can't sleep all day, even if it's Saturday!"

Then she slammed the door with a bang.

Josie opened her eyes again and sat up looking over at her brothers. Danny and Will were waking up, rubbing their eyes. Sometimes Josie wondered if they pretended to be asleep, too. She didn't dare to ask them, for then they would know she pretended to be asleep sometimes, and that was her secret.

Josie headed for the bathroom to dress. No dress needed today! Comfortable old jeans, an old pair of Danny's, soft and broken in. It was one advantage of wearing hand me downs. They were soft instead of stiff like new jeans could be.

Miss Eileen had poured coffee-milk for them and some stewed prunes and bread were lying out. Rye bread. Daddy loved rye bread. Josie preferred mushy soft white bread, but Daddy never bought it. "Too doughy," he'd say. But rye bread tasted so funny with jelly she'd complain to no avail. Daddy bought only what Daddy wanted. It must be wonderful to be grown up. To do whatever you wanted without thought of anyone else.

"Can we toast this?" Danny asked.

"You don't toast rye bread!" Miss Eileen snarled.

Danny shrugged. It had been worth a try. At least the prunes weren't too awful.

"Get done in there," Miss Eileen yelled from the bathroom, "so I can brush your hair!"

"I wish I could brush my own hair," Josie grumbled. "If it were straight I could." Then Miss Eileen would have no excuse to bully her every morning. *It's my hair,* Josie reasoned. *I should be allowed to brush it, even if it would look frizzy and funny.*

Once when her head had itched she asked Daddy if she could brush her own hair. He granted an okay. It had felt so wonderfully. Only suddenly Daddy had stared at her a shocked look of disbelief on his face.

“What in the h—!” he had yelled, unexpectedly. Josie had cringed in terror. He had gotten off the couch and loomed over her.

“You said I could, Daddy,” she started to cry.

Daddy stood there staring at her, frightening her. Then suddenly he had turned and walked into the bathroom, slamming the door behind him. She had felt so guilty, but Daddy had said it was okay.

When Daddy came out of the bathroom his face was red like he’d been crying. She hated it when Daddy cried. He’d hugged her a little.

“It’s only that you looked like—” he caught his breath. “You looked like your mother,” tears filling his eyes.

Josie had felt so torn between guilt for making Daddy so sad and joy that she looked like her mother. Her mother had been so pretty. Anyone could see that by just looking at her picture. And smart. Daddy always said that her mother had been smart, too. Only, if she’d been so smart why had she died? That hadn’t been smart at all.

Miss Eileen banged the brush on Josie’s head pulling through the tangles with unnecessary roughness. Josie didn’t react. If she cringed or cried out, Miss Eileen would only bang harder or jerk more violently. So, Josie endured the brushing, but smiled to herself at the memory of Miss Eileen running to the bedroom crying after she gave her a good shove. It gave Josie such a sense of power, knowing she could fight back as viciously as possible if she chose to. Today Josie chose not to.

After breakfast the three kids were to clean the basement. Danny and Will carried out the ashes from the furnace. Each took handles from the big metal baskets Daddy had filled with ashes during the week. They carried them down the back walk to the huge wooden ash box next to the alley. Then they opened the hinged lid and lifted the heavy loads to dump.

The dust was suffocating and by the end of the morning, their faces and clothes were covered with dust. The only basket not emptied was the one Daddy had filled that morning when he’d tended the furnace. A hot cinder left in among the ashes could cause a fire if dumped out where there was more air and things that could catch flame on the heat. One could feel the warmth on the outside of the basket even the next day sometimes.

Josie's job was to sweep the floor, making piles of the ashes and clinkers that had fallen. Danny or Will would hold the coal shovel using it like a huge dust pan while she swept up the piles. Then they bundled up the week's newspapers, tying them securely to be stacked until the annual paper drive at school.

All four of the families who lived in their flat used the same ash box. While the garbage men came more often, the ash men came about twice a month, opening the door that was on the alley side to the trash box and shoveling out its contents.

Once when Josie was little, Daddy had become angry because she hadn't put away her stuffed animals when he'd asked, so he made her throw them all away. It was no use to argue. She picked up her friends—the black and white dog with one eye, Panda, the bear with the frazzled ear from her rubbing it between her thumb and finger, Teddy Bear with his warm brown fur and red tie—and carried them out to the ash box and put them in.

Danny and Will had gone along, helping her carry the others that didn't matter so much. She kissed Teddy good-bye, fighting back the tears. *How would she spend her days now,* she'd wondered, *without her favorite friends to play with?* She'd left the box open so "they wouldn't be afraid of the dark," she explained to Daddy. He made her close the box anyway. He didn't understand at all or care.

Everyday, she'd go peek in at her friends. And day by day, they became more and more buried under everyone's trash until only an ear or a fuzzy foot was showing.

"I'm sorry," Josie would tell them. "I'm sorry I caused this to happen to you."

She felt so guilty, killing her friends like that. She had explained to them it was Daddy, not her, who had wanted them gone. Still it had been her fault. One day she went to peek in, to utter her apologies, and it was empty. The trash men had come, and they were gone.

Chapter Thirty-Two
Army Morning

"That's the way they do it in the army, sonny boys!" Daddy yelled.

Josie jumped. She was on her feet before she was quite awake. Danny and Will were lying on the floor tangled in their sheets and blankets, their mattresses half on the floor

"That's the way they do it in the army!" Daddy yelled again.

Will glared at Daddy. Danny looked like he was going to cry. Josie stood there by her bed feeling lucky that it wasn't her on the floor. She cringed a moment when Daddy looked at her and said, "You're a good soldier, getting up right away."

Of course, she had. Who wouldn't wake up at all the noise? *God,* she thought, *it could be me dumped on the floor*. Sometimes she felt guilty because it seldom was her. Daddy usually picked on the boys.

"That's because you're Daddy's little girl," Danny and Will would sneer at her.

Then she felt ashamed and guilty for being "Daddy's little girl." She wasn't any better than her brothers. In fact, they were so special, so wonderful.

"Clean up this mess and get ready for school," Daddy yelled.

"But Daddy," Josie said, knowing if her brothers said it they'd get hit, "Daddy, it's Saturday."

Daddy looked at her. She was afraid maybe he'd hit her anyway. Instead, he sort of blinked.

"Clean up the mess. You can't sleep all day just because it's Saturday," he said slamming the door.

Danny and Will slowly untangled themselves from the bedding. Tears ran down Danny's checks. Will's face was red.

"That's the way they do it in the army!" Will scoffed. "Only they blow a bugle first!"

Danny wiped his face on his pajama sleeve, then rubbed his shoulder where he'd hit the floor.

"I hate him," Will continued. "Someday …" He paused as he helped Danny put a mattress back on his bed. "Don't let him make you cry."

Danny just turned to pick up his sheets.

"It just makes him feel good to see us cry."

Josie started to help her brothers make their beds.

"Daddy's little soldier," Will sneered.

Josie felt funny. Maybe if she helped them her brothers wouldn't hold it against her. Wouldn't hate her because Daddy had been mean to them, but not to her.

"Don't bother, Daddy's little soldier," Will sneered again.

Josie didn't know what to do. She turned and made up her own bed while the boys continued putting their beds back together. It wasn't her fault Daddy had dumped them, but she really couldn't blame them for hating her for it anyway. After all Daddy *was* meaner to them. She did have it better.

Danny still hadn't said anything. He just continued cleaning up the mess with Will while tears filled his eyes and occasionally rolled down his cheeks. His silence bothered Josie. Will's anger was scary too, but the silence …it seemed so strange. Danny and Will usually chatted away even when Daddy did something. And Will, well, Will would make a joke and the three of them would laugh and all the sadness would sort of be forgotten.

Today was different. So different. She hated this scary feeling, never knowing what to expect next.

"Daddy's little soldier better go get dressed," Will shoved her, "before we get in trouble again."

Josie nodded. She gathered her clothes and went into the bathroom to dress. The boys dressed in the bedroom, but she always went down the hall to the bathroom. The bathroom was warmer in the winter, another reason the boys called her "Daddy's little girl." Dressing in a warm bathroom while they were in the colder bedroom. She felt so badly. She didn't want to be Daddy's girl. If she'd been a boy too, then Daddy wouldn't just pick on Danny and Will, he'd do mean things to her, too. Then at least the boys wouldn't be mad at her like this.

Josie put on her jeans. Last year they'd been Danny's.

At breakfast Danny and Will were more themselves, talking and laughing together. Josie began to relax a little. Daddy was sitting in the living room like he did when he was drunk, right arm propping up his head, maybe asleep, maybe not. They could never tell for sure. Just when they decided he was asleep, he'd pick up his beer and take a drink.

After breakfast, Josie swept the back stairs while Danny and Will cleaned the basement. They carried the trash out and bundled up the weeks' old newspapers. When enough newspapers accumulated, Daddy would sell them, and they would all split the money.

After a trip out to the alley, Danny and Will came in and told Josie the kids were planning a baseball game.

Chapter Thirty-Three
Boxing Lessons

"Make me stop! Make me stop, sonny boy! Make me stop!"

Josie watched as Daddy slapped Danny across the face, occasionally poking him in the stomach, repeating, "Make me stop!" over and over.

Danny held up his arms in the right stance, trying his best to protect himself against Daddy's increasingly harder slaps and pokes. The boxing gloves seemed so huge and heavy for Danny's skinny arms. He reminded Josie of the crawdaddies they caught in the creek.

Poor Danny. He was trying so hard to box correctly to please Daddy, but he just wasn't any good at it. Danny was so smart and wonderful, but he could "trip over his own shadow," as Granddaddy said.

"Make me stop, sonny boy!" Daddy's voice got meaner. He always called Danny "sonny boy" when he felt Danny wasn't "man enough." When he was mad at Will it was "baby boy." "Baby boy want his sugar bottle?" Daddy would sneer whenever Will appeared ready to show any hurt.

Josie could see the hurt in Danny's eyes as Daddy's slaps got harder. Try as he might, Danny couldn't block them. Without his glasses, Danny probably couldn't see them coming, but Daddy wouldn't let him wear them during their sparring.

"Whoever heard of a boxer wearing glasses?" Daddy would say. Besides, if they broke, it would cost money to replace them.

Danny was afraid, too, afraid of Daddy. You could see it. Not that she blamed him. She was, too. But she tried never to let anyone see her fear, especially Daddy.

"Sonny boy's a scaredy-cat!" Daddy laughed as he really let Danny have it across the face. Danny gulped hard and blinked quickly to push the tears back.

God! Josie thought. *If he cries Daddy will really get mad.* Daddy hated it when one of the boys cried.

But it seemed strange, considering Daddy cried himself. When she was little, he'd sit on the couch in "his corner," as he called it, tears streaming down his face. Josie didn't know why he cried like that, unless it was because he missed her mother. Daddy never said. Anyway, he hadn't cried like that in a while, and now he hated it when the boys cried. Maybe he wouldn't like her to cry either. Josie didn't know. Daddy never said how he felt about girls crying.

When Daddy had come home with the boxing gloves they were all so excited. Daddy had boxed when he was a young man and had decided to teach the boys "the fine art of self-defense," as he put it.

Will, who was exceptional at running and jumping and playing baseball, seemed a natural. Even Danny was excited to learn. Daddy had laced the gloves on the boys and shown them how to hold their arms and hands to keep someone from hitting their stomachs and faces. He showed them how to dance around, weaving and ducking. It was great fun. Josie had danced around, too, even though Daddy hadn't bought a pair of gloves for her. She was a girl and girls didn't box.

Danny and Will had zigged and zagged, pretending to hit each other. They were all laughing and jumping around, having a great time.

Then Daddy said to Will, "Hit him! Hit him!" Will just kept laughing and zigging around. Suddenly, Daddy was shouting, "D-mn it! Hit him! Think this is a g—d-mn dancing school? Hit him!" Danny and Will had stopped dead and looked at Daddy, puzzled, cautious. Daddy wasn't laughing at all. He was serious. Serious and about to become very angry.

Daddy glared at the boys. "D-mn it! The idea is to try to hit the other guy," Daddy shoved Will, "while not getting hit yourself! Now hit him!" Daddy jerked his head at Danny. Will just stood there staring at Daddy in disbelief. Then he hung his head a moment, thinking. "No," he shook his head. "I might hurt him."

Daddy was surprised at Will's refusal. No one ever refused Daddy. It was too scary to even consider. Josie was terrified at what Daddy was going to do.

"Well, of course you might hurt him!" The words sounded like an insult. "This is a man's sport, baby boy! People get hurt! Now hit him, d-mn it!"

Will just stood there. "He's my brother. Why should I hurt him?"

It was incredible! Daddy glared at Will, then turned to Danny. "Then *you* hit him!" he said.

Danny hesitated, looking from Daddy to Will. It was clear he wasn't sure what to do. To not hit Will would make Daddy furious. But to hit him for real, not just fooling around like when they wrestled, but a real hit with boxing gloves on, like a fight, was unthinkable! Danny just stood there. Daddy's face was getting red. It was clear he was about to blow.

"Then maybe you can hit me," he snarled. He started poking and jabbing at Danny.

Danny tried to dance around to fend away Daddy's pokes. He stumbled and fell on the grass.

"Oh, God!" Daddy looked disgusted as he turned to Will and began to poke him. "Make me stop!" he teased while slapping Will's face.

Will stood there a minute, then put one glove under his arm and pulled it off letting it drop to the ground. Then he pulled off the other one, throwing it across the yard as hard as he could. He walked away to sit on the back steps.

"What's the matter, baby boy? You yellow-bellied? Afraid I'll hurt ya, baby boy?" Daddy jeered.

In a feeble attempt to rescue the situation, Josie jumped up. "Let me, Daddy," she pleaded. "Let me try."

Daddy turned, staring at her as if aware of her for the first time. His anger faded. Josie picked up the gloves that Will had discarded, handing one to Daddy and pulling on the other. Daddy helped her get into the gloves and laced them. Josie danced around, jabbing at Daddy. Daddy half-heartedly jabbed at her a few times.

"Let's call it quits," he said.

Josie was torn between relief that Daddy hadn't hurt Will and disappointment that he hadn't really tried to "box" her like he had with her brothers. If only she had been a boy, too.

Since then each Saturday that Daddy had the time, he gave the boys a "boxing lesson." Will would go along until he was expected to hurt Danny or Daddy became too nasty. Josie tried to tell Will that Daddy wanted Will to hit him, that he wouldn't get mad if Will really socked him during the lesson. Will wouldn't listen.

"He just wants to show what a tough guy he is," Will complained. "It's just an excuse to bat us around."

"Sonny boy's going to cry!"

Daddy voice brought Josie's attention back to the present lesson. Danny did look as though he might start to cry.

"Sonny Boy's a crying yellow-belly. Boo-hoo! Boo-hoo!" Daddy was saying to Danny.

Danny, who was really so brave and fought Miss Eileen for them all and had been the first to try to make her stop hurting them, Daddy thought was a coward. Daddy never realized how brave Danny could be.

Josie jumped up. "My turn, Daddy!" she pestered. "My turn! My turn!"

Danny put his hands down, and Will came over to help him take his gloves off. Josie jumped around excitedly. Maybe if she was really good, Daddy would take her seriously, really spend some time with her. Josie took the proper stance as Daddy had instructed: slightly hunched, arms up, hands in front of her face, arms protecting her middle. She hopped around like he had shown the boys.

Daddy held up his open palms. "Try to hit them," he said quietly.

She jabbed away while Daddy kept moving his hands this way and that to avoid the blows. Then, as always, he said, "Let's call it quits."

"But Daddy," Josie began.

It was no use. Daddy had already started picking up the other pair of gloves. He tied the laces together and hung them over his shoulder. Then he unlaced Josie's gloves, tied them together and hung them over her shoulder.

"Come on," he said. "Let's go in."

Danny and Will, grateful to be done with the lesson, tore into the house running up the stairs to their flat.

Josie tried to hang back to let Daddy go in first.

"After you, Sweetheart," Daddy said as he held the door.

Josie shook her head, but Daddy insisted. "Beauty before age." he joked.

There was no choice. Maybe if she ran really quickly this time he wouldn't catch her. She darted through the door and up the steps. Maybe she had enough of a head start, but the pair of boxing gloves bounced on her shoulder, slowing her down. She could hear Daddy gaining on her.

Whack! Daddy got her. He swung his arm back and whacked her bottom again, so hard that she fell sprawling sideways on the stairs. She lay there as Daddy stepped over her, picking up the gloves as he went. Her right buttock was on fire and her left shoulder where she'd landed hurt.

"Just a love tap, sweetheart," Daddy said. But it sure hurt.

Daddy loved using physical gestures to show how much he loved her. Sometimes he'd flick his hand so just the nail of his middle finger snapped her. That hurt like the dickens, but only for a little while. When he whacked her like this it could hurt for days. Sometimes she made it to the top without him getting her. Today the gloves had slowed her down. But even if he hadn't gotten her on the stairs, it might have happened later that evening when she lay on her tummy listening to the radio or when she walked by his chair or even in bed when she was asleep. She never knew when Daddy might want to show her he loved her so much.

Josie picked herself up, her bottom really hurting, and limped up the rest of the stairs. The boys were already washed and at the table.

"It's about time," Miss Eileen snapped at her. "Get washed for supper."

Josie went to the bathroom and closed the door. Gingerly, she lowered her jeans and panties. Her bottom was flame red, Daddy's handprint clearly visible on it. She ran cold water on a wash cloth and held it on her injury.

God, it hurts, she sighed. *So much.*

Tears formed in her eyes. Josie forced them away.

"Get out here!" Miss Eileen yelled.

Josie pulled up her clothes, rinsed off her hands and hurried to the table. The boys were wolfing down their supper. She sat down carefully, trying to let her injured right cheek hang off the chair.

"Sit down on that chair properly," Daddy scolded.

Josie slid over putting her weight only on the left side, hoping no one would notice. It was very important to sit up and behave at the table. Daddy didn't like to be disturbed while eating. Josie picked at her food thinking supper would never be over. Her seat was a fire of pain. Her left cheek was getting numb taking all the weight.

Finally, everyone was done. Josie helped clear the table and then went into the bathroom again to check herself. It was beginning to feel better, the pain subsiding a little. At least she could move without the rubbing of her jeans hurting. It would be fine by Monday when she'd have to sit in school. Sister would have a fit if she fidgeted at her desk.

Danny and Will lay in the living room, playing checkers while Daddy listened to the radio and Miss Eileen mended. Josie read a book curled in the big chair. The big soft chair was so comforting, she'd pretend it was hugging her. This must be what sitting on a big lap felt like, she thought. A big, soft, comfortable lap.

She had started to nod off to sleep when Miss Eileen clapped her hands loudly to signal it was bedtime.

Josie settled herself under the blankets when she heard Danny sobbing quietly, trying to muffle the sound in his pillow. She listened a minute, then quietly eased herself out of bed. She crossed over to Danny's bed and crawled in with him. He lay on his left side, half curled in a ball. She snuggled up against his back and put her arm over his side.

"What's going on?" Will leaned over the top bunk. "What's the matter?"

There was no need to answer. Will figured it out.

"Let's get in Josie's bed," he said.

The three of them moved into Josie's tiny bed—Danny in the middle, Josie on his left, Will on his right. Josie put her arm across Danny to hold him. Will reached across with his arm. He grabbed Josie's arm, holding it tightly. The three of them together, holding each other, comforting each other. Her sore bottom seemed somehow less painful. Josie fell asleep surrounded by her brother's love.

Chapter Thirty-Four
Dreams

She woke with a start. The dreams still swirled in her mind, not quite fading completely, but becoming less vivid the longer she blinked in the darkness. Her arm felt as though it was still wrapped around Danny's waist, but as her jumbled sleep-drunk mind began to awaken, she realized her arm was touching her husband, Ted.

It was all a dream, she told her mind.

Childhood was a long, long time ago. People called her Josephine now. *Why do those dreams keep coming back?* her mind questioned. *Suppress them. Push them away. They're not reality anymore.*

She turned a lamp on and started getting ready for the day. The difficult news had come. Something had happened with Dad, but the hospital hadn't quite pinpointed it yet. They just said to come.

Cold fingers buttoned up her blouse and pulled on her stockings and boots. The wind outside caught wisps of snow from the piles that had been pushed up against the house to clear walkways. Josephine tucked her neck down into her scarf and grabbed Ted's arm to steady herself on the way to the car.

Life with Ted was so very sweet. They laughed so much. Their children were growing up on a farm, just like Ted had dreamed would happen. Sweet, chubby babies were added to the family, toddlers scurried underfoot, chickens and roosters squawked and clucked in the yard, and there was love—so much pure and unadulterated love to share and to have.

The nursing staff walked them to the hospital room where Dad lay. She should have brought a book or puzzle or something to keep their minds busy while they awaited instructions. Her father had changed so much since she and Ted had gotten married and started having children. He had mellowed, become sober, realized the value of the lives that were his grandchildren. Alcohol no longer made him a madman. For the last several years, life had been fairly peaceful. Sure, he had done everything in his power to keep her from getting married to Ted, including all-out fistfights in their home, but thankfully he was drunk when they went to get the marriage certificate, so he didn't know what he was signing. Now, he brought gifts every time he came over, cleaned up so nicely, watched his language. It was like he was a different person.

Now her dad lay there, helpless in his bed with nurses scurrying around him. "Stroke," they told her, including a lot of other medical information she could neither understand nor process. Somewhere in the explanation, they told her he might not be able to talk or recognize her. She prepared herself to be gentle and understanding.

Out of nowhere, Dad shouted. Cursed at a nurse, his hands swinging every way to try to hit anyone whom he might.

Her father's eyes locked onto her. *He remembered*. For the last several days, the staff said he had been unconscious and unresponsive. But now, in his moments of being awake, with the drugs and medications pumping around inside of him, he remembered. "Josie, you get over here!" he yelled. His eyes raged with fire. Fear gripped Josephine's heart. Fear she had long since felt, fear that was all too quickly remembered. He had reverted.

Josephine stood stuck in the corner. She was once again the little Josie, scared, timid, insecure, unsafe. Her hand woodenly reached behind her to touch the hospital wall and steady herself. She had to get out. *He can't hurt me,* she told herself. *He can't hurt me. He can't get up out of his bed.*

Ted, whom she had forgotten even existed for a few moments,

touched her arm and pulled her into the hallway. She couldn't think. She could barely breathe. The memories that she had so long suppressed, told herself couldn't be true, rushed through her mind—the pain that dug so deeply into her soul. She felt stifled. She had never told anyone. Ted, her best friend and the dearest man in her life, didn't know. He stood, looking confused into her eyes.

"Let's go home right now," he said. She nodded, unable to respond verbally.

The car ride was silent. Josephine tried to process. She needed to tell Ted; she couldn't keep this from him. He deserved to know.

They fixed supper and then put the kids to bed before Josephine felt she was ready to explain.

"I didn't want it to be true, so I made myself believe it wasn't," she sobbed uncontrollably as Ted held her. His quiet reserve didn't ask questions, didn't blame or fault her prior silence, just sought to understand and to listen.

She tossed and turned all night long, unable to remove from her mind the chaos of memories. She tried making sense of them all. How could someone cause so much damage? How could she cope with it all?

In the early hours of the next morning, Josephine tiptoed out of bed to make a pot of coffee. Once brewed, she hooked her fingers around the handles of two mugs and brought the whole pot back into her room and to bed. Ted stirred. Their morning habit always included the pot of coffee in bed before the children woke up. It was their quiet time alone, when they would chat before the day began and pray together and read the Bible.

Now, more than ever, she needed that quiet time. Before pouring her cup, before Ted was truly awake, she grabbed a journal and pen and began writing. At the very beginning, she started with her memories, the stories Daddy had told her of her mother. Moving her hand as quickly as she could, she spelled out the stories onto the pages. She didn't stop when Ted woke up. She forgot about the coffee. The children's rustling to get ready for school fell on deaf ears. And still she wrote.

Days and weeks passed, and she wrote, not for the purpose of reliving the joys and the nightmares, but to try to understand. Sadness enveloped her. Not depression, just sadness. And when she penned the final words, she sat back and looked at what was in front of her. It was her story. She closed her eyes and leaned her head on the back of the chair. But what now? What could heal her hurting heart?

In the quickness of a moment, a memory flitted across her mind's eye, a memory that, for the first time in weeks, had nothing to do with her childhood. She saw her children running around the farmyard with all the chickens. She smiled.

Another memory popped up. Her home was filled with other children—not her own, but her children's friends, those she had taken in and housed, some for days, some for months. Children whose parents had died, children whose mothers and stepfathers had been abusive, children whose homes were no longer safe. For years her home was filled with these new hearts to love. In her memories, she saw them walking home from school with her children, she saw herself tucking them into bed at night, sitting across the counter from them, listening to their hurts while she made them cookies. She understood them, she knew what they faced, she cried when they cried, she loved them through their hurts. So many children in the house even Ted couldn't keep them all straight.

Another memory settled into her heart: it was her first day in the church she and Ted had begun attending just before they got married. She cried through the service for fear she had not dressed properly. A lady approached her afterward to hug her. "We aren't worried about that kind of thing here, dear," she had reassured. Faith had become so real to her in her adult years. Not the staunch, cold, fearful faith of her childhood, but the true, genuine faith she had chosen herself, believing in the God who loved her, living in freedom instead of guilt. He was the God of forgiveness, the God of sacrifice, the God of truth. Her faith changed how she looked at her life every day. It made her relationship with Ted different, stronger, and more unbreakable. It gave purpose to the darkest moments.

A tiny bud of hope pushed its way past the ashes of painful memories and began to rise in her heart like a little flower. The flower continued to grow, blooming, opening its pure white petals to show a golden center, fuzzy and soft, that peeked up at the sun and laughed. It pulled nutrients from the ashes around it and from the rain of tears, and still it grew. A little daisy. And it was going to thrive.

She thought she could feel the very light of new life coming into her soul.

She opened her eyes and looked down again at her filled journal. It was her story, and yet, it wasn't who she was anymore. Her past did not define her or make her who she was now. The past had happened, and it was terrible and unfair and cruel and painful; she could not change that. But it was her *past*, not her present.

With every painful moment, every circumstance that hurts us, no matter our age, we are given a choice—a choice of what we are going to do with what has happened to us. We can choose to be life-takers or life-givers. We can choose to serve ourselves or serve others. We can choose hatred, or we can choose forgiveness. When we choose forgiveness, we choose freedom.

We are not meant to merely cope. We are meant to thrive. We cannot remove the hurts and pains that happen to us, but we can choose to live outside of them. We can choose to not be victims for the rest of our days. We can choose instead to be survivors.

The Story of Josie

Mary Wendland was Josephine. The lines she wrote after the hospital visit to see her father were the lines penned here. Based on the events of her childhood, only a few circumstances and characters were tweaked and changed. She worked on the book in between her other loves—serving people, being with her family, helping others who needed help, working in a florist shop and delivering bouquets. The book was not finished, though, before she became ill.

During the days and weeks before Mary passed away in May of 2003, she told Ed, her husband of almost 50 years, the last stories she had wanted to include in her book. The more she told, the more she remembered. For years, she had kept her stories and memories hidden in her innermost heart. Ed promised he would finish the book.

For years, Ed took up the typewriter and wrote down the stories she had told. He worked hard with his daughter, Shari, to type Mary's handwritten pages onto a computer and finish chapters where endings couldn't be found. He wrote and re-wrote a chapter that would have been the ending of the story she had told, but it wasn't a true book ending. It wasn't finalized. He couldn't seem to find the proper way to combine his wife's stories of pain with the life of freedom he knew she lived as an adult. What hope could be given to a reader after a book of childhood abuse and hardship?

In 2014, my husband and I, just married, moved into the upstairs apartment above Ed's duplex. I had a background of editing/proofing, and Ed began to give me projects to type up from his own book of memoirs. We worked on his biography, *A Kid Called Eddie,* as well as Mary's book of short stories and poems.

After four years of working together, Ed gave me *Stories of Josie,* at that point under a different title and with a different main character name. The original plan was to simply proof the book and get it ready for publishing. But it wasn't finished. After proofing through it with my sister, I called Ed. "Can I please finish this book? Let me write the last chapter. I think it will give you some closure." He told me yes, and I wrote the final chapter, combining both Mary's writing style and the values and priorities she carried in her life that Ed had so often talked about.

Grace Peters
Editor

About the Author

Mary and Edward were married for almost 50 years. During those years, they bought several farms, had five children, and lived out their dreams. When the children were grown, Mary went to work at a florist where she loved delivering to people and meeting new faces. She wrote not only of her childhood, but also her adult life and happenings in the forms of short stories and poetry, which have been compiled into one book called *The Ever-Circle of Seasons*. Being once a child with no advocate herself, her desire to help others who could not speak for themselves grew as she grew older. Within her writing, her value of and kindness toward those society sometimes calls "the helpless" (the elderly, special needs, children, etc.), especially, teaches true compassion and the value of all life.

Those who knew Mary agree that she had a quiet sense of humor, a deep faith that guided her actions, and open arms for anyone who needed help.

After Mary began writing as an adult, she became a founding member of the Watertown, WI, writer's group "Writers on the Rock." Her poem "Floodgate" won the first place Jade Ring Award for poetry at the Wisconsin Regional State Writers Association in 1998.

Mary passed away in May of 2003, and Edward has since finished her writings as a memorial to her life and to give others the ability to learn from her life and words.

Printed in the United States
by Baker & Taylor Publisher Services